TONI AT RANDOM

TONI AT RANDOM

The Iconic Writer's Legendary Editorship

DANA A. WILLIAMS

AMISTAD

An Imprint of HarperCollins*Publishers*

FIRST EDITION

Library of Congress Cataloging-in-Publication Data has been applied for.

ISBN 978-0-06-301197-7

25 26 27 28 29 LBC 5 4 3 2 1

Contents

Titles Edited by Toni Morrison
323

Acknowledgments
325

Notes
337

TONI AT RANDOM

CHAPTER 1

"We're All We Got"

A few minutes before 10 a.m., on Saturday, April 24, 1976, conference attendees hurried to their seats in the School of Social Work Auditorium at Howard University in anticipation of the final panel of the Second National Conference of Afro-American Writers. The conference, which was organized by the Institute for the Arts and Humanities (IAH), under the direction of the incomparable poetry scholar Stephen E. Henderson, brought together virtually all the major Black writers and critics for the second time in two years to discuss the state and future of Black writing in the United States. Themed "Beyond Survival: 200 Years of Black Literature, 1776–1976," a nod to America's bicentennial, the conference had one outlier to its list of standing panels on fiction, nonfiction, poetry, drama, literature for young people, and screenwriting. By popular demand, the organizers added a panel on publishing.

Haki Madhubuti, a longtime IAH staff member, opened the session with a tribute to fellow poet and publisher Dudley Randall, who had just celebrated the ten-year anniversary of his Broadside

Press, a stalwart of Black publishing. Joining Randall on the panel were poet and publisher Ahmos Zu-Bolton, founder of the newly established Energy Black South Press and a former IAH staffer; Charles Harris, the executive director of Howard University Press and former Doubleday and Random House editor; and the panel's moderator, Carole Parks, former managing editor of *Black World*, which, until a few weeks prior when publication ceased abruptly, had been the most influential Black literary magazine there was. But the room was not filled to near capacity on that unseasonably hot day in late April just to hear from Randall, Zu-Bolton, or Harris. Attendees were most anxious to hear from the woman whose presence commanded the room almost effortlessly—Toni Morrison, Random House senior editor and author of *The Bluest Eye* and *Sula*.

As Parks offered introductions of the panelists from the podium, Morrison seemed completely unfazed by the fact that she was the only woman at a speaker's table of men. No doubt, everyone noticed the limited interaction between the panelists as they waited for the session to begin. The room felt almost sterile, like there were unspoken truths that made the assemblage of these colleagues awkward or potentially combustible instead of logical and instructive. Perhaps out of nervousness about a tense written exchange she'd had with Morrison previously about who "discovered" the writer Henry Dumas, Parks, in her introduction of Morrison, stated that Morrison had earned an MA from Cornell in *1955* and an undergraduate degree from Howard in *1973*. As the crowd's whisperings became louder in response to the error, Morrison flashed her characteristically bright smile and feigned a look of self-satisfaction at the impossible achievement. She leaned her head to the side toward Zu-Bolton, who was seated next to her, winked her eye at him, and nodded as if to say, "I'm that good." Parks, feeling like a voyeur who had not been let in on a joke, went silent to try to read the room, which now muttered irrepressibly. Morrison sensed the need to come to her rescue. "You got the years wrong, Carole. You said I graduated from Howard in 1973." The room erupted in laughter, thankful for the release valve. Because she decided it would, the room now felt momentous yet light.

Despite Parks's blunder, she was spot-on in her introduction of Morrison as one of the few people who had earned the distinction of being a capable teacher, writer, and editor. Parks had worked as an editorial assistant at Doubleday Publishing Company in the 1960s, so she knew firsthand how rare it was for a Black person, a Black woman no less, to hold a senior editor position at a major trade publishing house. But here was Morrison, a Howard University graduate from Lorain, Ohio, commanding serious attention in the publishing world among Black and white editors alike. She was publishing books few other editors would have dared to take on and making it look easy.

Understanding that she had been invited to speak as an editor, not as a writer, Morrison focused her remarks exclusively on her work in publishing. There was no need for the coy warmth she worked so hard to exude as a writer while talking to an audience she was trying to convince to buy and read her books. Here, she donned a certain solemnity that was tempered by the familiarity of being on a campus where she had studied as an undergraduate (from 1949 to 1953) and taught as an English and humanities instructor (from 1957 to 1964). She had taken great care to look the part. Despite the rising temperature in the room, she resisted the urge to relieve herself of the jacket that completed the light-colored pantsuit she wore. Even for a Saturday panel, without the jacket, the V-neck top underneath might undermine her determination to look like the dutiful professional. Her Afro, more pepper than salt but salted no less, conveyed a certain maturity, while the large hoop earrings she wore said, "Yes, I am a career woman but not a dull one." Even the offhanded way she chewed her gum, no doubt a smoker's habit, had an element of performance meant to have a similar effect.

A hush came over the room as she approached the podium. Except for her voice, the silence remained for as long as she stood to speak. She confessed that she had two sets of remarks she wanted to give, and unable to decide between the two, she resolved to give them both. She wanted to talk, first, about the publishing industry and the ways it could be used as a source and resource for Black writers. But knowing that she had a captive audience of Black readers and writers, she could not resist the opportunity to talk about the responsibilities the Black editor and the Black writer had to each other.

"I think that the survival of Black publishing, which to me is a sort of way of saying the survival of Black writing, will depend on the same things that the survival of Black anything depends on," she stated, "which is the energies of Black people—sheer energy, inventiveness and innovation, tenacity, the ability to hang on, and a contempt for those huge, monolithic institutions and agencies which do obstruct us. In other words, we must do our work."[1]

Few editors could have made that kind of statement—one that was dangerously close to being patronizing—without feeling the wrath of the people in the audience, most of whom knew all too well the ways racial discrimination influenced the publishing industry and disadvantaged Black writers. And here was Morrison saying that the responsibility for the survival of Black writing did not depend on Madison Avenue or the United States government, or anyone else for that matter. It depended on the writers alone. But Morrison was no ordinary editor. She was a published writer who had also been warmly received by the establishment, so much so that hers had become a household name in Black literary communities and beyond. She was the editor of books by Black authors who would have likely continued to languish in relative obscurity absent her determination to get their work in print at a major publishing house, and the editor of writers like Huey P. Newton, Angela Davis, and Muhammad Ali, celebrities who were able to tell their stories in their own way. If the job of the publisher was to make money by investing in the creativity of writers, then the job of the editor, she told the crowd, was to take that creativity and translate it into something readers felt was alive and needed to be captured permanently on the page.

Morrison looked from left to right at the people in the crowded auditorium, turning her head ever so slightly in a way that made everyone in the room feel seen. She eventually fixed her gaze on the men and women standing against the wall to her left. As she leaned over the podium a bit, changing her cadence when needed, she employed facial expressions skillfully to bring home her point: Selling books was no easy task. A lot of energy goes into promoting a book, she declared. "All of this energy is to do one thing—make somebody get up out of his chair and walk to a bookstore and pay hard cash for it. Pick it up. You design a book so somebody wants to touch it. . . . Somebody moves, walks out of his way . . . do something inconvenient and buy that book. All of the energies are for that." As unlikely as that might be in some cases, she noted, it could happen, and it happened regularly. People bought books.

Simply put, she argued, Black folks have enough book-buying power to have some influence in the publishing industry. That power could be the counterpoint to every act of benign neglect of Black authors and Black subjects and to most industry choices that were or felt discriminatory. Publishers would feel obliged to publish more books by Black writers if the book-buying public demanded it. Detective novels proved this point, she chided almost in passing. "You publish thirty of them a year; they're all sold, every one of them. And it's a viable part of the industry."

She was a master storyteller, and she knew it. She was being at once authoritative and circuitous. On the one hand, she implied that the impetus for change in the publishing industry had to come from Black people, not publishers. But it was also true that publishers were driven almost exclusively by cold, hard facts. And the fact of the matter was they were interested only in getting the largest number of people to buy any given book. That meant that the book most likely to sell was the one that was most commercially palatable, if not mediocre, the one that received the most attention from book reviews or paid publicity, or the one that libraries would buy. The best she could do was to publish books she thought met Black people's high standards and to do so at a reasonable price point. Books were investments, after all, whether the author was Black or white. Though she laced the comment with humor, she was quite serious about how the cost of a book could help or hurt its sales. "I always make sure that it doesn't cost more than a fifth of whiskey or dinner. And if it does that, it might last longer than a fifth of liquor," she teased. "It would certainly last longer than a dinner."

The consummate professional, Morrison took liberties with this audience. This was a rare opportunity to speak freely about the practical and harsh publishing realities that impacted all writers, not just Black ones. Bookstores, except those on a university campus, were a racket, she claimed. But bookstores were also among the places publishers counted on to sell paperback books. "They began in small towns as a front. A small bookstore usually was a place where they had some books up front, and they played pool in the back or races or betting," she said furtively. Beyond the bookstore as front, small shops that sold books also sold other items that would move, like T-shirts and cards. To make matters worse, when books sat unbought or when the turnover was too slow, the bookstore owner returned the books. So, the publisher was left with selling books mainly in department stores and chain bookstores in larger suburban towns. This, no doubt, contributed to the conjecture that 70 percent of all books marketed were sold in and around New York, New Jersey, and Connecticut.

The deck was stacked against the writer, Morrison seemed to imply. But all was not lost. A good editor could convince a publisher to take a chance on a book and to find that book a readership. One might surmise, then, that Black authors needed more committed Black editors. Yes, but the survival of Black publishing, from Black-owned publishers to white companies publishing books by Black authors and on Black subjects, Morrison argued, would depend on collaborations among those who had the expertise in the field and Black people themselves.

"This is our work," she declared. "And if we do nothing more than to continue to build one, two, or three coherent, cohesive networks that exist among all the people in the industry that contribute in some way to the publishing of Black work, it must be done. There are no quick, fast solutions to the unbelievable economic situation, to the vestiges of racism." She went on. "This is the givenness of the situation. There must be Black independent publishers. White established publishers are what established things are: bases of operation through which Black people work and containing resources that Black people can use."

Long over her allotted time but holding the audience in her hands, she resolved, "What I want to leave you with is that we are the ones. . . . No Black publisher will fail if we buy his books. We are the ones who made it possible for Black music to contain only the best. . . . All of the mediocre people were destroyed right away. We must do the same thing with the books." As she hastened to her seat, she conceded that this kind of work was not easy.

> It is difficult. It is inconvenient. . . . Don't have it [the book]? Order it, call him [the bookseller] back, harass him. No, he doesn't want to order one book. That's too bad. That's his obligation as a bookseller. Order one, two, ten and go back. Go in the bookstore if he doesn't have it. Ask him why he doesn't have it. Why doesn't he have two shelves devoted only to the books that are of interest to you? That's not their industry. It's ours. It's ours.

Morrison's remarks were a mix of trade secrets and challenges to wield untapped power and influence. While she seemed to measure every word during her prepared remarks, during the question and answer period, the gloves came off. Someone asked what could be done to combat the dire situation. "Rather than waiting for the leader or waiting for the huge magical formula," she admonished, "what is needed is commitment." She declared matter-of-factly, "All the money in the world doesn't create commitment. You can have it [money] and shoot everything that walks on four legs and decorate your office. But if you don't have the commitment, if you don't love anybody, it doesn't make any difference." Morrison was, no doubt, taking this opportunity to critique publishing mogul John H. Johnson's lack of commitment to *Black World* magazine.

Johnson had founded *Black World* in 1942 as *Negro Digest*, a

Black corollary to the popular *Reader's Digest*. Under the editorial direction of Hoyt Fuller (and Parks as associate editor), *Negro Digest* was reimagined as *Black World* and emerged as one of the most impactful magazines of its time to convey cultural and political thought, artistic expression, and social action activities of interest to African American and Pan-African people. Earlier that year, however, Johnson had abruptly discontinued publishing *Black World* without explanation. The Black Arts community especially cried foul and expressed their dismay over Johnson's clear indifference to the role the magazine played in creating a space for public debate about Black Power and Civil Rights and, critically, for literature. As the audience laughed at Morrison's teasing reference to Johnson as Parks's friend, when he was actually the reason Parks was jobless, Morrison leaned back and smiled widely. "Well, I got a little passionate, but I hope I answered your question." In a way, the demise of *Black World* signaled that the gap between the promise of the 1970s' ideal of self-determination and the disintegration of that promise by the 1980s, when Morrison resigned her post as editor, would be great.

The next question came from an attendee dressed in a three-piece suit who had perfect enunciation. He clearly fancied himself as an erudite. Directing his question at no one in particular, he wanted to know "how to go about raising the intellect of the reading public." Halfway through his long-winded question, Morrison reached into her suit jacket pocket to retrieve a cigarette. Before she could locate her lighter, she looked quickly from left to right at her fellow panelists, then grabbed the microphone, which sat between her and Harris. "No one asked me to respond," she blurted out, "but we don't need that," punctuating each word. She added, "We know how to appreciate elegance. We always have. We have always been a *very* fastidious people." The problem, in her estimation, was getting the book to the audience, not the audience's response once they had the book.

For just over forty-five minutes, Morrison fielded questions alongside the other panelists until the question and answer period finally ended. Most of the concerns about publishing would be addressed with concrete action items during the business meeting, Parks noted. What Morrison made clear, with even more insistence than the other panelists, was that commitment and self-determination were the things in highest demand. The obstacles were outsize, yes, but they were not insurmountable. Somewhere between exasperation and entreaty, she insisted:

> While there might not be many stores that are stocking Black books . . . and while there may not be many Black bookstores, while there may not be many places where editors can get reviews for their books, while there may not be many places on television, radio, and so on, that will give us the opportunity to distribute or publicize our books, there is one other thing and there's always been that other thing. That's us! We're all we got!

Everything about Toni Morrison's distinguished editorship pointed to her understanding of that one truth—that any attempt to revolutionize the publishing industry to be more inclusive of Black authors and Black stories would require an army of people united by a belief in literary and artistic excellence in Black culture. While once-vibrant sociopolitical ties dissolved into gradual disconnection and the loss of support networks through neglect and design translated into a loss of the kind of collective identity that had formed in the late 1960s, Morrison never lost sight of the belief that Black people could be everything they needed.

She knew she was not alone in that belief. She enlisted some of the brightest Black minds to join her, and they got to work trying to make a revolution, one book at a time.

CHAPTER 2

Finding Her Form

White boys are circling. These four words were all Morrison's grandmother needed to say before finalizing her plan to pack up her family and leave the small farm where they lived in rural Alabama. Their destination? Akron, Ohio, a city where a confluence of roads met and offered varied paths to a better life. Importantly, too, in Ohio there would be more safety, relatively speaking, for her young but quickly maturing daughters.

This story of movement toward an uncertain destination and deft navigation of converging roads that enabled hopeful arrivals is an apt metaphor for Morrison's life as she moved between her roles as daughter, sister, mother, teacher, editor, and writer. While she has often repeated the claim that she became a writer as a way of keeping herself company after her divorce and an editor because she had no other job prospects, the truth is Morrison's move toward an art form that could accommodate all the pieces she was had far deeper roots. Unlike the titular character of her second novel, *Sula*, Morrison escaped the recklessness that would have surely ensued had she failed to engage her "tremendous curiosity and her gift for metaphor"[1] with meaning and purpose. To understand Morrison's self-fashioning as an editor and a writer is to understand intimately the formative experiences that helped shape her sense of self.

Born Chloe Ardelia Wofford on February 18, 1931, in Lorain, Ohio, Morrison was a child of convergences of the Jim Crow era and the Great Depression. Her parents, George Wofford and Ramah Willis Wofford, were among the millions of people who left the South during the Great Migration—her father from Cartersville, Georgia, and her mother from Greenville, Alabama. Like so many who fled the South during this period, the Wofford family's departure was fueled by racial violence. When George was fifteen, two Black businessmen in his hometown were lynched, and he had seen the scarred bodies firsthand. Racial tensions similarly motivated her mother's family to leave the South. One of Ramah's relatives had been shot for refusing to surrender land that was legally his. The fact that he had no recourse to protect or defend himself, his family, or his right to own property was one of many reasons the family decided to take their chances at finding a better life elsewhere. Their first stop was Kentucky.

When the Willis children came home one day excitedly noting that they had helped explain long division to their fellow students when their teacher could not, Morrison's grandparents John and Ardelia decided it was best for them to leave that town. They had no delusions that word about young Black children who thought themselves smarter than a white teacher would quickly spread and put the family in danger of a racist attack against them and their unacceptable intelligence. John made money as a traveling violinist. The money was good, but it left Ardelia home alone with the children and vulnerable in ways she could not withstand. The family's next move, Ardelia insisted, needed to be somewhere John could work without having to travel to provide for them. Like the Woffords, they settled in Lorain, Ohio.

Twenty-five miles west of Cleveland, Lorain was a steel town near Lake Erie populated mainly by immigrants. In the neighborhoods the family lived in over the years were Italian, Greek, and Polish people; Catholic and Jewish people; people who migrated from the South, as her parents did, and people who came from Canada. Just as Morrison's parents' families had, these families settled in Lorain for the employment opportunities the sturdy steel industry offered.

The year Morrison was born began with tempered hopefulness that the US economy was beginning to recover from the 1929 stock market crash that threw the world into the Great Depression. Following a series of banking crises in Europe that same year, however, the economic situation in the US worsened for all except those who held on to whatever cash they had. The Woffords had little to none.

For most of Morrison's young life, her father earned his living primarily as a skilled welder for US Steel, though he often had more than one job. He took great pride in his work, an ethic Morrison admits she adopted as an editor and a writer. He once told her that he left his initials in the steel when he welded a perfect seam. That no one would ever see it was irrelevant. The experience of doing his job well was what mattered most to him. Her mother was a homemaker who also worked small jobs outside the home when circumstances demanded, and circumstances often did. Steady work notwithstanding, life in Lorain for the Woffords was anything but easy. The family struggled financially. Between 1931 and 1946, the year George was finally able to purchase a home, the family moved at least six times—often enough for Morrison to understand that the inability to pay meager rent to landlords meant they were cash poor, even if they were not poor in spirit.

Whatever house they found themselves in, it was always filled with music, Morrison recalled. Her grandfather, who lived nearby and visited often, still played violin every chance he could. Her mother played piano, sometimes for movie houses, and she sang everything from opera and jazz to spirituals and blues in their home. As an adult, Morrison recognized her mother's singing and her song choice as more than entertainment. It was also a meditation and a way of probing her mind, a form of discovery. Storytelling was another ever-present pastime in Morrison's family. When Ramah tired of telling her children the same ghost stories they begged her to share—stories her mother and Auntie Bell had passed down to her—Ramah made up new ones. It would be years before Morrison would realize that storytelling and nurturing the storyteller's production were creative acts that fed her need for sustained discovery.

In the same way she learned the art of storytelling from her mother at home, Morrison learned reading at home from her sister, Lois, before attending school. When she and Lois began to write an expletive on the sidewalk with chalk and their mother raged about the first few letters, Morrison could sense the power of words. The notion that words must have some mysterious meaning only fueled her appetite for reading. She set out to discover meaning—in school and on her own. Exploring ideas in school proved to be more difficult, however, since she had the distinct sense, even as a child, that the school system in Lorain was inadequate. Most of her schoolmates, she thought, were dull. She would have to find other ways to feed her curious mind at home and at school.

While it might have been the case, indeed, that the schools Morrison attended did little to challenge her, it is also true that Morrison was a uniquely smart child. She was reportedly the only student in first grade who knew how to read. But there was more to her intelligence than an ability to read. Her readily apparent intellect contributed to her family's acceptance of her as one of them but still set her apart. No one objected strongly to her decision to convert to Catholicism or to her corresponding adoption of Anthony (after Saint Anthony) as her baptismal name, for instance, even though her mother was a faithful member of the local African Methodist Episcopal church. Rather, her family allowed her certain liberties that freed her imagination and fed her determination to be something other than what she was likely to become had she simply modeled her life after that of other young Black women in Ohio.

By junior high, a teacher sent a note home to Morrison's parents saying it would be a shame if they did not make every effort to send her to college. George and Ramah, already convinced that their daughter was intellectually gifted, resolved then to save enough money to do so. Her mother picked up odd jobs, and her father went against the rules and took a second union job. When threatened with firing for doing so, he declared that he intended to send his daughter to college and was allowed to keep both jobs. Morrison, who had worked odd jobs since she was twelve, also contributed to her college fund by working at the public library, a job that fed her curious mind. Reading on her own, she gleaned, did more for her than formal coursework. School, by that point, had more significance as a social outlet than anything else. In high school, she was on the honor roll, a member of the debate team, on the yearbook staff, and in the drama club. But she had no clear, compelling career path calling out to her.

At one point, Morrison was convinced she would be a dancer. For years, she had dreamed of being the next Maria Tallchief, the Native American dancer considered to be America's first major prima ballerina. Morrison knew she was a good dancer, and unlike her sister, Lois, who was too shy to dance in front of a watching audience, Morrison found public performance thrilling. It came easily for her. Realizing the severe limitations of a young Black girl's ability to earn a living as a dancer—one who had no formal training, no less—Morrison resolved to explore options for the right creative outlet in college. She wanted desperately to leave Ohio, so she never considered attending Oberlin College, which was nearby. Importantly, too, she wanted to learn at a place where there were other smart Black people, where she would not be the only one. She chose Howard University.

Morrison was a student at Howard from 1949 to 1953, during which time she assumed the nickname "Toni," reportedly in response to repeated mispronunciations of her name. An English major and classics minor, she was a good student who was also determined to have a good time during her college years. While Morrison had given up the dream of becoming a professional dancer, she did not discard the sport altogether. Instead, she joined the Modern Dance Club at Howard, a group organized by the women's physical education department. But she also expanded her interests. She joined Alpha Chapter of Alpha Kappa Alpha Sorority, Incorporated, the nation's oldest Greek letter sorority, and frolicked among campus queens, earning the title "football sweetheart" at one point. The one place at Howard she was most fond of, however, was the stage.

Morrison arrived on campus for the fall 1949 semester, just in time to experience the residual fanfare the Howard Players created as they set sail on the SS *Stavangerfjord* cruise ship on August 31 to begin their tour in Norway, Sweden, Denmark, and Germany. The previous autumn, the Players had presented Henrik Ibsen's *The Wild Duck* on campus. Officials from the Norwegian embassy attended one performance and immediately invited the troupe to perform the play and others abroad. Morrison joined the Players, making her debut performance in Alice Gerstenberg's *Overtones*, one of the productions mounted to celebrate the troupe's return to the US. In spring 1950, she was cast as one of five children in Ernst Toller's *No More Peace*, an anti-war satire that explored the vagaries of humanity during war and peace. Performing the highly intellectual play that resisted all aspects of fascism and dictatorship made a tremendous impact on Morrison's worldview.

By 1951, Morrison's studies and her sorority activities kept her busy, but she remained committed to the theater. The following year she was cast as Elsie in William Saroyan's *The Time of Your Life* and as Cynthie, "a regular patron," in Robert Ardrey's *Jeb*. The play had opened on Broadway in 1946, starring former Howard student Ossie Davis as Jeb. During the spring 1953 season, in anticipation of the June 2 coronation for Queen Elizabeth II, the Players produced William Shakespeare's *Richard III*. Morrison received excellent reviews for her performance as Queen Elizabeth in this production and was cast again as the queen when poet, playwright, novelist, and director Owen Dodson adapted the play for a television segment he titled "Richard and the Three Queens," which aired on WMAL-TV on June 25, 1953, in Washington, DC.

For a while, it seemed like performing in the theater would be the art form Morrison identified most intimately with. Her performances with both companies were consistent, and the drama faculty at Howard—Dodson in particular, and her philosophy professor Alain Locke—were well connected to theater houses in the US and abroad. Davis was making his mark on Broadway, after leaving Howard for Harlem in 1939. And in Morrison's senior year, Roxie Roker, who had also been a Howard Player and Morrison's sorority sister, went on to study acting at the Shakespeare Institute in Stratford-upon-Avon after earning her BFA in drama at Howard in 1952. There was a clear path she could take if she decided to pursue acting seriously. In the end, she decided against it, opting to attend graduate school instead. Still, a few weeks after graduation, Morrison joined the Washington Repertory Players, an offshoot of the Howard Players, and performed with them throughout the South all summer before becoming a graduate student at Cornell.

After four years in Washington, DC, Morrison had to adjust to the colder winters in upstate New York and to the smallness of the Finger Lakes college town. If anything, Ithaca reminded her of Lorain with winds off the lake and predictably heavy snowfalls in the winter. There would be fewer sunny days than in DC, but that also meant fewer distractions. Her undergraduate years at Howard had prepared her well, but graduate studies had a rigor that would require more focus and less time for nonacademic activities.

At Cornell, graduate instruction was largely individualized study. Morrison chose American literature—not dramatic literature or creative writing, both of which were options available to her—as her major subject area. Robert Henry Elias served as her thesis chair. Joining Elias on the thesis committee was John Gaywood Linn, an assistant professor who taught classes in dramatic literature and who would later author *The Theater in the Fiction of Marcel Proust* (1966). Linn's scholarship spoke to Morrison's attraction to theater. The fact that he combined two of her interests—dramatic arts and fiction—made him an ideal person to study with. But it was the burgeoning field of American literature that tugged at her imagination. Elias had earned a reputation as a leading scholar in the area of study and was, in fact, a cofounder of the American Studies Association of New York in 1951.

While studies on Woolf and Faulkner are commonplace now, Morrison's thesis—titled "Virginia Woolf's and William Faulkner's Treatment of the Alienated"—was a rather progressive one for the time. When American literature first entered the collegiate curriculum at the end of the nineteenth century, it was considered an inferior course of study, in part because it was still in its infancy comparatively. Elias was among the faculty who resisted this impulse, giving Morrison the green light to explore an American writer (Faulkner) and a "contemporary" writer (Woolf) and their modernist texts. Even then, Morrison was interested in thinking about the ways fiction told stories history would not. Her study of Woolf and Faulkner helped to facilitate this exploration and, no doubt, gave her the impression that she, too, could participate in the invention of her own brand of fiction.

Morrison completed the requirements for the master's degree at Cornell, but she had little enthusiasm about continuing her studies and earning a doctorate in English. As quickly as she could, she returned to DC and rejoined the Washington Repertory Players. Even at Cornell, she had kept in touch with Dodson and the three other faculty she had worked with in the theater— James Butcher, John Lovell, and Anne Cooke—and she fell right in when given the opportunity to be cast as Louka in the Players' production of George Bernard Shaw's *Arms and the Man*. But Morrison had come to see acting as a hobby, not a career path, though the interpretation and performance of other's words was never far from her imagination. Through her mentors' HBCU faculty network, Morrison learned of a teaching position at Texas Southern University. The English department chair, J. Marie Mc-Cleary, a fellow Cornell graduate, received Morrison's application with great interest and made Morrison an offer to join the faculty. Happily, Morrison accepted, and a day after her oral exams for her master's degree, she moved to Houston to begin her career as a professor.

It was not long, however, before she would find her way back to DC and to Howard after her former professor and department chair, Ivan Earle Taylor, offered her a position as instructor in the Department of English. She accepted it and began a new chapter—one that would include marriage, children, divorce, and the early pages of a book that would change her life. A year after she began teaching at Howard, Morrison married Harold Morrison, a Jamaican architect. The couple had two sons—Harold Ford and Slade Kevin—before they divorced in 1964.

As she struggled to avoid being overtaken by her failing marriage, Morrison began to write again. Whatever temptation there was to suppress her urge to be an artist was now gone. She joined a writing group and shared pages of a story about a young Black girl she knew who was convinced that God was not real because God did not grant her wish for blue eyes. The group's enthusiasm about the draft encouraged Morrison to begin to take her writing more seriously. All the experiences in her life up until this point were converging and bringing her the clarity she craved. She would not be a dancer, nor would she be an actor. While teaching had provided her with a fulfilling way to make a living, it did not do enough to engage her outsize curiosity. Only what she called "a trembling respect for words" could do that.

In the seven years she was on the faculty at Howard, she had married, birthed a son who required her attention (and prepared to share that attention with another on the way), divorced, and discovered that the thing that sustained her interest the most was word work. Her varied experiences were converging to offer a picture of what could be. In acting, she expressed others' words. Thinking about philosophy and poetry with students who dubbed themselves the "Howard Poets" allowed her to use language to explore ideas. Her graduate work marked the beginning of American fiction's evolution, hinting at her potential to invent her own narratives. Teaching involved guiding others in crafting sentences and stories, a process that helped prepare her equally to become a writer and an editor.

Jobless and now a single parent, she left DC, took a quick trip to Europe, and headed back to Ohio to live with her parents and to catch her breath until the future became clearer. The fact that she did not have a job was sobering, but it was far from disastrous. If nothing else, she was that much closer to finding her form. That clarity may have sprung forth largely from marital turmoil, but her potential for self-fashioning was always present, patiently waiting to be unearthed.

CHAPTER 3

There Needs to Be a Record

Being back in Ohio felt familiar to Morrison, too familiar in fact. More than ten years had passed since she had lived in Lorain. And while the city had not changed very much, she had. Being pregnant with her second son at the same time she was coming to terms with her divorce posed a personal challenge for Morrison for sure. The fact that she was jobless, however, foretold an impending financial crisis if she did not secure employment soon. Her mother and her sister, Lois, assured her that she would survive this time in her life, as she had all others and as the family had done many times over the years. Admittedly, Morrison appreciated being at home and having the care and attention her mother gave her during this pregnancy—something she sorely missed with her first pregnancy with Harold Ford. Worry would solve nothing. All she could do was write when she felt moved to do so and do the hardest thing of all: wait. Ironically, it proved to be the option that yielded the best result.

As the story goes, Morrison received three copies of the same issue of *The New York Review of Books* where an ad for an executive editor appeared.[1] "The position offers an opportunity to influence the literature and English programs presented in elementary and high schools throughout the country," the ad announced. Preference would be given to candidates "between the ages of 35 and 45, with a master's degree (PhD, if possible) in English, comparative literature, or education (psychology)." Employment rules related to age discrimination would not come for years. While the ideal candidate would have some teaching experience, it was not necessary. Knowledge of "content, curriculum and new education trends," however, was. The magazine's subscription department error (of sending not one but three copies of the issue) was not coincidental, Morrison's mother insisted. It was a sign that Morrison should apply.

The announcement had been placed by L. W. Singer, a small publishing house in Syracuse that had recently been acquired by Random House.[2] Morrison's master's degree from nearby Cornell was a notch in her belt. While the job notice did not say as much, the company was aware of its need to include books about Black people as a part of its varied textbook series. Internal Singer reports cited the need for books on (or commentary about) Harriet Tubman, Booker T. Washington, and Martin Luther King Jr., for instance, as a part of their "Leaders in Developing American Freedom" series; about George Washington Carver and Charles Drew in the "Leaders in Industry" series; about Langston Hughes, Louis Armstrong, and Marian Anderson in the "Leaders in the Arts" series; and about Jackie Robinson in their "Gentle Heroes" series. No doubt Morrison's experience as a faculty member at Texas Southern and at Howard made her an appealing candidate. She also had the benefit of an upcoming publication where she was one of four collaborators (along with Alice W. Grant, Joan B. Murrell, and Eleanor Traylor) for a textbook—*College Reading Skills*, which

Lettie J. Austin published with her Howard colleagues as a Borzoi Book with Knopf.

Not long after she applied by writing to Box Z at *The New York Review of Books,* as the notice advised, Morrison heard back from Singer. The publisher invited her to come to the office for an interview. Allowing their spirit of adventure to override any concerns Morrison had about moving so far away with two young children (she had, by then, given birth to her second son, Slade), she and Lois packed their father's Oldsmobile and made the trip from Ohio to Syracuse. Before midyear, Morrison received the good news that she would be jobless no more. But the idea of returning to Upstate New York with two young sons and no family to help her raise them was daunting. Though it had been years since she lived in Ithaca, only sixty miles from Syracuse, being paid to work with books all day was undeniably appealing. Reading came as easily to her as breathing. There was plenty of good work to be done. With the Civil Rights Movement in full swing, serious change seemed to finally be on the horizon for Black people in the United States. "I thought it was important for people to be in the streets," she noted. "But that couldn't last. You needed a record. It would be my job to publish the voices, the books, the ideas of African Americans. And that would last."[3]

In the same year Morrison joined Singer, Doubleday Publishing Company launched its Zenith Books series, which proved that it was possible to leave a lasting record, especially on the impressionable minds of young Black students who were hungry to see themselves in textbooks. As one of very few Black editors in publishing at the time, Charles Harris convinced Nelson Doubleday III and John Sargent to approve Zenith Books as a supplementary reading series, written on a sixth-grade reading level, that focused on African American history. Chicago,

Boston, New York, Philadelphia, the District of Columbia, and Los Angeles school districts adopted the books as supplementary materials. Over time, Morrison would follow Harris's lead in more ways than one.

A year later, in 1966, congressman Adam Clayton Powell chaired a subcommittee of the House Labor and Education Committee, which held a congressional hearing on "Books for Schools and the Treatment of Minorities." Powell's report confirmed Morrison's belief that textbooks, like so much literature and sociology, could not be trusted to help Black people know the truth of their own cultural sources. But it also inspired other publishers who were further along in their planning than Singer was to announce their minority readers' series and to release their first books in the series. Textbook publishing, when done well, could be lucrative. And most firms intended to stake their claims. By 1967, there were six series—Follett's Great Cities Reading Program; Macmillan's Bank Street Readers; Doubleday's Zenith series; Benziger's Land of the Free; Holt, Rinehart and Winston's Holt Urban Social Studies series; and Webster, McGraw-Hill's Skyline series—that set the pace for multiethnic textbooks.

As hopeful as Morrison was about adding Singer to the list of publishers that had a series expressly for minority readers, she would not get that opportunity. Her work at Singer was limited instead, by and large, to literature anthologies for grades nine through twelve, including work with the St. Thomas More poetry and prose series. With six new series in the mix, Random House could not justify allowing Singer to establish a competing one. And the initial plan Singer had involved adding Black trailblazers in various fields to their existing classic American series, not launching a new one. Another consequence of Random House's acquisition of Singer was also in play. Singer was finally closing and being fully absorbed by Random House. A few years earlier, immediately after the acquisition, Random House founder Bennett Cerf had sent his second-in-command, Robert Bernstein, to check on the textbook division at Singer. While there, Bernstein met Morrison and was struck immediately by her intellect. When the time came to close the Singer offices in Syracuse, Bernstein remembered the brilliant young woman whom he thought would be a good trade editor and made certain that she was among those invited to join the team at Random House in Manhattan.

Morrison was reluctant to raise her sons alone in a big city, but she knew the likelihood of creating a lasting impact would grow exponentially if she agreed to join one of the largest publishers in the United States. Critically, too, she was writing more and more. As a writer, being in New York City would be a great boon. She and her ex-husband remained estranged, and she had little interest in his input. The decision was all hers to make, and she felt good about the opportunities she and the boys would have there. By the time she moved her family to Manhattan, she had completed a draft of what would become *The Bluest Eye* and had successfully pitched it to an editor at Holt, Rinehart and Winston. When the novel received a generous review from famed *New York Times* critic John Leonard, her anonymity as a writer was compromised. Chloe the editor and Toni the writer became one. The critical success of *The Bluest Eye* prompted Bernstein to recruit one of his editors to join the firm as an author. Recognizing Morrison's talent in both regards, Bernstein suggested she talk to two people—Jim Silberman, editor in chief at Random House, and Robert Gottlieb, editor in chief at Knopf. She took Bernstein's advice and met with both men. The choice was easy. Gottlieb had read and admired *The Bluest Eye*, so he would be her editor. And she would cut her teeth in trade while working with Silberman, becoming the first Black woman senior editor at Random House in the process.

Random House's liberal approach to book acquisitions, coupled with Bernstein's steadfast admiration for her apparent talent, made Morrison's introduction into editing trade books (books that could be sold widely to a general audience) unusually easy. Unlike other houses, Random House did not require editors to present their books to a committee. If an editor could convince the editor in chief that a book was worth pursuing, so be it. And with Charles Harris's surreptitious resignation from Random House—tensions were high when he left to become the founding director of the newly established Howard University Press, an inverse of Morrison's move from Howard to Random House—Morrison was on track to become the preeminent editor for the firm's list of Black authors. While it meant that she would be without another Black editor to infuse more diversity into the firm's roster of employees, Harris's departure provided a rare opportunity for Morrison to move up the ranks quickly. She met the occasion with confidence, even as she was troubled by the sense that her rise was a direct result of Harris's fall. She was all too familiar with practices that allowed only one minority to succeed at any given time in white corporate culture.

Far from feeling adrift in her new position, Morrison embraced the fortuitous opportunity to help guide a major publisher during the period when the Black Studies movement in academia was in full swing. Books that could provide critical frameworks for analyzing systemic racism, empower readers through shared knowledge, and inspire communities to advocate for social justice were vital. She was at the center of a significant historical and cultural moment with little warning, and she stepped into her role with no hesitation. The culture at Random House offered her a unique opportunity to do this work.

As an imprint of the larger publisher of the same name, Little Random reflected the vision of its founders, Bennett Cerf and Donald Klopfer, and the ambition of the Knopfs after Random House acquired the publishing house of Alfred A. Knopf in 1960. In the 1930s, Cerf not only began to sign leading literati authors; he also won the right to publish an uncensored version of James Joyce's *Ulysses*. When Random House published the novel in 1934, following a favorable court ruling declaring that the novel was not obscene, it was the first edition of *Ulysses* to be printed in the United States. Then, in 1947, the firm began publishing reference books, starting with the *American College Dictionary*. This financially lucrative title gave Random House great flexibility in terms of pursuing the books that might not be immediately profitable but would feed the editors' taste for high literary art. Even if Morrison was not aware of Cerf's practice of giving his editors free rein, she benefited from this legacy.

Like Random House, Knopf had a history of publishing progressive titles. Founded by Alfred A. and Blanche Wolf Knopf, the firm, for its earliest days, was committed to publishing young, emerging writers who were less likely to find a home at older publishing houses because of these houses' resistance to diversifying their pool of authors. During the Harlem Renaissance, for instance, more titles by Black authors appeared on the company's list than on any other publisher's. The fact that Blanche Knopf often acted as a de facto literary agent for the firm's Black authors, helping them place their shorter works in journals and magazines during the Renaissance and afterward, suggested that the Knopfs' relationship with Black writers involved something more than capitalist interest. While Knopf's actions were not purely altruistic, their willingness to publish and promote Black authors' work at a time when other houses did not cannot be denied. Many years later, Morrison would be on the receiving end of this liberality as a writer at Knopf and as an editor at Little Random, both of which Random House owned.

By the time Morrison joined Random House, the firm was caught in the crosshairs of the failed attempts at racial integration that characterized the 1950s and Black people's growing intolerance for the slow pace and modest gains of the Civil Rights Movement. The period was ripe with demands for racial justice and buttressed by upstart Black journals and Black presses that reflected the sentiments of a Black populace unwilling to sacrifice Black life and culture for the sake of America. The Black Power Movement, as the more radical offshoot of the Civil Rights Movement, ushered in an unparalleled period of cultural transformation that mainstream publishers could not ignore. Morrison saw her job as documenting stories that might otherwise go untold. There would need to be a record.

CHAPTER 4

Escaping the Chrysalis

Morrison wasted no time jumping into the Black Studies fray. On November 21, 1968, a group of Black students occupied the president's office at the University of Wisconsin–Madison, demanding a more racially diverse campus. Ninety-four students were arrested and expelled. With tensions high, the university scrambled to address some of the concerns the students raised. A subcommittee on new curriculum in the American Institutions Program quickly developed a course to be offered for an Afro-American concentration. Professors Fred Hayward in political science and John Willis in history were designated as co-ordinators. The press release announced:

> The University of Wisconsin will offer an experimental course titled Afro-American Cultural and Intellection Tradition beginning with the second semester, open to all undergraduates for three credits. . . .
>
> Guest lecturers already signed up to meet with the class include Hoyt Fuller, editor of Negro Digest; Prof. Hollis Lynch,

director of the Black Studies Program, State University of New York at Buffalo; Kenneth Goode, assistant to the chancellor, University of California, Berkeley; Prof. Adelaide Hill, Boston University; Claude Brown, author of *Manchild in the Promised Land*; Chloe A. Morrison, author and senior editor at Random House; and Andrew Billingsley, associate professor of social welfare and assistant chancellor for academic affairs, University of California. Others will be announced later.[1]

The visit to Wisconsin was not just an opportunity for Morrison to reconnect with her former student, Claude Brown, whose novel *Manchild in the Promised Land* she had edited informally while he was a student at Howard. It was also an opportunity to see firsthand how the Black Power Movement spurred students' desires to have more opportunities for formal intellectual engagement with Black traditions on college campuses. It had been more than five years since she had left her job as a full-time English and humanities instructor at Howard, which had its own student protest and demonstrations over Black curriculum a few months before the Madison campus erupted.

Of the thirteen demands the students presented at the conference they organized and held on February 3–8, 1969, four focused on the establishment of a Black Studies department and employment of twenty Black faculty to organize the department and to develop Black Studies courses. Even before her scheduled visit to the campus, Morrison had been thinking generally about the kind of books she could propose, especially books that had general audience potential in the trade market, that would speak to the demands for new Black Studies courses—courses being mounted nationwide—students and faculty were making. The first book Morrison had in mind that spoke to this need was one she was confident she could edit well as a former literature professor but one that would stretch her in terms of content awareness. What was needed at a foundational level was a book that could course correct the assumption that Africa was without a rich cultural heritage. An anthology of African literature could do this as well as anything. A less confident person might have been concerned that choosing an anthology—essentially a textbook—as her first trade book would be construed by her peers as proof that she was not yet ready for the big leagues, that she would rely on what she knew rather than jump into the fray. Morrison, however, saw the decision as a first opportunity to prove that she could expand the limits of what publishers thought would appeal to a general audience and, by extension, would sell well enough to meet the profit expectations of trade books.

The idea for the anthology came to Morrison after being drawn to African literature during visits to Africa House, a cultural center in New York. Books by African writers were everywhere. The more she read, the more she realized how free these writers seemed to be—free most especially from the need to respond to racism. Even as the burden of colonialism persisted, the writers seemed to be talking to other Black people, not to white colonialists to whom the authors had nothing to prove. "Whatever these African writers were talking about," she told *Black Issues Book Review* founding editor Susan McHenry, "it wasn't about color."

> They weren't explaining anything to white people, though they may have commented on social conditions under colonialism. In one of Chinua Achebe's stories, for example: A man leaves his home and saying goodbye to his wife, he touches her hair—a very small subtle gesture you'd never see in Black writing in

America back then. I realized that with all the books I'd read by contemporary Black American writers—men that I admired, or was sometimes disturbed by—I felt they were not talking to me. I was sort of eavesdropping as they talked over my shoulder to the real (white) reader. Take Ralph Ellison's *Invisible Man*: That title alone got me. Invisible to whom?[2]

Morrison had begun to execute this project of dismissing the white gaze in her own fiction. But taking up this work in her editorship required far more nuance. Publishers wanted books that appealed to general audiences, and textbooks were the most conservative in this regard. Teaching some and reminding others that African literature was a long, rich tradition that far exceeded the stereotypical ways Africans and their literature were presented was delicate work. So when she visited Madison and learned about a summer language program featuring eight African languages—Swahili, Hausa, Amharic, Yoruba, Berber, Wolof, Fula, and Sango—being organized in response to the student demands, she made a point to scout faculty who could do the delicate work well and whom she could recruit to serve as editors of the anthology she had in mind.

After extended conversations with Edris Makward, who was slated to teach Wolof in the program, Morrison was certain she had found her first collaborator. At the time, Makward was a new assistant professor of African literature—having earned an MA from the University of Paris–Sorbonne and a PhD from the University of London. As was the trend then, the African languages and literature department at the university had a virtually all-white faculty, with Makward being an important exception. His position as junior faculty notwithstanding, he was already an established figure in national African studies conversations. He was very active in the African Studies Association (ASA), the major professional organization for African studies professors at the time, and he was a published author. A Gambian by birth, Makward had written the foreword to *Growing Up African: Black Africans Recount Their Childhoods in Tribal, Colonial and Independent Africa*, which Jay David and Helise Harrington edited and William Morrow published. He had also written the introduction to Collier Books' 1970 reprint of Ferdinand Oyono's *Houseboy*.

When Morrison suggested to Makward that he select a coeditor for the project, he invited Leslie Lacy to assist. Like Makward, Lacy had an established reputation in the field of African studies. A graduate of the University of Southern California for BA and MA degrees; the University of California, Hastings, for a law degree; the University of Ghana for an MS degree; and the University of London for a PhD, Lacy had lectured in African history, politics, and literature at Howard University, New York University, and the New School for Social Research. In 1969, he published the secondary school textbook *Black Africa on the Move*, a sixty-four-page book that described the people and culture and provided a brief history of African countries south of the Sahara and their continuing struggle for independence. And in 1970, he published *The Rise and Fall of a Proper Negro: An Autobiography* with Macmillan and *Cheer the Lonesome Traveler: The Life of W. E. B. DuBois*, a young adult book illustrated by James Barkley and published at Dial. As a member of the Black American expatriate community in Ghana during the Kwame Nkrumah years, Lacy had met DuBois in Accra in 1963 and counted among his peers Maya Angelou, Julian Mayfield, Tom Feelings, and a host of other well-known artists who fled the United States and racial discrimination for the newly independent African nation.[3] Morrison agreed that Lacy was an excellent choice.

While there had been anthologies of African literature published as trade books, as a textbook, *Contemporary African Literature* was one of the first of its kind. The target audience for the book (which had an accompanying instructor's manual) was senior high school and freshman college students. Morrison was clear about the book's appeal. She told Jim Smith of the college department that the "anthology should have a great deal of appeal for teachers of Black or Afro-American studies, world literature, world cultures, and humanities. Although primarily intended for eleventh- and twelfth-grade students." Though the material was generally appropriate for upper-track tenth-grade students, she argued that "possibilities [we]re also good for college sales."[4] As one of many books developed in response to public school integration and to demands that public school curricula at least begin to try to reflect diverse cultures, the anthology, Morrison knew, would fill a gap immediately.

There was no denying that the current interest in Black or Afro-American studies was strong and growing. That interest was rooted in and pre-supposed a curiosity about an African heritage. But, by and large, attentiveness to that heritage had been obscured. An anthology of African literature could help correct this. Morrison mapped the need this way:

> The fact that African literature has been largely neglected can be accounted for by the fact that the educational and literary community has been very slow to discover that African literature is something more than a collection of primitive folktales.
>
> The purpose of this anthology will be to gather in one volume twentieth century African literature which 1) reveals the talent, points of view, interests and culture of contemporary African writers; 2) complements the African history text in

preparation by the Social Studies Department; 3) extends the awareness and perception of American students (both Black and white) to African people, their literature, traditions, problems, and culture.[5]

Heightened interest in Africa and its cultures had reached its peak during the 1960s when Black Arts Movement artists began to reveal the ways the look to Africa could empower African Americans, many of whom were beginning to consider Africa as their homeland. The African independence movements of the 1960s, too, rejected stereotypical portrayals of Africa and offered, instead, a view of African cultures as rich and diverse. What the anthology made clear was that African literature, both written and oral, existed long before a colonial presence and that much of the varied literature that emerged after this presence did so on its own terms rather than in response to a white gaze.

"Africa was discovered by Africans," Makward and Lacy wrote, making the point that Africans could write for and to themselves quite explicitly. There was also the understanding that *Contemporary African Literature* could not discharge its teaching function. "The popular view of Africa in America is distorted," they noted in the book's introduction; "it varies from a cloying romanticism to staggering ignorance, and a vague fear of that which is remote. . . . If we are to get on with the real discovery of Africa we must listen to Africans."[6] And so the Africans speak. The book's impulse to get on with the real discovery of some truth by allowing peoples to speak for themselves is emblematic of Morrison's editorship in many ways. She and the editors made no effort to limit the texts to those written to a white audience or to those that could be easily understood in a Western context. Rather, the tales, fiction, poetry, drama, and nonfiction alike were informed by social, political, and cultural experiences and traditions that challenged the primacy of Western ideals as universal. Ideally, this approach would prompt readers to understand that there were multiple worldviews, that Western ways of thinking and being were one among many.

Morrison also challenged Makward and Lacy to choose selections that revealed the diversity of African thought. Each section featured literature that exposed a range of social, political, and cultural circumstances as dictated by geography. As they decided with more specificity what intellectual work they wanted the book to do, Morrison, Makward, and Lacy committed to having the anthology explore critical questions that were emerging in relation to African literature. In what languages should the texts be written and to what end? Who was the primary audience for African literature published in the West? What was the African writer's duty, with respect to the self and to the legacy of colonialism? (E.g., what happened and what was lost?) What exactly should African literature reach for, and how might the internal conflict about its aspiration best be resolved? The anthology was as invested in philosophical impulses as it was in artistry.

As Makward and Lacy noted in their introduction, part of the work of the anthology was to "unstick the romanticism" of Africa, "to curtail the ignorance" about the continent and its literature, and "to eliminate the fear" Americans associated with all things remote. They reminded readers of Chinua Achebe's declaration that African societies "'were not mindless but frequently had a philosophy of great depth and value and beauty, that they had poetry and, above all, they had dignity.'"[7] Makward and Lacy were also careful to point out the variety of approaches African writers took in writing literature—some reflective of the old, oral literary tradition of Africa, some fully aware of the ancient tradition of African literature before the invasion of white settlers, some influenced by Negritude, and some focused largely on the literary search for historical, cultural, and traditional roots. Significantly, though, all the authors included in the anthology were "writing from a context that [was] essentially different from that of any European or American writer we may be tempted to compare them with." The reader was to bear in mind, the editors warned, that the texts they included were "describing social, cultural, and political relationships which may not exist in the West."

While preparing the book, Morrison, Makward, and Lacy talked often, sent proofs back and forth via mail, and met several times in New York to discuss the selections for the anthology. Morrison's input on the textual selections was significant. And the choice of illustrations for the book was singularly hers. Random House agreed to fund a trip to Africa for Makward to get images he imagined best corresponded with the book's selections and objectives, but he was unable to take time off from teaching to do so. So, Morrison—working closely with the design team, which comprised Herb Lubalin, Walter Norfleet, and Shareen Brysac—made the selections for the thirty-six photos that introduced the book's different sections and the cover art from a library of images available to her for use. Perhaps because it was a textbook or because it was her first book and she was so intimately involved in its conception, Morrison was cited in the book's prefatory pages as the "project editor," an oddity in the publishing world where the in-house editor typically goes unacknowledged in a book's credits.

The anthology contained sixty-five selections—five tales and legends, sixteen short stories, six novel excerpts, thirty poems, two drama excerpts, and six essays. The tales and legends featured previously published stories that honored African traditions and their tendency to reveal the ethic of living in community. The questions at the end of the first section prompted readers to think about the norms of good behavior and the morals of the cultures represented, to consider how people come to understand human nature, and to identify the allegories and symbolism in the tales and myths. While the tales and legends were anonymous, the short stories included were written by emerging and established writers from Ghana, Kenya, Morocco, Sierra Leone, South Africa, and Zimbabwe. There was similar range in the style and form, from satire to abstract to realist coming of age.

The novel excerpts included sections from Camara Laye's *The Radiance of the King*, Ferdinand Oyono's *The Old Man and the Medal*, James Ngugi's *A Grain of Wheat*, Mongo Beti's *The Poor Christ of Bomba* (*Le Pauvre Christ de Bomba*), Ousmane Sembène's *The Money Order*, and Chinua Achebe's *Things Fall Apart*. Following Morrison's advice, the editors introduced most of the novel excerpts with a headnote that summarized the novel, first, then provided a preview of the excerpt. The section concluded with questions that challenged the reader to put the novels in conversation with each other and to explore various aspects of African culture as portrayed by the novel's protagonists. The photographs between the fiction and poetry sections, all of which Morrison selected, paralleled the geographical variation that characterizes the poets' nationalities. In the thirty poems, the editors include poets from Angola, Congo, Gambia, Ghana, Madagascar, Malawi, Mali, Nigeria, Senegal, Sierra Leone, South Africa, and Uganda. It was important to Morrison and to the editors that the whole of African literature be considered. So, there were poems of love, of resistance, of identity, and of conflict.

While the drama section was much shorter than the others, including excerpts from just two plays, the inclusion of Wole Soyinka's *The Strong Breed* and Athol Fugard's *Blood Knot* was meant to introduce the reader to the primacy of theater in attempts to dramatize the colonial situation all over Africa. If we consider performances at festivals, rituals, and cultural expressions, African theater's rich history predated colonialism by thousands of years. But the editors were also keenly aware of the richness of theater that emerged in Ghana, Nigeria, and South Africa especially during African independence movements. The anthology's final section on nonfiction included essays from John S. Mbiti, Chinweizu, Lewis Nkosi, Achebe, Es'kia Mphahlele, and Léopold Senghor. The essays took up now familiar themes—varying points of view on Negritude; distinctly African concepts of time, progress, and history; the question of human dignity; views on using English to write African literature; and articulations of the relation of language to culture. While Chinweizu is the only author in the anthology Morrison later worked with as an editor, the impact of the anthology as her first publication as editor was tremendous. *Contemporary African Literature* quietly announced Morrison's editorial aesthetic to bring to as large an audience as possible explorations of interior Black life with minimal interest in talking to or being consumed by an imagined white reader.

If the anthology brought lesser-known writers to readers' attention, another book Morrison secured a contract for that year was one that had a waiting audience. It was a proposed collection of previously published essays by the jailed Black Panther leader Huey P. Newton. Aware of how interested the reading public was in hearing from and understanding the Black Panther Party, Random House published books by a number of Panther affiliates between 1969 and 1972: Eldridge Cleaver's *Post-Prison Writings and Speeches* in 1969, Bobby Seale's *Seize the Time: The Story of the Black Panther Party and Huey P. Newton* in 1970, Stokely Carmichael's *Stokely Speaks: Black Power Back to Pan-Africanism* and the volume of essays *Look for Me in the Whirlwind: The Collective*

Autobiography of the New York 21 in 1971, George Jackson's *Blood in My Eye* and Huey P. Newton's *To Die for the People* in 1972, the latter of which gave Morrison the opportunity to shape the narrative about a critical figure in the Black Power movement.[8]

Morrison's work with Newton began with her light editing of the statement he prepared for the Revolutionary Memorial Service for George Jackson, which was published as the afterword for *Blood in My Eye*. Random House's interest in signing Newton up for a book preceded his contribution to Jackson's book, however. In December 1968, while Newton was still in jail for allegedly killing Oakland Police Department officer John Frey, executive director John Simon wrote to Raymond Procunier, director of the Department of Corrections in Sacramento, requesting that "reportorial privileges" be extended to *Ramparts* journalist Robert Avakian, whom Random House had assigned to work on a book on Newton. Procunier wrote back shortly thereafter that Avakian might be allowed to conduct one interview with Newton at some point in the future, pending approval from Newton's warden. The request for a series of interviews was denied not only to Avakian but to all "authors of books, producers of television documentaries, magazine writers, and free lancers," supposedly because the interviews that were conducted in the months prior "had an adverse effect on his [Newton's] [institutional] adjustment." Newton had been "quite cooperative with institution authorities prior to these interviews," Procunier claimed. "He assumed his current uncooperative posture immediately thereafter."[9]

Newton's storied battle with police officers and correctional authorities dated back to 1966, when he cofounded the Black Panther Party with Seale. The Party grew quickly from a local organization in Oakland to a national organization garnering media attention. On May 2, 1967, not quite six months after its founding, the Party made national headlines when a group of Panthers took up arms, appearing before the California state assembly carrying rifles, pistols, and shotguns to protest the Mulford Act. This act repealed the law that allowed people to carry loaded weapons and made the Panther Patrols (which observed police to deter abuse, among other things) illegal. The Panthers alerted the media in advance of their intent, and coverage was comprehensive. Surely, there would be immediate ramifications for the stunt.

On October 28, 1967, Officer Frey alerted dispatch that he was about to stop a "known Black Panther vehicle." It was regular practice to use these stops to issue tickets or to arrest a member with an outstanding warrant. At some point during the stop, Newton was outside of the car. An altercation ensued, and Frey was killed. Another officer, Herbert Heanes, who arrived on the scene after Frey made the stop, was wounded. Newton was shot before he was arrested. The defense claimed that Newton was unconscious when Frey was shot. Newton speculated that perhaps Frey had been shot accidentally by his fellow officer. Newton maintained that he had no weapon, only a lawbook, which the Panthers kept with them to remind the police that they knew their rights. According to the defense, an angry Frey shot Newton in the abdomen and in the thigh. Newton said he remembered nothing other than the sound of a volley of shots after having been shot himself.

Even without knowing exactly what happened at the scene, many assumed that the Panthers' notoriety would create bias against Newton. The Party, in coalition with the Peace and Freedom Party, which was largely an anti-war political organization, launched the "Free Huey" campaign on February 17, Newton's birthday. The campaign kicked off with a five-thousand-person rally at the Oakland Auditorium to support Newton and his legal defense fund. Stokely Carmichael, H. Rap Brown, and James

Forman—prominent members of the Student Nonviolent Coordinating Committee (SNCC)—spoke at the rally, making clear that the less militant civil rights group supported Newton as well. When Newton's trial began on July 15, 1968, thousands of demonstrators gathered to show their solidarity with him. But on September 28, 1968, a jury found Newton guilty of manslaughter, and he was sentenced to two to fifteen years. Coordinated rallies at federal district courts in twenty major cities were held on May 4, 1969. Newton's image as a national figure who could not be ignored was solidified. When the California Appellate Court reversed the conviction and ordered a new trial and two subsequent trials ended in hung juries, resulting in a dismissal of the charges, Newton was released. Interest in a book explaining his positions was more desirable than ever. For Newton, the money earned from book sales was also a motivating factor.

In October 1971, Party attorney David G. Lubell sent a manuscript consisting mainly of a selection of Newton's previously published essays to editor in chief Silberman, suggesting that a letter from George Jackson (who had just been killed while allegedly attempting to escape from San Quentin prison) could provide a dramatic introduction to the book. Lubell knew that Random House was a publisher sympathetic to the Panthers. But he also knew that he needed a specific angle when he pitched the project. The essays would work well as a book, he argued. Newton's political and philosophical development became clearer "as one proceeds chronologically from one essay to the next."[10]

Morrison's review of the draft after a quick read was mixed. The early pieces were "naïve . . . awkward, and inaccurate," she suggested to Jim Silberman, who had invited her to read the draft. "But some of the later ones are good. . . . All together [the essays] show the development of his thought (and it *does* develop, mature) and there is some wide-open criticism of his own party. Very healthy."[11] She recommended deleting the weak essays that were submitted and editing all of those that were to be included, even those that had been previously published. Morrison felt strongly that "the Panthers and their prose should be given the benefit of editing and thus be shown in its best light." The introduction, she noted, "must be strong and strongly analytical of both the party and the prose."[12]

Morrison and Newton's corresponding relationship was convivial, and the production of the book was collaborative, even beyond necessity. Perhaps concerned about the limits of his burgeoning intellect, Newton frequently asked Morrison to assist with syntax in short pieces he sent to make them read better. In addition to making the edits as needed, Morrison helped select the pictures to be included in the book, at one point directing Gwen Fontaine, whom Newton later married, to send specific images Morrison had seen in a supplement of the *Black Panther* newspaper. She also worked with Joe Kraft in the legal department to address those elements of the essays that could be deemed libelous. Among the comments about which she was most concerned were those in the essay "On the Middle East," where Newton claimed that Stokely Carmichael was a CIA agent, and those in the essay where Newton discussed Eldridge Cleaver's defection from the Party. Kraft and Morrison considered every angle regarding statements that might land them in court. When they could, they weighed the risk and possible damages against Newton's conviction that his interpretation of the truth should be told. The fact that the statements had already appeared in print made their decision easier.

Even amid complaints that a curious public knew too little about him as a person, Newton convinced Morrison that *To Die for the People* should focus on the practice, theory, and ideology that informed his thinking and the Party's essence instead of using the book to offer personal reflections. In this way, the collection reinforced characterizations of Newton as highly disciplined in his published writing and speeches, even if the same was not true of his day-to-day life. He and Morrison kept in focus the goal of the book, which was to collect in one place a map of his thinking. He was determined to shift the Party's focal point from armed revolution to the survival programs ("survival pending revolution"), and the book could help him do that. The Party understood the racialized lens through which Black Americans rightly viewed the world, but Newton knew that coalition and international politics were necessary elements of the revolution. To help make this point, Morrison helped him arrange the book to reiterate the idea that revolution is a process that must be practiced in community with others, not just analyzed or theorized in relative isolation.

Because of Newton's notoriety, Morrison did not have to worry very much about marketing the book the way she would have for an unknown or lesser-known author. Still, she sent copies of the bound galleys to the usual suspects—editors at *Library Journal*, *Kirkus*, *Atlantic Monthly*, *Harper's*, *The New York Times Book Review*, *Book World*, *Saturday Review*, and the *LA Times*. And she sent out appeals to editors of almost fifty Black outlets Random House had on its list of venues that attracted Black readers. With minimal editorial work to do on the book, since the essays were already complete, Morrison could focus on shaping the reading public's understanding about the book's importance.

She announced the book this way on its editorial fact sheet: "More than a series of position papers, this collection 1. calls into question the institutions, values, and systems that undergird the American Empire and 2. traces the development of the Party's political raison d'être from Self-defense to Nationalism to Internationalism to 'Intercommunalism.'" Morrison was determined to position Newton as both reflective and critical. "With rare candor," she wrote, "Newton acknowledges internal struggle and rivalries within the Party, describes what he believes are errors in judgment in the Party line behavior, and proposes courses of action to rectify these errors." This was important work in Morrison's estimation. His ideas were not all smoothed out; rather, they were sometimes at odds one with another. "Contradictions are useful," though, she opined. They "clarify and advance the struggle": And in Newton's view it was only this posture of honesty, reanalysis, and the acceptance of the changing nature of reality that will keep the Party relevant and healthy.[13] She thought the range of essays was impressive. There were formal pieces that were authoritative, less formal pieces that were more humanistic, and speeches and interviews that were more conversational. There was something for every type of reader.

When *To Die for the People* was published, Morrison wrote to Newton commending him for a job well done.

My feelings about the book . . . are that it is one you should be very proud of. The most striking feature is its reflection of the many facets and strengths of the party.

All in all it is truly a remarkable collection and should do a great deal to educate the public about this country, this world as well as the Party. It was a genuine pleasure working with you and all of those who helped.[14]

Despite the positive exchanges between Morrison and Newton and those who assisted with the book, Newton published his autobiography a year later with Harcourt Brace Jovanovich, not with Random House. Losing Newton to another publisher through no fault of her own stung. But she could not help but to be pleased with the fact that *To Die for the People* was among the first three nonfiction books she had published as a trade editor—and all in one year.[15] These were books of which she could be immensely proud. She had stepped into her new role ready to meet the challenge before her. Each manuscript was different, but she approached each with the same skill—guiding the author toward clarity and shaping the manuscript to help it achieve maximum impact. With a strong sense of purpose as her guide and opportunity as her fortune, Morrison was more confident than ever that she could leave an indelible mark as an editor on a publishing industry that was not yet quite sure what to make of her ambition.

CHAPTER 5

Taking Flight

Much of the editorial groundwork Morrison laid in the previous two years while she worked on the first books on her list continued to bear fruit in 1974 when she published Boris Bittker's *The Case for Black Reparations*, Melville Herskovits's *Cultural Relativism: Perspectives in Cultural Pluralism*, and George T. Land's *Grow or Die: The Unifying Principle of Transformation*. The relationships forged and manuscripts cultivated in these early years of her editorship reflected Morrison's agenda to publish books that could enrich the cultural landscape while addressing important social issues whenever she could.

As editor in chief, Silberman had deep respect for editorial autonomy and did what he could to match Morrison's interests with projects he thought the firm would do well to pursue. So when Bittker sent a letter and table of contents for what would be published as *The Case for Black Reparations* to Random House in the fall of 1971, Silberman thought of Morrison immediately since she had expressed to him an interest in working on books especially relevant to Black history and culture. And the fact that she was still building her list allowed him to pass the inquiry along to her without concern that she was already overrun with manuscripts. Bittker's proposal also had two points of connection that prompted Silberman to offer her the project. First, the reparations conversation was part and parcel of the Black Studies curriculum Morrison was attentive to, and Bittker had developed his course in response to students' call for a more diverse curriculum following the infamous 1970 New Haven Black Panther trials. Relatedly, Morrison's work on *To Die for the People* around the same time Bittker engaged Random House established an evident synergy Silberman wanted to take advantage of.

Once she reviewed Bittker's materials, Morrison quickly responded, expressing her interest in a book on the problem of group compensation for slave labor. If the book offered a way to break the stronghold of white supremacy through a legal argument proffered by a scholar, she was all for it. Bittker was a tax law professor who taught at Yale at a time when "Yale Law School was at the epicenter of struggles over the place of the university and law in the maintenance of . . . the 'white power structure.'"[1] When New Haven prosecutor Arnold Markle charged national Panther leaders Ericka Huggins and chairperson Bobby Seale for the torture and murder of suspected informant Alex Rackley by the New Haven Panthers, arguing that those who carried out Rackley's murder did so under the command of Huggins and Seale, the Party dispatched nationally recognized speakers to New Haven to support a three-day fundraising campaign. The city quickly became a hub of radical protest.[2]

The trials, which by then had become a part of the larger discourse on American racism and counterculture taking place nationally and at Yale specifically, were held close to Yale's campus. Bittker was among the faculty willing to use his position to effect change.

When students demanded courses that could speak to the concerns of civil rights and activism, Bittker offered a seminar entitled "The Role of the Black Lawyer." He also began to write about how the law could speak to historical injustices against Black people. The subject matter for the book he proposed and the milieu that informed Bittker's professional reality drew Morrison in quickly.

When he first proposed the book, Bittker was calling it *Black Reparations: An Inquiry into a Second "American Dilemma."* He purposefully wanted to reference the Gunnar Myrdal title, *An American Dilemma: The Negro Problem and Modern Democracy* (1944), since Bittker's argument was that the persistence of racism long after slavery had ended, more than slavery itself, provided justification for Black reparations. While Myrdal was clear in *An American Dilemma* that white people's historical and ongoing oppression of Black people meant that the "American Creed" did not apply equitably to Black people and that the circumstances of Black people needed to be improved, he did not suggest a remedy for the deep-seated economic segregation and inequality. While the Civil Rights Act of 1964 made key components of segregation illegal, it focused on discrimination in the future but resolutely preserved incumbent jobs obtained through segregation practices. Accordingly, inequality would persist, even after the *Brown v. Board of Education* decision. Bittker's argument was that some remedy would be necessary if inequality were to be diminished.

Early on, Morrison referred to the book as *The Case for Black Reparations*, a title Bittker opposed. That title, he argued, would give a "misleading impression of the overall tenor of the book."[3] Bittker did not feel that the book actually made the case for Black reparations; it simply addressed its possibilities and the legality of the proposition. He then proposed *Black Reparations: The Case and the Dilemma.* Morrison and Bittker agreed to use that one for the pre-sales meeting. But the use of a subtitle was rejected. Morrison found herself straddling the academic and the trade markets, with the sales team reminding her that trade books needed titles that could make the unassuming buyer think that the book is accessible. A subtitle would connote textbook and create unnecessary immediate resistance. Hearing this, Bittker pushed for *Black Reparations* sans any subtitle, before Morrison convinced him that *The Case for Black Reparations* was the best and only real option.[4]

By all accounts, Bittker was a progressive thinker undaunted by the silence that too often hovered around the topics he was most interested in. He was among the first to speculate about the implications racial integration would have on governmental land use policy.[5] And when there was no serious response to James Forman's "Manifesto to the White Christian Churches and the Jewish Synagogues in the United States of America and All Other Racist Institutions," Bittker began to draft what would become *The Case for Black Reparations.* He chose one of the most radical students at Yale, Mark Tushnet, who went on to clerk for Justice Thurgood Marshall, as his research assistant.

Forman introduced the idea for the "Manifesto" on April 26, 1969, at the National Black Economic Development Conference (NBEDC), before commandeering the pulpit at Riverside Church in New York on May 4, 1969, and demanding $500 million from white Christian churches and Jewish synagogues for their role in slavery and its residue. He was not a member of NBEDC, but he spoke on behalf of the group, which was composed mainly of business and church leaders. In the "Manifesto," Forman outlined why Black people deserved to be compensated and how the money would be used. Not surprisingly, most of the white community publicly declared outrage over Forman's demands, though some religious leaders expressed sympathy for Black people without conceding that reparations were in order. But as Bittker commented in the first chapter of *The Case for Black Reparations*, what was most notable, though not at all surprising, about the public response to the "Manifesto" was the dearth of analysis of the demands. "Most commentators addressed themselves solely to Forman's tactics," Bittker wrote. "Few had anything to say about reparations as a concept of social justice."[6]

Forman's demands were not, of course, without precedent. What was without precedent prior to Bittker's book, however, was a critical response from a mainstream scholar to the question of reparations on the basis of a theory of legal responsibility or liability. Part of Bittker's objective, in fact, was "to bring the concept of Black reparations out of its ghetto." It would be years later, only after Ta-Nehisi Coates's "The Case for Reparations" appeared in *The Atlantic* in 2014, before this would happen though. One of the ways Bittker thought he could do this was to contextualize the absence of any serious consideration of reparations amid Myrdal's limited commentary about reparations, compensations, or restitution in an otherwise comprehensive study of the "dilemma" of race in a "moral" and "democratic" America. For Bittker, there was just cause to move beyond Myrdal's tentative suggestion that the US might make parcels of plantations available to formerly enslaved people via long-term installment plans.

Basing his argument principally on Title 42, Section 1983, of the US Code (which allows damage suits for deprivation of civil rights), Bittker used *The Case for Black Reparations* to make the legal argument for reparations, specifically for the inequity Black people faced during what he referred to as the Plessy period (1896–1954). Morrison found Bittker's argument interesting and compelling. While Bittker did not answer the complicated question of who exactly would be cited as the liable party, he did make clear that the injured party—anyone deprived of constitutional rights—could pursue legal action as an equity remedy. The book, which expanded two lectures Bittker had given at Ohio State in 1971, offered two possible approaches to reparations— federal funding by Congress or a federal court's decision in favor of a plaintiff whose federal rights (in segregated public housing or public facilities) had been violated. The law asserted that when public officials conform to state law but violate a person's federal rights, payment of financial damages is the proper remedy. But it would be difficult to litigate the latter, making legislative action to address the matter more feasible.

Federal funding was similarly challenging, though, so the second half of the book focused on the sticky issues that constituted, in Bittker's estimation, a second "American dilemma." He posed and explored the same critical questions that inform today's controversial reparations debates: Should reparations be paid to representative groups or to individuals? Should all individuals be paid the same amount? How would eligibility, in terms of racial classifications, for potential recipients be handled? Are racial classifications constitutional? What priority should a reparations program take among other national goals, especially in relation to poverty across races? Morrison and Bittker agreed that the strength of *The Case* needed to rest in its robust contextualization of social welfare and justice issues that explored the question of reparations legally and morally. For Morrison, even if the book could not completely make the legal case, it could do the hard work of fostering a national debate on the topic. To avoid the trappings of the respectability politics that would make Bittker's commentary as a white Yale law professor more palatable than Forman's, Morrison and Bittker agreed to include Forman's "Manifesto" as an appendix to remind readers that the call for serious consideration of a reparations program was made by a Black man and predated Bittker's book. For Morrison and Bittker, the payoff would be in its effort to help shift the conversation, at least in some circles, from spectacle to serious debate.

Reviews of *The Case for Black Reparations* in popular venues were generally favorable. *Kirkus Reviews* argued that Bittker "succeeded with unusual force, suggesting the book would unquestionably receive the close attention it deserves from racial partisans and the academic and legal communities." Similarly, *The New Yorker* opined that Bittker's argument was closely reasoned and that it put "a case for reparations to American Blacks on solid grounds in American statute and legal precedent." The *Stanford Law Review*, however, contended that "as a legal argument, Bittker's book is superficial, if not deficient, in a number of respects, but his goal is clearly broader than provision of a legal brief of reparations." Indeed, the book's goal, as the review noted, was to "foster a national debate about the subject, redirecting the public response to demands for reparations from criticisms of tactics to considerations of substance."[7] It was to be a catalyst. Even as a catalyst though, critics contended that *The Case* came too late. In the late 1960s, *The Case for Black Reparations* might have commanded a much wider audience. But with the Nixon administration's efforts to dislodge Lyndon B. Johnson's Great Society anti-poverty campaigns and, to the extent that they were still relevant, Roosevelt's New Deal programs, reparations were not all that likely. The fact that Black people were seemingly, if not in reality, better off than ever also hurt the argument *The Case for Black Reparations* made—that slavery was followed by a century of racial inequality that kept Black people in a position of inferiority.

Years later, Morrison realized that the book had not come too late. It had come too soon. It would be years before the national debate Bittker hoped for would come to fruition. When *The Case* was reissued in 2003, its promotional material heavily featured the fact that Morrison had edited the book when it was first published. Her role was also underscored on the front and back covers. "His [Bittker's] work is more than significant—it is vital," the short quote on the front of the book announced. The longer quote on the back cover concluded with that line but was preceded with a nod to her work as editor: "Publishing Boris Bittker's *The Case for Black Reparations* in 1973 seemed to me an important contribution to the fledgling reparations debate." That the author of *Beloved*, *The Bluest Eye*, *Sula*, and *Playing in the Dark*—the Morrison books the publicity team decided were most relevant to *The Case for Black Reparations* (or perhaps best known)—had published the book gave it its bona fides. The description read: "Published by Toni Morrison when she was an editor, the book came from an unlikely source: Bittker was a white professor of law at Yale University who had long been ambivalent about the idea of reparations." Through his research on the use of laws to compensate groups who had experienced injustice, he came to see that the case for reparations could be made indeed. As public opinion shifted from a "crazy, far-fetched idea" to one that needed to be taken seriously, Morrison and Bittker were affirmed that the work they did together left a record of what was possible for those who joined the conversation almost two decades later and then again in the twenty-first century.

In the same way *The Case for Black Reparations* prompted readers to recognize historical injustices and the enduring impact of slavery on individuals and communities, the second book Morrison prepared for publication that year—Herskovits's *Cultural Relativism: Perspectives in Cultural Pluralism*—invited readers to acknowledge the role historical and cultural contexts play in individual and communities' practices of morality and, by extension, their application of concepts of justice. Morrison began to work with Frances Herskovits to publish a collection of Melville Herskovits's essays in October 1971. Here, again, the opportunity to publish a book that was primarily done and only needed to be pulled together provided Morrison the chance to have books on the list for the year with limited effort. Herskovits was an author whose books would sell largely by reputation. She also had the added benefit that publishing *Cultural Relativism*, like *The Case*, was more akin to the textbook, academic market she was familiar with than it was to publishing trade books.

Herskovits was an authority in the field of anthropology. In 1938, he became the founding chair of the Department of Anthropology at Northwestern University and the first chair of an African studies department in the United States in 1959. Prior to joining the sociology faculty at Northwestern, Herskovits had been an assistant professor of anthropology at Morrison's alma mater, Howard University, where he took full advantage of his access to Black people to gather additional anthropometric data for his research. Among his peers at Howard was Lorenzo Dow Turner, the famed linguist who, like Herskovits, studied African retentions in American culture.

A white scholar, Herskovits's research was in direct opposition to that of the Black sociologist E. Franklin Frazier. Frazier, who would later work at Howard as well, though not at the time Herskovits was at the university as a National Research Council fellow, argued that the American Negro was fundamentally American and had no notable cultural connections to Africa. Herskovits's well-known intellectual debate with Frazier was emblematic of the fact that Herskovits's understanding of African retentions, while commonplace today, was the source of much debate then. As well-respected as Herskovits was in his day, he was also a problematic figure in the field of African studies if for no other reason than his prominence as a white scholar often came at the expense of scholars of African descent who received less attention while making similar arguments. The American academy was biased toward white scholars, while Black scholars, who were also teaching the next generation of researchers, too often labored in obscurity at small institutions with meager resources. It would be years before this would change, and even then, the changes were modest.

Herskovits published fourteen books between 1928 and 1972, the most notable of which were *The Myth of the Negro Past* (1941) and *Man and His Works* (1948). A number of these books were published with Knopf, including the last single-authored book he wrote, *The Human Factor in Changing Africa* (1962). Before he died, he sent the table of contents for *Cultural Relativism* to Knopf's then–editor in chief Harold Strauss, with whom Herskovits had worked on *The Human Factor*. Years after his death in 1963, his wife, Frances, began to correspond with Morrison about pulling together a collection of previously published essays that would show the evolution of his thinking while also showing important continuities. Because she and Morrison knew each other personally and because Morrison was familiar with Melville Herskovits's work, their professional relationship was an easy one.

When Frances wrote to Morrison about the manuscript Frances referred to then as *On Cultural Values and Cultural Relativism*, she provided Morrison a bit of context. "The papers on Social Selection and the Formation of Human types, and the review entitled Rear-Guard Action," she wrote, "are included by special request of colleagues in the Afro-American field; and Some Approaches to Myth and the last essay from The Human Factor in Changing Africa by request of Africanists interested in literature and the arts."[8] The two spoke not long thereafter and agreed to ask Sidney W. Mintz, who was on faculty in the Department of Anthropology at Yale University, to write one of two introductions to the collection of essays. The tone of the introduction, Morrison told Mintz, would not be one of endorsement since Herskovits, by then, was an authority on the topic and since the essays were not wholly original. What she and Frances hoped for, instead, was a serious evaluation of the essays collectively.

Mintz declined the offer, citing other writing obligations and reluctance about being able to do the work justice. She wrote:

I have thought very hard about my capacities and limitations with regard to this undertaking. I have to conclude, very reluctantly, that this is not really the job for me. . . . I do not feel that I have given the kind of thought to the relativistic point of view that it deserves, were one to undertake to write an introduction to the papers. I say this advisedly, even though I am generally in agreement with the view Herskovits advanced.[9]

When Mintz declined the offer, they made an overture to Alan P. Merriam, an ethnomusicologist at Indiana University, before deciding that an introduction by Donald T. Campbell, with whom Herskovits had collaborated on previous publications, as the lone prefatory writing, was more than adequate. By year's end, a few short months after she sent Morrison the manuscript, Frances Herskovits received a contract for the book, and she and Morrison met over the Christmas holiday to talk about the project and to share vermouth and cinnamon ice cream.

With all the writing done, Morrison and Frances focused their attention on determining which essays to include and how to group them. Surprisingly, it was not an easy task. "I am having the greatest difficulty trying to group the essays thematically," Morrison wrote.

> The most obvious categories, Cultural Relativism in Economics, Art, Science and Myth, don't seem to work because the distribution is so uneven—one piece on art for example. So, I am inclined to alter our original plans for the material to something simpler and I hope just as satisfactory: A two part division perhaps, one group made up of those pieces focussing on economic and political development—another on human relationships. That may not work either because there is the beautiful harmony in Melville Herskovits' thought— the important relationships between art and economy or myth and "science"—that makes dividing the pieces into groups so hard.[10]

Frances concurred. "I fully agree with you that thematic grouping of the essays presents difficulties," she wrote, "since we are dealing with occasional papers, for special occasions, and special audiences."[11] She suggested three such groupings—"Definition of Culture and Cross-Cultural Values: Affirmations, Ambivalences, Polemics," "Economics and Cross-Cultural Values: The Modern World and Tradition," and "Expressive Arts: Ideologies and Realities in Cross-Cultural Perspective."

Ultimately, the two themes that organized the book were cultural relativism and cultural pluralism; and the four groupings were "Culture: Definitions and Values," "Ethnocentrism, Racism, and Peace," "Economics and Values: The Modern World and Tradition," and "Expressive Arts: A Cross-Cultural Perspective."

The structure of the book determined, Morrison pondered several options for the title, which proved to be similarly challenging. "I have been trying to find a title that would be as striking as all of the Herskovits titles are," she noted in a letter to her friend. "I haven't succeeded but think I've come close: CULTURE, PERCEPTION, AND PREJUDICE, Essays on Cultural Values and Relativism." Morrison understood the work titles must do and, similarly, the way words can make or break a title. "I'm a little weary of 'prejudice' as a word that means anything to anyone," she noted. She needed to find "one word suggesting how culture influences perception and, in fact, determines the extent of our biases."[12]

Beyond the title, there was the issue of the headnotes, which Morrison thought could do some of the heavy lifting of guiding the reader. She identified quotations for some of the pieces and invited Frances to review those Morrison chose and to suggest others. Frances responded immediately with suggested quotations and a promise to send the proofread manuscript with several footnotes. Before she could send them, however, she became deathly ill. Serendipitously, she managed to complete the manuscript with the headnotes, the sequence of essays and titles of the subsections, and the editorial changes to be made before dying unexpectedly in May 1972.[13]

Even as debates among sociologists, anthropologists, and philosophers about the "truth" of cultural relativism had by then intensified (especially in human rights' circles), the book did not garner very much critical attention. The *Choice* review suggested that the book should be "read by all social scientists who are concerned with ethical issues, the misuse of anthropology, and the relationship between cultural diversity and the world order." Herskovits's collection, the reviewer imagined, would help clarify the matter. The *Library Journal* review alerted readers of the book's consideration of the implications of critical relativism for understanding "culture contact, acculturation, culture change, cultural dynamics, racism, and the expressive arts." The brief *Kirkus* commentary focused on the collection's strenuous call for mutual respect of all cultures when judging different societies and labeled students as the book's primary readership.[14]

The longest and also the most coveted review, however, came from noted anthropologist Margaret Mead and was published in the *American Journal of Sociology*. Mead opened the review with a nod to Frances Herskovits and, perhaps unknowingly, to Morrison: "*Cultural Relativism* is the product of magnificent editorial judgment. There should be more books like it—books in which an editor thoroughly conversant with the lifetime of a scholar's production selects pieces on distinctive themes without loss of context."[15] Mead took great care to explain critical elements of Herskovits's work, including offering a corrective for those who wrongly believe "attacks on cultural relativism as denial of all values." Campbell's introduction, Mead argued, was misleading and evidence that, despite his long association with Herskovits, Campbell did not fully understand the position of the fieldworker and overemphasized Herskovits's articulation of cultural anthropology as more of a humanities discipline than a social science. For Herskovits, Mead claimed cultural anthropology was both. No one, though, could argue against the fact that the book was proof of Herskovits's full, productive scholarly life that stood against Eurocentric views of culture and race and revealed the ways African culture contributed to global societies in rich and complex ways. Undoubtedly, this is what Frances Herskovits and Morrison set out to achieve.

It would seem in retrospect that each of the books Morrison published in 1974 turned on the notion that accepted ideas needed to be challenged. Much in the same way Herskovits's collection upended long-accepted ideas about race and culture, the final book Morrison published that year, Land's *Grow or Die: The Unifying Principle of Transformation*, decried conventional wisdom and prevailing business practices and promoted, instead, proactive approaches to organizational change and growth. At the core of Land's argument was the claim that risk aversion and safe decision-making were guarantees for stagnation and death. Of the three authors she worked with whose books were published that year, though, Land was the one she found least amendable to her preferred way of working with an author. Consequently, he was also the author who helped unleash a part of her personality that left no room for debate about who was in charge in the author-editor relationship.

Morrison and Land began to work on the manuscript in November 1971, even before the book was under contract. She knew better than to invest a lot of time on the project without a contract because there was always the possibility that once the book was in better shape, in no small part because of her efforts as the unofficial editor, the author could easily take the manuscript elsewhere to sell it. She made an exception with Land and pushed him to improve the book in the three or so months she worked on it with him. By May 1972, their working relationship evidenced tension, which they eventually resolved but which made clear that Morrison had little patience for insolence. Morrison insisted that Land's writing suffered "from overweight: two words where one will do; deadwood phrases; inexact adjectives and connections." Her frustration with his effusive prose was palpable. His ideas and his data were sharp, but his language was unrestrained. The tone was just as challenging. "It sounds too often like advertising copy," she lamented, "the overuse and emphasis of 'new,' 'prime technique.' . . . Too salesman-y."[16]

Dissatisfied with her pace and injured by her critique of his writing style, Land arrived unannounced in Morrison's office in early summer. He expressed feelings of distrust of her and Random House. She cautioned him, first, against attempting to publish a book with an editor or company for which he had contempt. It was a fool's errand. She followed up with a letter to make sure he got the point. She warned:

> I cannot be strong-armed. It is simply an ineffective tactic because it makes me angry and uncooperative. Also it rips the thread of trust I assumed existed between us. . . .
>
> We have been working on this since last November. I am excited about it, but very apprehensive about the turns your impatience have [*sic*] taken. None of this has to do with anything other than human frailty and the structures of vanity—mine and yours, but I think it terribly important to articulate these things at the precise moment they can be helpful.[17]

Morrison and Land were able to work through their personality challenges but only after Morrison made it clear that they were both authorities, each differently so. While he knew more about the book's content, she knew more about how to make the book better. What she would not tolerate, however, was a temperamental author who had convinced himself that he knew more about book publishing than she did.

Back in 1965, Land had established a research institute that examined ways creative performance might be enhanced. He conducted a study of 1,600 children to test their creativity when they were three to five years old, when they were ten years old, and again when they were fifteen years old. The study revealed that as the children aged, their levels of creativity waned—from 98 percent at age five, to 30 percent at age ten, and 12 percent at age fifteen. When his research revealed that the creativity level for adults who took the same test was 2 percent, he concluded that noncreative behavior is learned.

A seminal development that emerged from the various studies of his research institute was his transformation theory, which integrated principles of creativity, growth, and change. In a presentation of transformation as a general system theory, *Grow or Die* explored the three stages of growth—forming, norming, and integration—and applied them to a variety of disciplines and contexts. Its eleven chapters examined the origins of behavior and evolution, patterns of growth, and the achievement of growth in the future. Land's theory of transformation argued that organizations that cannot resist the impulse to return to their old ways during the improvement phase move toward obsolescence before ultimately dying. At the center of this failure, he argued, was the tendency to reinvent and improve rather than to create and innovate. The creativity that informs the start-up/invention phase dissipates, and the adaptive theory used to improve products and processes is mistaken for growth.

In some ways, the book's message was relevant for Morrison, too—either her success as an editor for a mainstream publisher during the early years in this role would grow or her career as an editor would die a swift death. Publishing Land's book, which was as controversial as it was acclaimed, counted as a growth in her editor's column. Having reoriented their relationship on the grounds of mutual respect, Morrison advised Land on the revisions he needed to make while she worked with the design team on the book's layout. He reviewed the galleys, while she finalized the copy for the jacket and the publicity team. Once the book was published, in May 1973, Morrison tried hard to get it as much attention as possible. She went back to Margaret Mead, whom she had been in touch with a few months earlier, with an invitation to write a review essay about Herskovits's *Cultural Relativism*, this time asking for a promotional blurb on Land's behalf. Mead's endorsement of *Grow or Die* was added to the book's cover, announcing the book as "a magnificent synthesis that deals with the question of cultural change in evolutionary terms more effectively than any other synthesis [she had] seen." Mead contextualized Land's work among Zero Population Growth advocates who, in the 1960s, cautioned that too much growth would hasten the destruction of civilization. Contrastingly, Land argued that such fears were oversimplified, that survival actually depended on concurrent growth, and that growth could make a new consciousness that could usher in a new world civilization.

Morrison's promotional efforts paid off when *Grow or Die* was chosen as a main selection of the national *Saturday Review*'s Science Book Club and nominated for a Pulitzer Prize in the science category and for the National Book Award. Perhaps too prescient for its own good, however, it received far less critical attention than Random House hoped for, despite having an excerpt of the book published in the *Journal of Creative Behavior* the same year it was released and despite several nominations of the book for major awards. Indeed, Morrison and Land had survived their first publishing foray together, but for Morrison one venture with the author was all she was willing to suffer.

During the years 1972 and 1973, Morrison's editorial identity began to take shape more clearly as she published eight books, four in each year.[18] Her editorial choices reflected her belief that books could provoke thought and foster critical discourse. Her assumption, one that would persist through the years, was that a good editor could collaborate with the author to produce a book that revealed a writer's individual achievement alongside the book's more general efforts to shift perspectives. The nonfiction books she edited during these years foreshadowed her interest in publishing books that engage directly with social and cultural reorientations. Far from a disparate hodgepodge, these early books helped craft an editorial identity that positioned her as a serious professional, as one with a gift for helping authors on her list render complex and uncomfortable topics more legible, and as one committed to using her role as a tool for social change.

Morrison took risks publishing voices some deemed marginal and, by extension, challenged Random House to remain true to its legacy of prioritizing artistry and quality over market trends around the same time publishing conglomerates had begun to drift toward privileging commercial viability above all else. Pure profit motives might be their agenda, but it would not be hers. Ironically, there was one idea she wanted to pursue that just might trouble this debate about what would sell and what would not. She had not yet determined all its contours. But she did have a title in mind. She would call it *The Black Book.*

CHAPTER 6

The Simplest Life
Is a Triumph

Making *The Black Book*

*T*he Black Book* took shape in Morrison's mind years before she secured collaborators to complete it. The resolve to finally do it—and to do it well and with fanfare—was a function of her obstinance, a personality trait that had always served her well. "I . . . remember sitting in a sales conference," she noted. "One of the salesmen says, 'We can't sell books on both sides of the street,' meaning there's an audience of white people and, maybe, an audience of Black people. But they don't merge. So, I thought, 'Well, I'll just solve that, and I will do something that everybody loves, particularly Black people.'"[1] Her confidence in her ability to solve a perennial problem like building a book-buying audience, one that was multiracial no less, was indicative of her firm sense of self on the one hand and of her belief in the universal attractiveness of Black people's consumable culture on the other.

As was frequently the case, ideas she pursued in fiction made their way into her work as an editor. Just as *The Bluest Eye* set out to interrogate the life of a young girl who did not ascribe to the 1960s rallying cry "Black is beautiful," Morrison intended for *The Black Book* to function, at least in part, as an interlocutor to the refrain, which she felt was "an accurate but wholly irrelevant observation if ever there was one."[2]

> The slogan provided a psychic crutch for the needy and a second (or first) glance from whites. . . . The phrase was nevertheless a full confession that white definitions were important to us (having to counteract them meant they were significant) and that the quest for physical beauty was both a good and worthwhile pursuit. . . .
>
> When the strength of people rests on its beauty, when the focus is on how one looks rather than what one is, we are in trouble. When we are urged to confuse dignity with prettiness, and presence with image, we are being distracted from what is worthy about us: for example, our intelligence, our resilience, our skill, our tenacity, irony or spiritual health. And in that absolute fit of reacting to white values, we may very well have removed the patient's heart in order to improve his complexion.

The Black Book, then, was to focus on the heart—"the old verities that made being black and alive in this country the most dynamite existence imaginable."

Controversially, Morrison suggested that in the determination to exalt beautiful things (and to manage how white people saw us), meaningful things were lost. When little statues of Black jockeys were deemed derogatory and hidden behind sheets until they could be removed, the preeminence of the Black jockeys who won fourteen of the first twenty-seven Kentucky Derby races was also covered up and lost. While the NAACP argued that "Amos 'n' Andy" was a "gross libel of the Negro and distortion of the truth" and offended the sensibilities of Black people, Morrison shared the position of the surviving Black cast members, who thought that the program did not deal in stereotypes as much as in genuinely funny characters. *The Black Book* set out to explore the full history of Black people in America—the good, the bad, and the ugly.

Once the idea for the book morphed into a plan she could sketch out on paper, Morrison set out to find the ideal person to help construct it. At the top of her list were collectors, people who would have raw material that could be included and, more importantly, who had an outsize regard for the fullness of Black history. As she talked about the idea for the book among friends, all roads led back to one person, Middleton "Spike" Harris. While doing research of his own family's history, which he traced back to the colonial period, Harris began to collect original documents, books, and newspapers. That collection expanded to include photocopies of documents he gathered during research trips to libraries, museums and societies, and the National Archives.

As Morrison would soon find out, Harris was more than a collector. He was probably the best-known and most highly regarded self-taught Black historian in New York City. Under the auspices of the Negro History Associates (NHA), which he cofounded with fellow collectors, Harris created exhibitions, audiovisual presentations, manuals, and monographs. NHA also published *A Negro History Tour of Manhattan* (1967), which boasted on its cover that its author was "Uncle Spike, the Negro History Detective," and erected plaques on city buildings of significance to Black history in New York. A New York native, Harris had earned his BA from Howard University and his master's degree in social work from Fordham University. Over the years, he worked for several local and state agencies in New York, including the Boys and Girls Club, the YMCA, the Emergency Welfare Association, and the parole division of the state executive department. He had also served as the field director for the American Red Cross in the Southwest Pacific during World War II. By the end of their first meeting, Morrison was convinced that Harris's extensive collection, the range of his experience and expertise, and a "ruthlessness in his pursuit of material"[3] made him the ideal person for the venture.

She trusted him to assemble the team he needed to get the work done. Harris's first recruit to the project was his friend Morris Levitt. A retired teacher and sports enthusiast, Levitt served as a consultant for NHA and could lend his organizational skills to the undertaking. At their first meeting in May 1972, Morrison, Harris, and Levitt agreed that getting the book done quickly was both desirable and feasible. Since Morrison had just finished the final draft of her second novel, *Sula* (1973), and could devote a significant amount of time to the project, she proposed an October delivery date, giving them five short months to organize the book. To do that, they needed another pair of hands with specific expertise in Black culture. The trio agreed to add Roger Furman to the team. Furman was a playwright, director, actor, and lecturer who had founded a street theater, the New Heritage Repertory Theater, in Harlem in 1964. He had also cofounded the Black Theatre Alliance, an organization of performance groups.

Morrison tasked Harris and Levitt with delivering the first one hundred items within two weeks and outlined the sixteen categories under which they would group their items: Armed Forces, Battles, Education, Music, Patents, Dreams and Numbers,

Obituaries, Advertisements, Recipes and Root Medicine, Sports, Theater and Film, Science, Name Origins, Language, Literature/ Journalism, and Cowboys. Other categories, they agreed, could be added as the book took shape. Furman, as a Black culture aficionado, would focus more on folk and popular culture items in these categories—roots, medicine, recipes; early Black films and old minstrel theatre; beauty aids; snuff and tobacco; race records and Louisiana Black Code; Marie Laveau, Dr. Buzzard, Black prophets (Mother Horn, Prophet Jones, Elder Micheaux, Daddy Grace, Father Divine); American Indians and Blacks; secret societies (Odd Fellows, Masons, Elks, Eastern Stars); and Marcus Garvey and A. J. Rogers.

Even though no one at Random House was completely clear about what the book would be exactly, Morrison managed to get a contract drawn up a few weeks after her meeting with Harris and Levitt. The book would be like the *Whole Earth Catalog* but different, she suggested, more like "the kind of record somebody might have kept in his trunk if he had lived from Pre-Middle Passage Days to just before WW II."[4] It would include "old timey photos, patents of inventions, little known facts, folklore, magic, dreams, filmwork, advertisement posters, heroes, adventurers, recipes, medicine and much much more."[5]

Morrison and Harris spent hours in his Croes Avenue apartment in the Bronx poring over old newspapers to find source material. They reveled in stories about Thomas Jefferson's supposed indifference to an escape attempt by an enslaved man he allegedly fathered while it was also credibly rumored that he allowed his daughter to be sold to a trader headed to New Orleans. Among countless other things, they looked for historical references to Columbus's observations of trading, with minted coins, between Native Americans and Africans, and for an old

Georgia charter that prohibited slavery in the state. Excitingly, the fast-approaching delivery date seemed reasonable and unobscured.

The book was assigned a designer, Jack Ribik, and a production manager, Dean Ragland. These two and Morrison began to work on the format and pitched to each other ideas about how the book would be set and by when. But by March 1973, Harris became ill, Furman was preoccupied with other matters, and Morris left New York. To avoid having to postpone the project indefinitely (and to keep the trio from defaulting on the contract), Morrison added Ernest Smith, a resort owner in upstate New York and a collector himself, to the team and extended the delivery date to April 12, 1973. The original team was falling apart, but the project itself was coming together. The motley crew (which now included Ribik and Ragland) had two things in common that mattered to Morrison: They were all collectors of Black memorabilia or Black culture enthusiasts. And they had a passion fueled by something other than careerism.

Delays and personnel changes aside, Morrison's enthusiasm for the project never waned. Rather, she took even more ownership of it. While the design and layout teams completed their preproduction work, she tapped into her network of friends to invite Bill Cosby to write an introduction for the book. Cosby's bona fides as a popular Black television personality were unmatched. Importantly, too, he was also gaining a reputation as an activist-educator. Morrison knew that his endorsement would give the project the kind of star power that could offer an extra lift with marketing and promotion. By this time Cosby, who had started as a comedian, had become a successful actor. His role as Alexander "Scotty" Scott in *I Spy* made him one of the first Black actors to star in a mainstream series.

Somewhat audaciously, she wrote to Cosby, describing the book as "joyful, painful, and astonishing" and outlining its contents.

For months I have been trying to get hold of you and finally asked Max Roach to presume on his friendship and call you. You were still in France, I think, and now he is off in K.C. somewhere. So now I am writing a letter—which is desperate and hurried—to ask for your help. . . . I am convinced you will enjoy this and will agree with me that the project is immeasurably valuable and worth your effort and energy. . . . I can, if you like, come to where ever you are and give you more details, show you the book in page proof, tape your remarks, receive them in longhand—whatever.[6]

Morrison was careful to be both professional and familiar in her letter. She needed to be clear that she had inside information, but she also had to concede that getting in touch with him through drummer Max Roach had not yielded the result she needed just yet. "It is a wild book—an authentic book, a highly educational book," she wrote. And because it had "no precedent, no corollary in publishing," the book needed a succinct introduction that could clarify its contents with serious good humor and flavor. Cosby was one of a few people, in her view, who could strike that balance.

In 1968, following the assassination of Martin Luther King Jr. in April and, subsequently, a summer of racial unrest, Cosby had narrated "Black History: Lost, Stolen, or Strayed," an episode of the one-hour series *Of Black America* that CBS News presented as a way of exploring Black history and the contributions Black people have made historically to the development of the United States. He was a regular cast member of *The Electric Company*, a popular educational program for elementary school children. And

Fat Albert and the Cosby Kids, the show he developed and debuted in 1971, was wildly successful and innovative—with a group of inner-city Black kids who met every challenge they faced with imagination and good character. An introduction from Cosby could strike just the right chord, Morrison imagined. Importantly, too, it could serve as an entrée to her intention to recruit him as a Random House author whom she would edit.

Though they shared a mutual friend, which she no doubt hoped would encourage Cosby's favorable response, Morrison ended the letter with a trace of humility. She set that modesty aside quickly, however, and reinforced her letter with honest bravado, concluding with a final pitch about her confidence in the book.

> I suspect this letter should include some information about myself—something to prevent you from ignoring this letter— but that's probably presumptious [*sic*] if not just a waste of letter reading time. Let me just say . . . : I want to publish books about us—black people—that will make some sense—to give joy, to pass on some grandeur to all those black children (born and unborn) who need to get to the horizon with something under their arms besides Dick and Jane and the Rise & Fall of the Roman Empire. . . . I have already published some books that I believe do that. I know the one I have described to you will do more.[7]

The pitch worked as Morrison hoped it would. Cosby accepted the invitation and agreed to record five scripted spots to be played on radio stations all over the country. Each advertisement was humorous, some more than others. But each did the work necessary to appeal to Black audiences specifically.

The first announced his excitement about a different kind of

"black book"—not the little black book men kept women's contact information in. This black book was a folk journey of Black
America, he noted, one that was "beautiful, haunting, curious, in-
formative and human." The second suggested that everyone was
talking about the book and that it had something for everyone,
including people who did not like to read. The third spot was
short and whispered that Black people had something serious to
share—a book that would be helpful in revealing who was passing
(for white but actually had Black ancestry). Morrison knew that
this ad especially could be tricky. But it was in the tradition of the
material included in *The Black Book*. Done well, the spot would be
humorous. It struck the insider's chord she was more than comfortable with.

The fourth spot would be a counterbalance of sorts. Like the
third, this one also claimed to share a secret. But this time the
secret was inside information about a hip book that would make
its owners seem impressive. "Now, if you don't ever have another
book, if you have *The Black Book* on your shelf," Cosby cajoled,
people will walk in your room and say, "Hmmh, he's heavy." A
Black audience would recognize the line as a colloquial affirma-
tion of high intellect. The final spot declared that the book was
one you must have before dying. "Now don't pass right away," he
joked, "because we want you to see *The Black Book* before you pass
away. And when you look at it, tears will come to your eyes and
you will say, 'Yes, Lord, I remember that happened to me and I
remember this and that.'"

Since the book was released at the end of February, the promotional materials noted the upcoming holidays for which the book
would make a great gift—for Easter, Mother's Day, and Father's
Day. Beyond holidays, though, every man should have a copy to
take to the barbershop, Cosby declared: "When you go . . . take

The Black Book with you. You won't lose no arguments, now."[8] Each ad was designed to grab and keep the listener's attention—a decidedly Black listener. The language choice and cultural references made this clear, but then, so did the book's title. It was a book about Black life in its most complex and simplest forms.

While Morrison was looking to prove that well-conceived and -designed books could indeed sell "on both sides of the street," she was foremost committed to making sure that *The Black Book* sold well among Black people. Proving that Black people bought books of interest to them was a fight she intended to have one time only. Her proof had to be so compelling that she would gain the same authority in sales conferences that she had in editorial meetings. Convincing other editors to allow her to pursue certain ideas was easy, relatively speaking. But for a book to do well in every regard, it took more than the green light to acquire a title and hearty preproduction work from an editor. You also needed the full support of the design, marketing, and sales teams. Design and marketing were in-house jobs. She could redirect or nudge those teams along when needed simply by leaving her desk and going to theirs. But the work of the sales team happened on the road, where she had little control and even less access. The demand for *The Black Book* had to be so high that even the most recalcitrant salesperson would have no choice but to fall in line.

Everything about *The Black Book* was a collective experience. Morrison had put off for months the challenge of publishing a book with no clear single author. She had begun the project with Harris, but his collection was propped by sources from disparate places. Wherever she went, she talked about the project excitedly. And everyone who heard about it told her about some unique lore she thought should also be included. Contributions came in from all over. Now that the project's layout was almost done, she had to decide how best to represent the full complement of contributors. In the end, she decided that Harris would be cited as the primary editor, and she would add the line "with the assistance of" to be followed by the names of Levitt, Furman, and Smith. Other contributors were mentioned by name on the acknowledgments page with special thanks to Mary Singleton, Donna Woods, Ramah Wofford, George Carl Wofford, Vertamae Grosvenor, June Rephan, and Eleanor Charles for the "stories, pictures, recollections, and general aid" they provided. "Above all," Morrison wrote, "our thanks to those millions of black people who lived this life and held on." At the core of her belief in the book's meaningfulness was the notion that every aspect of Black culture was a testament to Black joy and survival.

Over the course of eighteen months, the team worked to assemble *The Black Book*. With the heavy lifting done, Morrison began to ramp up prepublication promotions by contacting 175 radio stations with Black programming and every Black writer, celebrity, and news outlet she thought would be helpful. She released the Cosby spots to Black radio stations first. Then, she sent review copies to everyone from Barbara Halliday at the *Detroit Free Press* to Don Cornelius at the popular TV dance show *Soul Train*. Anybody who might garner attention for the book received a copy, along with a letter from Morrison expressing her enthusiasm for the book. "I've so far brought six copies into my home and every friend that comes to visit takes one away, calls me the next morning and says, 'Thanks. Believe it or not, I read it from cover to cover,'" she claimed.[9] She also secured advance praise blurbs—which she promptly added to the book's promotional assets—from public figures Muhammad Ali and Angela Davis and highly respected Black authors Gwendolyn Brooks, Ishmael Reed, Paule Marshall, and Clarence Major.

When *The Black Book* was published February 26, 1974, it had received enough critical attention to create great anticipation. The book scored prime real estate in a December 10, 1973, *Publishers Weekly* article, and Morrison published "Behind the Making of *The Black Book*" in *Black World* for the magazine's annual history issue in February. The book had a range of audiences, and Morrison played well to each of them. The *Black World* article, which spoke directly to Black people, was the most revealing, however. For almost two years, preparing the book had consumed most of her time. "All of the other publishing ventures I was involved in got secondary treatment," she admitted. "I was scared that the world would fall away before somebody put together a thing that got close to the way we really are."[10]

The one project that had not been put off by her work on *The Black Book* was her second novel, *Sula*. Knopf had published it a few months earlier. And it was getting a lot of early attention. Happily, she agreed that every time she promoted *Sula* as an author, she would also promote *The Black Book* as its editor. Attention for one book was free publicity for the other in many cases. As much as Morrison was invested in building her reputation as an author, she still saw editing as the work that paid the bills. And she was determined to do that work extraordinarily well. The publication of *The Black Book* would be an event, if for no other reason than she had a point to prove.

Days after the book rolled off the press, Morrison threw a launch party to celebrate its publication. Each contributor gave her a list of people to invite to the soiree, which she managed to secure a reasonable budget for. Random House did not offer financial support freely, but Morrison had convinced the publicity team that everything about the book's publication needed to be an event. The invitation, which featured images from the book, declared the

March 4 party at Charles's Gallery in Harlem a "can't miss" event and promised good dining, good dancing, and good times.

Barbara Campbell covered the party for *The New York Times*. She wrote:

Last night influential blacks and black celebrities crowded into Charles's Gallery at 315 West 125th Street, a popular Harlem discothèque-restaurant, to celebrate the publication of "The Black Book." . . . Many who had received an advance copy said what touched them about it was the same thing that would touch every black—that it at last documented their history with the actual artifacts, minutia and writings of the time.[11]

Among those present, Campbell noted, were playwright Ed Bullins, film director Melvin van Peebles, Mrs. Countee Cullen, and David Dinkins, whose political career was then on the rise. Furman, one of the book's collaborators, hosted a second party in late June at his New Heritage Repertory Theater, on East 125th at Madison Avenue, with Soul of the People providing live music. The events surrounding the publication became an opportunity for old friends to reunite and new friends to meet, all in celebration of the book's achievement.

A few months later, in August, Morrison scored a long piece she titled "Rediscovering Black History: It's Like Growing Up Black One More Time," in *The New York Times*, where she articulated the need for the book in her view. The article chronicled the development of *The Black Book* from an idea she had to a completed project and extolled its virtues. As popular as the book was among Black audiences, Morrison took care to show how white people were buying the book, too. In the March *New York Times* article that corresponded with the book launch party, Morrison told

Campbell that white people, too, found the book fascinating: "One white woman I know, who is as indifferent to blacks as anyone can be and still have a clear conscience, told me, 'I can understand what you mean about the book. It's alive. When I put it down hairs curled on my arms.'"

In the August article she authored, Morrison moved deftly between the claim that Black history was not, by and large, invested in whiteness while also noting that "a major part of American history is the history of black people." The economic history of the country was inextricable from its history of forced free labor, for example. And America's legal history was related almost wholly to the effort to restrict Black people. To her surprise, she wrote, *The Black Book* helped her see that there was connecting tissue between Black history and white history: "The two histories merge in the book, as in life, in a noon heat of brutality and compassion, outrage and satisfaction."[12]

The book sold well from the start, eventually reaching number nine on *The New York Times* trade paperback list and earning attention from radio DJs all over the country, who read from the book on the air. It also became a favorite among faculty teaching Black history, including those who taught in prisons. One of the letters that moved Morrison the most, in fact, was from a prisoner who had one copy already but who requested two additional ones. He needed one to give to a friend, he noted, one "to throw up against the wall," and one to hold close to his heart.

In March 1975, *The Black Book* was among the ten books nominated for the National Book Award in the Contemporary Affairs category. In April that same year, it was nominated for *Publishers Weekly*'s Carey-Thomas Award. It did not win either, but the nominations helped create more attention for the book and helped Morrison make the point that a book about Black life, when done well and marketed effectively, could be both a popular and critical success. For a short time, it seemed like the book would score another boon with a television show. Ray Hubbard Associates, a firm known for its promotion of educational and socially conscious programs, attempted to get networks to dramatize *The Black Book* in a ninety-minute television show that would include "a musical revue of songs, dancing, and readings based on material from the book."[13] NBC agreed to do it as a part of its *Big Event* series. But when the executive in charge of the series was fired, the deal fell through. CBS liked the idea but would only agree to do it if a sponsor signed on to underwrite it. But, by 1974, the commitment that emerged after a summer of racial unrest in 1968 to represent more of Black life on television had already subsided. Unable to secure a sponsor, the serial rights team relented, and the TV project never came to fruition.

More than any other project, *The Black Book* defined Morrison's editorship. It encapsulated, in a single book, the whole of her feelings about what a book about Black life could do—celebrate the pride of Black accomplishment and acknowledge the joy and pain of three hundred years of Black life. The universality of Black experiences (and its particularities) informed her editorial and artistic conceit at every turn. In her view, this had to be done without overt regard for white people. "I remember when black people refused to let the enemy—'the man'—get to them, down there, in that private place where we lived and where we exercised skill and power," she wrote.[14] *The Black Book* navigated with skill the irony of the need to be appealing to white people while also preserving enough distance from them to maintain Black privacy. Ultimately, even as anyone could read the book, it operated on the assumption that Black people understood uniquely if not exclusively the relation of our anger, frustration, and hope one to another. Everything about the book captured Morrison's belief about Black people—that even "the simplest life a black person has lived is a triumph."[15]

CHAPTER 7

The Two Tonis

When Morrison explained to Bill Cosby what she wanted to accomplish with *The Black Book*—to offer Black children something other than Dick and Jane to tuck under their arms as they moved toward the horizon—she admitted that she had already begun to publish books that did just that. The one that did it most brilliantly at that point, indisputably, was Toni Cade Bambara's short story collection *Gorilla, My Love* (1972).

When the two Tonis, as Bambara's mother referred to them, found each other in 1970, both women were fascinated by the fact that they had not met before. They had plenty of friends in common. They frequented many of the same places in New York City. Their books—*The Bluest Eye* and *The Black Woman*, both released that year—had been embraced by the same readers. How they had missed each other except through encounters between the reader and the page was a grand mystery they could not be bothered to solve. They were together now, they declared. While they had plenty in common, the two women were also quite different temperamentally. Bambara had the uncanny ability to make people feel comfortable immediately. Morrison, on the other hand, tended to be more reserved, especially when it came to her willingness to mix business with pleasure. But something about Bambara was different, compelling Morrison to ignore the line she typically drew between editor and friend.

"From the beginning I knew we would be friends," Morrison told Linda Janet Holmes, Bambara's former student and biographer.

> I didn't know we would hang out, but the connection was instant for me. . . . I just found her serious. But, what I found mostly was that her writing was unbelievable to me—so fresh, so pointed, so witty, so strong and also beautiful. There was no question ever in my mind about publishing anything she had written.[1]

The two Tonis had Hattie Gossett, their mutual acquaintance, to thank for their introduction. At the time, Gossett was Bambara's agent and had arranged the meeting with the hope of securing a contract for her new client.

Bambara and Gossett had been friends for years, the two of them among the many Black artists who hung out at the gathering spot Pee Wee's, on Avenue A between 12th and 13th Streets. Gossett had been an editor at women's magazines, *True Story*, *Redbook*, and *McCall's* among them, and at theater magazines. She had also taught courses on Black women writers at Rutgers. But she had not made a mark as an agent. No Black woman had, really, especially in terms of securing a contract with a mainstream publisher for an author. Gossett's inexperience in that regard had no effect on the way she approached the meeting with Morrison. Quite the contrary. She and Bambara made a lasting professional and aesthetic impression on Morrison. "They were both fierce and seemed so clear," Morrison noted.[2] Their short hair, "like crew cuts," Morrison recalled, accentuated their natural beauty and affirmed their cultural confidence. The idea of three Black women controlling their own publishing fates was more than enough to inspire Morrison to accept the challenge of trying to sell a collection of short stories by an author who had a limited publishing profile.

Even before Bambara made her way from her apartment in Harlem to the Random House office on East 50th Street for their meeting, Morrison was familiar with Bambara from her edited volumes *The Black Woman: An Anthology* (1970) and *Tales and Stories for Black Folks* (1971). Bambara had also published more than a dozen stories in popular magazines and journals. Between 1959 and 1971, her short fiction had appeared in the full range of outlets—the scholarly journal *The Massachusetts Review*; the University of Nebraska–Lincoln literary magazine *Prairie Schooner*; leading Black cultural journals like *Negro Digest / Black World* and *Liberator Magazine*; two short story collections published by Scott Foresman; and the popular women's magazine *Redbook*, where Gossett had been a staff editor. As prolific as Bambara had been as a writer, she did not have a book where she was the lone author. The fact that her first two books were edited collections that showcased the work of others instead of her own exclusively reflected Bambara's lifelong commitment to community over individualism. Gossett knew Bambara well enough to know that she would always choose community over self. Part of Morrison's job as her editor was, in fact, convincing Bambara that she did not have to choose.

While critics lauded and readers embraced *The Black Woman* as a sort of collective Black feminist manifesto, its significance rests perhaps in its unwillingness to embrace or advance male/ female dichotomies and individualism. Like Bambara, Morrison had a healthy skepticism about oversimplifications of the so-called "women's question" and the ways that set up competition between race and gender and self and community. Even as Bambara agreed that women must approach "the complexity of ourselves in a fearless way," she saw no dilemma in the ways being a Black woman intersected with being a race warrior. As she told Beverly Guy-Sheftall,

> It's not as if you're a Black *or* a woman. I don't find any basic contradiction or any tension between being a feminist, being a pan-Africanist, being a Black nationalist, being an internationalist, being a socialist, and being a woman in North America. I'm not sensitive enough to people caught in the "contradiction" to be able to unravel the dilemma. . . . My head is somewhere else.[3]

Morrison found that level of complexity and sophistication of thought refreshing and imagined that readers would as well. She was certain that Bambara could do work in service of the community and share her work as a writer publishing at a mainstream house. The success of *The Black Woman* helped on both fronts.

Two months after *The Black Woman* was released—the book was designed to be small enough to fit in your pocket and to cost less than $1—it needed a second printing. Bambara boasted: "That book was everywhere. There were pyramids of *The Black Woman* in every bookstore."[4] It sold well beyond its publisher's expectation. This helped make the point that Black women's manuscripts that got a fair hearing with publishers could sell. Bambara had white friends from school who worked in publishing and speculated, with good reasons, that there were fabulous manuscripts by Black women that "end up on the sludge pile," supposedly because "there was no market for black women's work."[5] She and Morrison found common ground yet again in their determination to undermine the myth. Morrison, of course, would be at the center of this deconstruction, publishing her own work and that of other Black women writers, Bambara the first among them.

While she had not been an editor for very long, Morrison had learned quickly what factors helped editors secure contracts for books they wanted to publish. Morrison would need to be strategic in her pitch. A year after publishing *The Black Woman*, Bambara published a second edited collection, *Tales and Stories for Black Folks*, with the Zenith Books series at Doubleday. It had only been on the market for a short time, but it showed no signs of being as popular as *The Black Woman*. If Morrison used the publication of *Tales* at Doubleday as a point of note, its early low sales numbers could hurt her case. Unqualified impudence was the approach in the end. Bambara had a track record for selling books, she was a talented writer who had well-crafted stories published in reputable venues, and she was willing to accept a small advance. The latter point was crucial. The publisher had nothing to lose, Morrison argued, and everything to gain. If the collection did well, financially or critically, it would be a win. If it did not, the loss would be so minor that the opportunity to add Bambara to Random House's roster of authors would offset the loss. No one could argue with this rationale. By the end of the week, the contract was being drafted, even though every publisher, including Random House, was reticent, if not obstinate, about offering a writer a contract for a short story collection.

While Bambara worked to polish the stories she had in draft, Morrison prepared the editorial fact sheet. In the "Sales Point" section, she noted that *The Black Woman* was in its fourth printing and that sales were at four hundred thousand. Surely, the "first collection devoted exclusively to her [Bambara's] own work" would be enthusiastically received. "The amount of Black *fiction* on the market is still unbelievably slim," Morrison decried, "in spite of the tremendous interest in it. This book should satiate some of that hunger."[6] Morrison's emphasis on the lack of Black fiction available was a not-so-subtle reference to the ways poetry was the preferred genre of the Black Arts Movement, which, by 1970, was in decline.

In Morrison's view, the stories were evidence of Bambara's talent. "Perfection seemed effortless in the writing," Morrison would later remark. That kind of rhythmic prose was what she was looking for as an up-and-coming editor, "not that struggle to say something ornate, or the struggle to say something simply."[7] In that sense, editing the stories was easy. The biggest challenge Morrison had was finding the right titles. Bambara's titles, Morrison joked, tended to be cavalier or foolhardy. The title of the collection needed to be provocative but ambiguous enough to convince the reader to pick up the book to see what it was actually about. Once the book was in the reader's hands, the dust jacket copy, which Morrison would ensure was pitch-perfect, could do its work. They decided on *Gorilla, My Love*.

The title story was, among other things, a critique of adults' unwitting but no less hurtful betrayal of children. Hazel, the lead character and narrator, confronts adult duplicity every opportunity she gets. She is quick-witted and honest, unlike the adults in the story. When she and her brothers go to see the film *Gorilla, My Love* but the man in the booth plays *King of Kings* instead (because it is Easter), she protests, eventually starting a fire at the candy stand that causes the theater to close for a week. As the storyline of Jesus's crucifixion plays in *King of Kings*, she resists again by decrying the onlookers' weak-willed response to Jesus's death on the cross. If it were her brother who was to be crucified, she thinks, her parents would have been defiant. Her mother and her aunt Daisy would have hit the Romans with their purses in reprimand, and her brother would have been off the cross and playing with his friends. Long after he had been freed, her family would continue to find ways to undermine if not eliminate the Romans' state-sanctioned violence. For Bambara, no mythology was sacrosanct. Every act of violence could be interrogated and revised to show that another, more caring reality was possible. While all the stories share themes, they are executed with ample variation.

In "My Man Bovanne," Bambara explored the generational tension among community activists to make the point that everyone has a role to play in the struggle and that everyone must be cared for instead of discarded. "Raymond's Run" turns on Hazel's recognition of her disabled brother's running talent after years of focusing exclusively on her own. "The Hammer Man" comments on policy brutality against a man who is mentally unstable and on the ways social services often stereotyped Black families. A critique of capitalism informs "The Lesson" as the reader goes on an outing with young people and their teacher, Miss Moore, to FAO Schwarz and the kids think about how a $1,195 toy could feed them all for at least six months. Adult narrators in "Mississippi Ham Rider," "Talkin Bout Sonny," and "The Survivor" help round out the collection by offering personal stories that have communal implications.

Morrison admired all that Bambara accomplished with the stories in *Gorilla, My Love*. She excitedly sent the collection out in galleys to secure promotional comments. Lucille Clifton's response to Morrison's request for a blurb was telling. It echoed Morrison's sentiments about how the stories revealed Black life uniquely. Clifton wrote:

It is so good to be reading about real Black people who are doing what Black people really do; that is, dealing with life. She has captured it all, how we really talk, how we really are; and done it with both love and respect. I laughed until I cried, then laughed again. I loved it! She must love us very much.[8]

What Morrison knew was that Bambara loved Black people very much, indeed.

Morrison also knew that Bambara's craftsmanship was on full display throughout the collection. The book's critical reception affirmed this, scoring points for Morrison and Bambara alike. As one of five judges that year, Walker Percy recommended it for the 1973 National Book Award. While *Gorilla* was not selected as a finalist, its nomination was an achievement for an author publishing her first single-authored book. A favorable review of the book on October 15, 1972, in *The New York Times* certainly suggested that it was an important one. Commenting on Martha Foley's *The Best American Short Stories of 1972*, Bambara's *Gorilla*, and Norma Klein's *Love and Other Euphemisms*, C. D. B. Bryan outlined exactly what it takes to make a short story successful, at least in his judgment. "Either a short story works, or it doesn't work, and that is really all there is to it," he wrote. "No other literary form is more demanding of a writer's skills . . . [or] requires greater control, a higher polish, or more acuteness. The short story must contain everything the reader needs to know, but not one word more."[9] A good writer, he argued, provides a "flash of lightning" without overtly teaching or condescending. He then cites Bambara's "The Lesson" as one of only two short stories (along with Jose Yglesias's "The Guns in the Closet") that triggered that flash for him.

In celebrating Bambara, however, Bryan did not miss the opportunity to condemn other Black writers: "I am tired of being shouted at, patronized, bullied, and antagonized by Black writers. . . . I dis-like being told I'm an insensitive, arrogant, ofay honky who won't listen." Bambara's stories, he argued, avoided doing that. They were disturbing in their accuracy about race and capitalism, among other things, but they were "always entertaining" and impactful. In the end, ironically, he realized, "by God, [he was] an insensitive, arrogant, ofay honky after all." But he came to realize it without epithets and through Bambara's being "an articulate, intelligent and sensitive writer who happens to be very funny, hip, warm, and unmistakably her own Black woman." Bryan's review echoed Morrison's sentiment about books she wanted to publish. A good writer, in Morrison's view, could show the foolishness of racism without talking to or about white people at all. Authentic representations of Black life in America could do that work without remark. All in all, Bryan's was a strong endorsement, in a review of the best books of the year no less, and proof that a Black writer could write about Black life with no regard for the white gaze.

Morrison's determination to galvanize critical attention for the book was so effective that it was reviewed in the *Times* not once but twice. Pairing *Gorilla* with Julius Lester's *Two Love Stories*, Anatole Broyard opened his review with a disclaimer of sorts: "These two books by Black authors read as if they were revolutions apart."[10] Yet, they are forced together. Years later, Morrison would recall this forced marriage and chose release dates for her Black authors that would conflict the least with the release of other books by Black authors since she knew they would likely get lumped together, no matter their differences in content and style. Perhaps because Bambara mentioned Lester's *Black Folktales* in her collection *Tales and Stories for Black Folks*, Broyard offered the tongue-in-cheek suggestion that "Miss Bambara reads as if she had written her stories to offer a deliberate and shocking contrast to Mr. Lester's."

Miss Bambara gets pretentious once in a while—pretty often, in fact—both in trying to turn Black English into a staccato primitive poetry and in putting on airs with the king's English when she comes over all literary. Most of the time, though, her prose has a lot of jump, a fair amount of strut and an idiomatic authenticity uncluttered by the ethnic clichés of the Black chapter of the Angry Young Men.

Broyard's was a mildly favorable if stereotypical review. While the seeming juxtaposition of Bambara's use of Black English to mimic "primitive poetry" against her impervious (at least to him) use of the King's English made her pretentious, Broyard, like Bryan, thought she was to be lauded for resisting the anger of the Black Arts Movement. Published so closely to the undeclared end of the movement, *Gorilla* muddied the porous boundaries between Black Arts Movement literature and literature published after 1970. Even as she avoided the inflammatory style and language of some Black Arts Movement writers, Bambara was similarly committed to using writing for its transformative, activist, and interventionist impulses. By the end of the review, Broyard seemed aware of his own folly: "It's not certain that the difference in quality between these two books can be generalized into a broader statement about Black writers." Bambara, he imagined, may have simply come closer to "doing her thing." Her thing, as it related to her fiction, ironically, had more in common with the Black Arts Movement than either Bryan or Broyard realized.

With critical enthusiasm for Bambara's first short story collection high, Morrison worked to issue a second contract for the author, this time without Gossett as Bambara's agent. By June 1976, Bambara informed Morrison that her professional relationship with Gossett had ended, though the two were still friends. All future royalties for *Gorilla* and the advance for her next collection were to be sent directly to her. Morrison made the adjustment in her records, and the two went to work planning the content for the next collection. Four years had passed since *Gorilla's* publication, and Morrison was anxious to get Bambara's next manuscript in hand. Absent Morrison's frequent prompting, Bambara was content to write when she could find the time amid her many other obligations or when she was struck by a moment of inspiration.

Having sold just over 6,400 hardback copies of *Gorilla* and the book's paperback rights to Bantam, Morrison signed Bambara up for a second collection, which they referred to initially as *The Organizer's Wife and Other Stories*. The keynote on the editorial fact sheet announced the book as "a second collection of tough, warm and witty stories depicting Black life."[11] The description, which Morrison later excerpted for the book flap, declared that the book was

> written with Ms. Bambara's characteristic vigor, sensibility, and winning irony. The stories range from the timed and bumbling confusion of a novice "community worker" in "The Apprentice" to the love versus politics crisis of an organizer's wife and the dark and bright notes of "The Seabirds Are Still Alive" about the passengers of a refugee ship from a war-torn Asian nation. Young girls, weary men, lovers, frauds and revolutionaries— Toni Cade Bambara handles them all with expertise, passion and huge talent.

In the "About the Author" section, Morrison continued to rely on the success of *The Black Woman* and its reported four hundred thousand copies sold and on the demand for Bambara to give lectures and readings. Favorable reviews for *Gorilla* did not hurt either. "As a Chicago reviewer said," Morrison wrote on the same fact sheet, "Mrs. Bambara grabs you by the throat . . . she dazzles, she charms."

The early table of contents included titles for fourteen stories. By the time it was published as *The Sea Birds Are Still Alive: Collected Stories* in 1977, they had narrowed the stories down to ten. Like the first stories collected, these required minimal editing. But, once again, her titles needed Morrison's attention. "The Apprentice" was originally titled "Am I Spoiling Ya?"; "A Tender Man" was "The Father"; and "Medley" was "The Mother." Morrison contended that calling a story "The Father" or "The Mother" would do little to distinguish it from other stories of similar titles and even less to garner the reader or the critic's attention. They intentionally kept the title of "A Girl's Story" generic, however, to reinforce the point Bambara made in the story, that the character could be any girl. The order of the stories also needed to be adjusted. They were content to keep the last five stories as arranged, but the order of the first five changed a number of times before they settled on replacing the title of "The Winds of Change" with "The Sea Birds Are Still Alive" and making this the title story. The four stories they deleted—"Carnivale," "Ballad for Two Ladies," "Signorina Lumumba," and "The Salt Eaters"—became source material for Bambara's first novel, which Morrison encouraged relentlessly.

Both Morrison and Bambara recognized a shift in her writing between the two short story collections. Unlike most of the stories in *Gorilla*, which had a young girl narrator or a young girl character who seemed to guide the narrator's focalization, the stories in *Sea Birds* had a more mature but no less astute life commentator. In *Gorilla*, the narrator adopted the language of the people whose stories are being told, creating the sense of an absent or nonintrusive narrator on the one hand or the false sense that the narration is always first-person on the other. The seeming absence of a narrator (or author) was not an absence, however. Rather, it was the presence of a narrator whose voice was not distinct from the characters (or its author, for that matter). That quiet presence of the narrator (and by extension the authorial voice) persisted in *Sea Birds*. What changed was the narrator and characters' use of the vernacular. The narrator was still one with the people, which Bambara insisted on. She rejected outright the tradition of having a narrator whose language was feigned superiority. But the characters were now adults trying to make sense of life after incremental but no less critical positive sociopolitical changes happened domestically and abroad. Publishing *Gorilla* helped her get what she referred to as "the kid stuff" out. This cleared her thinking for other topics and approaches. Because *Gorilla* answered the question she had been asking herself for years—*How do we ensure space for our children?*—she could ask a new question with *Sea Birds*—*How are we faring now that the energy is shifting?*[12] Morrison supported this change in focus because it showed Bambara's range and moved her more toward the novel as form.

Bambara had published three books in three years, but for her, the act of creating was more a by-product of her commitment to a way of living than a function of her desire to be published for financial gain. Morrison had tried all along to convince Bambara that there need not be a separation between her writing and her activism, but it was a trip to Cuba in 1973 that helped convince her that writing could be used in the service of political struggle, to which she was foremost committed. When her trip to Vietnam was delayed, she used the time to revisit the stories that were included in *Sea Birds*. She described the turn of events to Louis Massiah:

In the spring of 1975 I was part of a delegation called the North American Academic Marxist-Leninist Anti-Imperialist Feminist Women. . . . We were invited by the Women's Union of North Vietnam to come as a delegation. . . . We were invited in the spring . . . but they had the victory in the spring, which was unexpected, so the Women's Union needed to go around and visit the socialist camp and thank people for their solidarity during the struggle. So we were put on hold. . . . I sat down and wrote, and that became *The Sea Birds*.[13]

Though most of the stories had "been hanging around the house," she had not taken the time to polish the ones that were almost publication ready.

"Sea Birds" is structured as a series of vignettes about the people involved in conflicts of war and war's resolution. The story opens with the critical recognition that newspaper reports of the war could not be trusted. Each newspaper, representing different constituents, would claim victory for the same battle. We see the movement of refugees, vendors, and foreigners as they try to survive the day. When a young girl throws food, of which there is none to spare, to screeching sea birds, a researcher thinks to himself that the birds will become vicious having been fed at one point and ignored thereafter. We learn that this same researcher had been handsomely rewarded at his university with a named chair and by "people that mattered" for a study about Afro-Brazilian personality and racial character. When his colleagues challenged him to suss out the difference between coping mechanisms of the oppressed and racial character, he declared their jealousy and doubled down on his thesis: that, like the sea birds, natives who have been "supported by foreign aid, sustained, educated, taught a superior way of life" fight back in adolescent fury when abandoned. Their fatalism, work ethic, irresponsibility, and absent sense of time explained their poverty, not colonialism and its legacy.

The title story stretched the short story genre and embraced certain features of script writing. In Bambara's mind, this story, like a number of stories in the collection, lent itself to performance as much as it did to the written page. "Medley," in fact, was written with performance in mind. When the actress Ruby Dee read "Witchbird" (which first appeared in *Essence* magazine) and "Medley" (which she read to review *Sea Birds* for *Freedomways*), Dee could see immediately how these stories could be performed. She adapted the character Honey from "Witchbird," portraying the actress/singer whose sass and spunk sustain her beyond life's challenges on the public television series Dee cohosted with her husband Ossie Davis. For "Medley," Dee created a one-woman show, where she portrayed Sweet Pea, the story's manicurist who is almost single-minded in her ambition to make a better life for her daughter. Morrison encouraged the performances since they gave unique insight into the work the stories tried to do and because they gave Bambara a new audience.

Beyond the performances, *Sea Birds* also enjoyed ample critical engagement in a wide range of venues, from *The Washington Post* and *Essence* to the *Chicago Tribune* and *Ms.* magazine. Bambara was a master of showing how Black experiences had universal appeal, a review in *Booklist* announced.[14] Dee's *Freedomways* review declared that Bambara "brings blurred, ill-defined ideas and characters into sharp focus. She writes like a fine poet who makes every word count because there's so much to say."[15] Barbara Mahone reviewed the collection for *First World*, where she observed its "great versatility in both style and subject." Reviewing *Sea Birds* for *Newsweek*, Margo Jefferson celebrated one of the collection's strengths: The variety of stories made space for all kinds of people "struggling to trim the rhetoric of their wishes to the smaller, tighter fit of reality." Robie Macauley included *Sea Birds* in his review of short story collections that offered "new feminine talents, new feminine concerns" for the March 27, 1977, issue of *The New York Times*.[16] Macauley thought that some of the stories were stronger than others, but "Sea Birds" and "Witchbird" were undeniably good. Not all the critics agreed, however. The review for *Choice* objected to how much the reader had to struggle to understand the stories and argued that Bambara's insights into the Black world were heavy-handed. Some of the stories were unrealized, the reviewer opined. To achieve the kind of universality she seemed to be after, the stories needed to be expanded to a full-length novel.

Bambara and Morrison might have agreed with the *Choice* review, at least in part. Bambara thought the stories were too long and too dense. Morrison, who was anxious to get Bambara to publish a novel, encouraged the length and suggested the density would likely be addressed with added length. She thought Bambara needed to exercise the muscles needed to write long fiction, even if this was a short story collection. In a November 1975 letter to Morrison from Bambara about the collection in preproduction, the story she was calling "The Salt Eaters" was at the center of the conversation.

> Am readying my manuscript to send off to you. Have on hand 10 of the 13 stories for new collection. Remaining 3 need editing and retyping. . . . The collection's called "The Salt Eaters" and the average length of stories is 14 pages. The title story is a novella.

They agreed to pull the story from *Sea Birds* and use it for the long-awaited novel. Even before Morrison secured a contract for it, Bambara tried to explain what she thought the novel was about principally. It unfolded, she told Morrison, in the space of the ten short minutes it takes Minnie Ransom to heal Velma Henry, the novel's main character. In Bambara's view, the novel was about one thing—an exploration of the struggle for wholeness—but it involved many other things as well: the love story between Velma and Obie; the love story between Palma and Marcus; an allegory about Black *potencia* and a freed-up colonized spirit; a blueprint and rationale for integrating political and psychic forces and for forgoing scientific certitude; and a group story about the Seven Sisters troupe and the Brotherhood of the Academy of the Seven Arts (in the tradition of John Dos Passos). "I don't know how to describe the damn thing," she wrote, "except to say it's rolling toward a conclusion."[17]

As if the uncertainty was not enough, another problem was Bambara had recently lost two typists. One had just had a baby, making her unavailable for work; and the other misplaced the book's first two chapters, forcing Bambara to re-create them. Morrison offered to have the manuscript typed in New York, thus eliminating this challenge while also incentivizing Bambara to keep writing. Bambara initially declined this option. She needed someone familiar with her drafting style and, ideally, someone close by to whom she could clarify any questions about her handwriting and the directions she drew all over the pages. But the situation now was desperate. She would try her luck and hope the person could read "what kin and friends called deranged hieroglyphics."[18]

As comfortable as she was with alternative realities, she had never had a writing experience where the characters took over the story beyond her imagination. She wrote to Morrison for advice:

About this novel business, Miz [*sic*] M. How is it done? I have now 5 chapters, some 250 typed pages and haven't a clue as to whether it is a novel or what. It's like I never never saw one much less read one in my whole life. Weird. . . . There's this 77 year old sassy woman who heals and stuff that keeps dying every 30 pages or so. Perhaps you could have a talk with her and maybe explain that I am new at this so lighten up a little. I shall need some hard headed directives.[19]

One way to make sense of *Salt Eaters*, Morrison suggested, was to read it through the lens of the three Black-led institutions in Claybourne, Georgia, the fictional town where the novel is set—the Academy of the Seven Arts, the Seven Sisters of the Pleiades, and the Southwest Community Infirmary. The gap the Academy of the Seven Arts tries to bridge is the one between the medicine people and the warriors. Velma's well-meaning husband, Obie, is the focal point of this effort. The Seven Sisters, who represent the possibilities for Third World coalitions, attempt to bridge the gap between political and artistic worldviews. The Southwest Community Infirmary offers us an example of an attempt to eliminate the gap between traditional and modern medicine practices. At the center of this convening work is the community organizer, Velma among them.

When Bambara submitted the first complete draft of the manuscript to Morrison, Bambara was not satisfied that she had found the language that could accommodate the psychic and spiritual existences of everyday life—the very thing *Salt Eaters* explores. She was satisfied, however, at her effort. Even the attempt to question assumptions and to articulate the challenge for community organizers of bridging gaps was an accomplishment in her view. She also assumed that if the novel was not readable, Morrison would direct her in the revision process.

Editing *Salt Eaters* required a level of attention even Morrison was unaccustomed to. Working on the short stories had been effortless. But editing the novel was undeniably hard, in part because its structure was so tight. Years later, Morrison told Valerie Boyd just how hard it was to make even the smallest change in the manuscript. She could not take anything out "without the whole thing collapsing." Bambara was "very, very intricate, and almost cunning in her structure," Morrison noted.

> I used to complain a lot because I said she never waited for the lame and the halt, the reader. If they weren't with her, she left them behind. . . . Once you surrendered to it and just did it (as a reader), you were amply rewarded, but it's hard any way to get readers in large numbers to put in that kind of service.[20]

Their best shot at it would be to work closely on the revisions in a focused way and without interruption.

Morrison had just moved into her new home on the Hudson, and Bambara joined her there for three days as they went back and forth with edits and revisions to ready the book for publication. "She'd write and I'd edit some," Morrison recalled.

> She would go upstairs and work, then she'd run down the stairs and say, "What about this?" Then I would sit down and go over that, then she'd run back up the stairs. It was the most amazing— but certainly extremely efficient, for us—way to do it, because she was so clear. She could focus immediately. I would just have to grunt and point and she knew exactly what I was suggesting.[21]

Once Bambara was done, Morrison began the prepublication work required to prepare for the novel's release.

Morrison announced the book on the editorial fact sheet as a "brilliant first novel by Toni Cade Bambara" whose "reputation as a writer should take a magnificent leap" with the publication of this book.[22] She also made it a point to have Bambara's name on top of the title of the book jacket.[23] While it was Bambara's first novel, she did have name recognition. Beyond placement of Bambara's name, Morrison also communicated explicit instructions to the design team, via an interoffice memo:

> Design of the interior should be very like the type and page make up of the stories in *The Sea Birds Are Still Alive*. I would just as soon not have heads or feet—just folios center top or center bottom. A nice open face with generous margins. . . .
>
> For the jacket I think a strong and colorful type jacket with special care in the choosing of the type of design will be best. The Salt Eaters refer to a large group of Black people of many backgrounds and interests who all have eaten salt, i.e. protected themselves from the snake, but neglected to protect themselves from the serpent. The book is about the healing of one individual, Velma, and also about the healing of an entire culture.[24]

As they waited for the mock-ups, Morrison pushed Bambara to get the final pages to her. Their time together in New York was productive, but Bambara felt more was needed to finish the draft. "Time's up," Morrison wrote to Bambara: "I need the last three pieces yesterday. Soon you will lose prepublication energy, excitement and money. Bullets follow along with love."[25] Morrison wanted success for the book as much as her friend did. Timing was everything.

Even after she submitted the final pages, Bambara still needed to decide about the placement of certain parts of the manuscript and to craft a new chapter from excised excerpts from another. She also needed to add a dedication page. So she traveled to New York in August to join Morrison in a final consultation with the book's copy editor to handle these details. Even with the late changes and additions, Morrison managed to avoid a long delay of the publication (the date was pushed back from January to April), and by mid-November, Morrison began to send review copies out with an introduction to the book, under her signature. The note extended the theme of anticipation: "After years of acclaim as one of our finest short story writers, Toni Cade Bambara has written a show-stopper of a first novel."[26]

The Salt Eaters was finally released on April 1, 1980. Publicity for the book included a series of book parties, especially in places where Bambara was well known or was scheduled to lecture; pitches to magazines, journals, and newspapers to review the book; and ads in the major national outlets and smaller outlets with a known Black readership. Bambara created a short list of readers to whom galleys were to be sent and then a very long list of nearly two hundred names with whom an announcement of the novel's publication was to be shared. Between March and May, she was scheduled to visit Hampshire College, Amherst College, University of Massachusetts, Colgate University, Tuskegee Institute, Livingston College at Rutgers, Cayuga Community College, and Cornell University. She also did readings and interviews at restaurants, libraries, neighborhood centers, and museums all over Atlanta. Morrison could not have asked for a more well-adapted author, one who understood book promotion as well as Bambara did and who had a following of people who would buy her book.

Morrison took every opportunity to get attention for the book, too. When Michael Dirda, deputy editor for *The Washington Post's*

Book World, invited Morrison to review for the outlet, she agreed to consider a review of *The Wayward and the Seeing: A Collection of Writings* by Jean Toomer if Dirda would return the favor. "I might be persuaded," she wrote. "Send it and I'll let you know. Now it's my turn. Read *The Salt Eaters* by Toni Cade Bambara which I am publishing in the spring (it is magnificent) and do some serious deputy editorship."[27] The not-so-subtle prompting worked, and Anne Tyler was assigned the review, which appeared in the March 30 edition of *Book World*. Tyler, like most reviewers, noted the book's ambition and the work it required of the reader. But, she argued as Morrison had, that the effort enabled the reward. In addition to getting standard appraisals in places like *Library Journal*, *Booklist*, *Publishers Weekly*, and *Kirkus Reviews*, *Salt Eaters* was reviewed in *The New Yorker*, *Vogue*, *The Boston Globe*, *Chicago Tribune*, and twice in *The New York Times*, once by John Leonard and again by John Wideman. While sales were modest at best, the book was well reviewed.

Adrienne Rich penned a substantive two-part review of *Salt Eaters* for *New Women's Times Feminist Review* in which she wrestled with the challenge of having white women critics talk about books by Black women. Articulating, repeatedly, her position as a white lesbian and feminist, Rich worked to avoid claiming an authority she could not earn while still examining the novel's political, spiritual, and social commentary. Undeniably, Rich's was among the most probing and thorough reviews of the novel. Her enthusiasm for *Salt Eaters* was so compelling that the Women's Press in London offered to bring out a paperback edition with one stipulation—that Rich's *New Women's Times* essay be used as the introductory piece to their edition.

Bambara was incensed by this heavy-handed offer. Rich was sympathetic to Bambara's annoyance, especially in light of Rich's constant refrain that white women are wrongly given authority over Black women's texts. Bambara shot off a letter to Stephanie Dowrick, cofounder of the Women's Press, after hearing about the offer.

> As I have said to both Random and Ms. Rich, I think the stip-ulation is hasty-headed if not downright rude, unshrewd, and racist. It is at least a stunning misreading of the very position Ms. Rich so painstakingly takes in her two-part essay vis a vis Black women's writings and white women reviewers. That a woman's press, presumably a feminist press, would overlook or mis-see/ appreciate the stance she is taking in the contxt [*sic*] of a feminist movement that has yet to fearlessly counter the undeniably vi-cious tradition of cultural imperialism is bewildering, shocking.[28]

Because she was still willing to discuss a Women's Press edition, Bambara offered alternatives to the Rich essay. These included Bambara's essay "What It Is I Think I'm Doing Any-how," previously published in Janet Sternburg's *The Writer on Her Work*; the interview with Kalamu Ya Salaam, "In Search of the Mother Tongue," published in *First World*; a new essay she would write for a British audience (which she presumed consti-tuted "an Afro-European" and Euro-American readership); or Eleanor W. Traylor's "My Soul Looks Back in Wonder," a review that also appeared in *First World*.

Of all the reviews of *Salt Eaters*, Traylor's was the most reveal-ing and intelligent in Bambara's view. Bambara often described Traylor, a professor and literary critic (and a close friend to Bam-bara and Morrison), as "the best reader/seer we've got."[29] After reading Traylor's review, Bambara had more clarity about what the book was doing. She admitted to Justine Tally:

After the first version of Eleanor Traylor's critical discussion of *The Salt Eaters* . . . I went and sat down and read the book again. Every time I read it, it is an act of discovery, but I particularly enjoyed it once she had organized that discussion [of the book as a jazz suite] around it. . . . That's what a good critic does. A good critic feeds it back to you and tells you how it's read, tells you how it is threaded, how they thread and read it. Then you can go back to it. Because you are not consciously thinking, "I will now set up a scene that does this and that."[30]

Part of Bambara's attraction to Traylor's critical eye also involved Traylor's effort as a critic to collaborate respectfully with the author rather than to impose the critics' view and language on the text. Her appreciation of Traylor's attentiveness was so strong that she wrote to Morrison that "Eleanor T [will] do whatever intro piece there'll be. . . . They can go fuck themselves."[31]

In that same letter, Bambara lamented the loss of another victim of the Atlanta child murders, the subject of the final book Morrison would edit on behalf of her friend. Between 1979 and 1981, in the city of Atlanta, more than forty African American children, teens, and young adults were kidnapped and murdered, their bodies discovered days or weeks after their disappearance. By the time *Salt Eaters* was released, at least six victims had been killed. But the police had found no connection between the cases. When the mothers of the children who had been killed began to protest police inaction, the community began to organize itself to investigate and to try to stop the killings, all of which were brutal—strangulations, stabbings, bludgeonings, and close-range gunshot wounds. Bambara was among those organizers. Like so much of her published work, *If Blessing Comes*, as she was calling the book at the time, started as journal entries. She kept notes about the murders as the tragedy unfolded and initially imagined the book as nonfiction before deciding that exploring the larger theme of global disappearances and the silences that enable them could be done using the novel as form. That novel was published posthumously as *Those Bones Are Not My Child*, in large part because of Morrison's interest in seeing it released.

When she finally did complete it in 1987, she felt she needed to let it sit before trying to edit it. By then, Morrison had left Random House and was no longer Bambara's editor. That change, along with the self-professed madness that attended living through the experience of the murders she was writing about, proved to be too great a challenge for Bambara to overcome. "I stopped going out, I stopped bathing, I stopped washing my hair, I became a lunatic," she told Louis Massiah.[32] Her daughter, Karma, who was thirteen years old at the time, insisted that she get it together. It did not help that her script for the screenplay of Morrison's *Tar Baby* was rejected during this time as well. She would later describe the creative block she was experiencing during these years as the early warning signs of the colon cancer to which she would eventually succumb on December 9, 1995.

Shortly after Bambara's death, Karma, who was by then an adult, enlisted Morrison's assistance to publish a final collection of essays and stories, *Deep Sightings and Rescue Missions* (1996). Morrison introduced the collection with a preface and shortly thereafter began to work on the novel, a task she committed to publicly at Bambara's Philadelphia memorial. Morrison had secured the contract for the book before resigning from Random House. Some twelve years later she ensured the book's publication, taking three months off from her own project to complete final edits for the book that was finally published as *Those Bones Are Not My Child*.

Editing *Those Bones* was a salve of sorts for Morrison, who was devastated by Bambara's death. When she began to work on the draft, Morrison realized the first page was missing.

> I had some old pages of this book from various stages—you know, parts of it: 200 pages here, 200 pages there. Anyway, when I got the manuscript, after the prologue comes the first page of the text, right? That wasn't there. The first page. I called up everybody. Who typed it? Nobody knew this, nobody knew that. I had the second page. (Laughing) You can fudge a lot as an editor, but you cannot fudge the first page. That has to be there! So, I thought, "What kind of trick is she pulling on me?"[33]

Morrison finally located an early draft of the book. Fortunately, the fifty pages she found were the same as the first fifty pages of the draft Bambara considered final. With a full draft of the manuscript now intact, Morrison began the work of cutting the novel from 1,800 pages to 669. But doing so was a difficult task. With this book, she could not separate reading it from editing it. So she enjoined an in-house editor who could read it without her "baggage and seduction."

That editor assembled a team to do research—to review the spelling of names for accuracy and consistency, to figure out what the acronyms stood for (even harder since some of the organizations referred to were defunct), and to check street and community names. "And I just would not let them [the editorial team] off the hook," she professed. "We just had to find out. The novel part of it, the fiction part . . . , that family has *got* to rest on publicly verifiable information. Otherwise, it doesn't work."[34] In the end, she had a very simple litmus test once the cutting—which required some rewriting—began: *What would Bambara say, and how would she say it?* The task was to make sure that Bambara's voice was clear, that the book reflected what Bambara wanted it to, and that the editing and rewriting work was focused supremely on what the book was demanding.

On one of the few occasions Morrison spoke explicitly and at length in print about what her work as an editor entailed, she described the work this way:

> Editing sometimes requires restricting, setting loose or nailing down; paragraphs, pages, may need rewriting; sentences (especially final or opening ones) may need to be deleted or recast; incomplete images or thoughts may need expansion, development. Sometimes the point is buried or too worked-up. Other times the tone is "off," the voice is wrong or unforthcoming or so self-regarding it distorts or misshapes the characters it wishes to display. In some manuscripts traps are laid so the reader is sandbagged into focusing on the author's superior gifts or knowledge rather than the intimate, reader-personalized world fiction can summon.[35]

None of this editorial work was necessary with Bambara as author, Morrison noted. Quite the contrary. "Entering her prose with a red pencil must be delicate; one ill-advised (or well-advised) 'correction' can dislodge a thread, unravel an intricate pattern that is deceptively uncomplicated at first glance—but only at first glance."

Bambara appreciated that delicacy from her friend and editor. In one letter, she slowed down long enough to say so.

> Occurs to me I need an agent.[36] I realize I expect/load an awful lot on you, Toni. And while I thoroughly/deeply appreciate your beyond the call of duty support, I mean damn TCB, lighten up.

In case you didn't know—you are a superb editor. I've just checked off items in the middle of your page 2 (middle of my page 300 and somp'n) and cracking up (laughin rather than ravin) over your shorthand language. Perfect. . . . Thank you, Toni. Really, truly truly.[37]

For Morrison, editing Bambara was so much more than work. It was an opportunity to witness, up close and personal, a writer with remarkable talent, a writer who was "just outrageously brilliant."[38] Working with Bambara was also confirmation for Morrison that there was a market for writers who took chances in their fiction, not unlike she did in her own.

Morrison imagined that fiction by Black authors could reflect the sophistication of Black culture in both style and content and that it could speak directly to Black people in affirmative ways rather than as a response to whiteness. Having Bambara on her author list helped clarify how Morrison could uniquely impact the tradition of African American literature after the Black Arts Movement. Recruiting Bambara in her early years as editor was all the good fortune she needed to prove to herself and to her fellow editors that she was up to the challenge of convincing others to join her cause.

CHAPTER 8

Leon Forrest and the Collective Complexity of Blackness

It is hard to imagine that Morrison could have chosen a more challenging manuscript than what would become *There Is a Tree More Ancient Than Eden* by Leon Forrest to make her mark as a literary editor. Publishing Bambara's short stories made clear that she could recruit and edit successfully talented literary artists. But Bambara had already established herself as a writer with the publication of the anthology *The Black Woman* and the publication of her short stories in mainstream magazines and journals. Notably, too, her stories needed little more than light line editing. Morrison's input as an editor for Bambara's collection *Gorilla, My Love* had more to do with the selection and arrangement of the stories. Forrest, however, was trying his hand at long fiction for the first time with his novel. What both authors did have in common, however, was a real interest in being edited. Over the years, Morrison would learn that such was not true for all the authors with whom she worked.

Forrest grew up in Chicago and was heavily influenced by Black culture there as a rendezvous point for Black people who moved to the city during the Great Migration. After high school, he served as a public information specialist in the army from 1960 to 1962, following troop training in Germany, and wrote about GIs who had curious or unique stories. He then secured a job back in Chicago as a journalist for the *Englewood Bulletin*, a community newspaper, and later with the Woodlawn Organization, a community-based nonprofit group with social, cultural, civic, and institutional interests. In 1969, he began to work at *Muhammad Speaks*, the official publication for the Nation of Islam, where he wrote feature articles and served as an associate editor until being promoted to editor in 1972.

As much as Forrest appreciated a paying job, his ambition was to write fiction. He would later realize the advantage his work as an editor at *Muhammad Speaks* gave him. Being an associate editor of the paper helped him understand how to put a story with many disparate but related parts together. It turned out that the organizing principle required to put a paper to bed was transferrable to fiction. His work at *Muhammad Speaks* also facilitated a number of key connections that positively impacted his literary career. A fellow writer at the paper who knew Forrest was drafting a novel connected him with an editor at Holt, Rinehart, and Winston, who later directed him to Morrison. He met Morrison for the first time while on assignment in New York for *Muhammad Speaks* to review Melvin van Peebles's play. And he gave Ralph Ellison a copy of the *There Is a Tree More Ancient Than Eden* manuscript while interviewing Ellison in 1972 for the paper.

The meeting with Ellison would prove to be almost as important as his meeting with Morrison. As it turned out, working at *Muhammad Speaks* was an on-ramp, not a detour.

When Morrison and Forrest first met, he had published a short piece titled "That's Your Little Red Wagon" in *Blackbird* magazine. Part of this story was eventually integrated into chapter 3 of his first novel. He had also published "Ezekiel, Notes Towards a Suicide; Poem" in *Negro Digest* and produced his three-act play, *Theatre of the Soul*, at a community theater in Chicago.[1] Still, he was largely an unknown as a writer. He had been working on his first novel for quite some time. He had not completed it, but he was convinced it was time to begin to try to sell it.

He initially sent the manuscript to Holt, Rinehart, and Winston, where Morrison's *The Bluest Eye* had just been published. The editor there who read it claimed to like it but could not make sense of it fully. He suggested that there was an editor at Random House, whose new novel also rejected a traditional plot structure, who might be interested in the kind of book Forrest's manuscript in progress was shaping up to be. Forrest called Morrison directly, a common practice in those days. When she answered, he pitched the novel to her. The next time he was in New York, Morrison told him he should come to her office to talk more about it. They arranged a meeting and talked for hours about topics ranging from literature and music to the church and politics. Meeting Forrest was like meeting every one of your relatives—old and young, alive and ancestral—in a single person, Morrison joked.

After their meeting, Forrest sent Morrison the draft in progress he had described to her over their lunch meeting. He framed the pages he shared with what he thought was necessary context for the draft.

Enclosed are chapter-portions of material from the planned
trilogy novel. . . . As you can readily see most of it is rather
dated and immensely provincial. Also, I believe that I have absorbed whatever strengths or resonance it possesses, into the
larger concerns and frame work of *wakefulness*. But if these two
chapters-portions can be of aid, in terms of an after accident report (smile) or personally help you concerning the inteelligence
[*sic*] centers and motif bundles within the finished product—
well fine.

. . . again I feel very lucky that you have found something of
value in [the] novel.[2]

Morrison read the pages quickly and was overwhelmed by
Forrest's language and innovation. The fact that he was a first-
time novelist was only a minor concern. She, too, after all, was
a recent first-time novelist. The fact that the book was the
opposite of what readers had come to expect from novels authored by Black writers, however, outweighed any concern she
had. The daring experimentation of a book steeped in Black
culture encouraged her tremendously. It was not another "fuck
whitey" treatise, she thought.[3] It was undeniably critical of racism throughout, but its critique was folded into literary imag-
inings. She found this kind of book immensely appealing. The
challenge would be to convince others at Random House to take
a chance on it.

There Is a Tree More Ancient Than Eden is a fantasy novel.
It explores the consciousness of its main character Nathaniel
(Turner) Witherspoon—the narration often adds "Turner" in
parentheses as an homage to the character's namesake—as he
struggles to come to terms with his mother's death. To understand his new reality as a motherless child, he reviews his fa-

milial and racial history to use this history to construct a viable self-identity. The novel experiments with form and turns on Nathaniel's seemingly random but loosely connected thoughts during his mother's funeral procession. It has more characters than the typical novel and no traditional plotline to be neatly followed. Instead, it hangs on the balance of imagery and emotion. While Morrison appreciated the format of a loose, almost absent plot, the book needed something to offer readers a point of entry. She suggested that Forrest add an introduction, not just for the reader but also for those she needed to convince at Random House that, with her guidance, the novel could be developed for publication.

Heeding her suggestion, Forrest wrote a new section titled "The Lives," which offered a brief description of the characters the novel develops at different points and with varying depth. Morrison assured Forrest that adding this section helped to ground the novel. She also expressed to him how much she appreciated how carefully he considered and responded to her recommendations. "Thanks for being such a 'professional' and working so well with me on the manuscript," she wrote. "For me it was essential. Now I can proceed—rather easily, I think—with the editing."[4] She felt she needed to get a handle on the story first. With that done, she could better help him determine what to move, what to cut, what to clarify, and what to reconsider. Importantly, too, she had enough coherent pages to pitch the idea to Jim Silberman, her editor in chief. Trusting Morrison's confidence in Forrest, Silberman approved a contract for the untitled novel in November 1971 but offered only a minimal advance, $2,500.

Morrison sent Forrest a copy of the manuscript with notes in June 1972. She alerted him that while she had taken her first pass editing the draft, she intended to do a second edit while he considered the pages she returned to him. She held no punches about what she thought worked and what did not work in the drafts. When Forrest sent new pages for her to review in July, Morrison responded curtly:

> This has to be *drastically* cut. It is quite out of hand. Can you reduce it to some 5 pages to include the revelation of Jamestown at the throttle, the ticket request and the fact that the narrator had none?
>
> The rest of the editing is completed and I am continually re-impressed with things I am discovering in the manuscript.[5]

In addition to recommending that he delete passages "that wander or are repetitious," she helped Forrest order the narrative (into five parts with eleven chapters) and tightened the language in the novel as needed. Their affection for one another's skill was mutual, and Forrest seldom pushed back on Morrison's edicts. He was one of the few male writers who did not challenge her authority as an editor, in fact.[6] When he sent her the next version of the manuscript, his attending letter read:

> I've pruned *our* common tree to eden/tree to heaven, as per your wise directive. I've clunged [*sic*] desperately and "drastically" to some of the wounded flesh upon the wishbone of Nathaniel to keep his personal/symbolic Passion afloat. . . . However, I won't feel castrated or lynched (smile) if you decide to prune away a few winter-frozed [*sic*] fussy limbs of dead wood.
>
> Miss Toni its [*sic*] difficult to imagine a more perfect EDITOR, who the hell needs Edmund Wilson! (smile)

Her editing, he remarked, was tantamount to translating the novel into readable English, such that the book was now "damn near coherent."[7]

To help Morrison see the novel's point of crisis, which he saw as Nathaniel's attempts to reconstruct a viable identity, Forrest reminded her that

> before and during the dialectic between these two titans . . .
> Nathan is pretty close—symbolically—to the tender floundering
> seed babe of democracy—about to be dipped into the hell-fire
> of many times retold, ritualized, most awesome western myth,
> as it is refined, as you might say, through Blackness. . . . Perhaps
> Nathan's "discovery" is important if we look at the book as much
> as a narrative poem, as novel.[8]

Their back-and-forth about the narrative arc, a function of Morrison's sharp editing, helped them both understand what the book was about. In the description for the editorial fact sheet, Morrison suggested that the book was about Nathaniel's confrontation with five "major modes of black life." The first mode was captured with his family—with Jamestown, a "tragic artist turned con-man"; his aunt Hattie, who had seen the face of God and lived; and Madge Fishbond, his and Jamestown's relative who had watched her mother set fire to their house. The second mode conflated the nightmare of his mother's death with the nightmare of racism. The third mode examined "the confrontation between the sons and fathers, the republic and its leaders, the believers and their God." The fourth commingled Jesus's crucifixion with a lynching, and the final confrontation explored "the moral implications of being black."[9]

Even with this clear summary of the novel, *There Is a Tree More*

Ancient Than Eden was still different enough from a traditional plot- and action-driven novel that she knew the early readers needed to be among the most sophisticated. She sent galleys to J. Saunders Redding, a leading Black literary critic; to Quincy Troupe, a poet and friend she would later edit; to Toni Cade Bambara, whose intellect she respected; and to Ralph Ellison, the legendary writer whose efforts to represent Black life complexly were as layered as Forrest's. Redding was impressed with the novel and declared that even as a first-time novelist, Forrest took his place beside established authors Ellison and John Edgar Wideman, Ishmael Reed, and up-and-coming writer Barry Beckham.[10] Troupe described the novel as "a sort of sustained poetic sermon dealing very effectively with the universal question of man's search for himself." Forrest's vision, Troupe declared, "opens up the lost door of our collective Black and humanistic consequences." Bambara marveled at Forrest's ability to blend "personal mythology, collective consciousness and biblical legendary all in one" and commended Forrest for showing writers "how powerful a motif/image/conceit can get when there is theme and theme control."[11]

Then on February 8, Ellison sent two pages of comments about the novel. The highly regarded writer seldom gave endorsements (only two in many years, Morrison claimed), yet he provided pages of praise for a first-time novelist. "The Ellison introduction is sensational," Silberman wrote to Morrison. "Please be sure that it is circulated [to the sales and marketing teams] with a note telling clearly what it is. . . . I also think we should make the introduction into a four page leaflet to be sent to all the reviewers plus any critics, writers, etc. that you think would be useful."[12] Morrison suggested that such a "pointed, articulate and unequivocal" statement by "the undisputed Dean of Black letters" who was known to be "very fastidious about the objects of his compliments" be included in the book as a foreword and that the phrase "with a foreword by Ralph Ellison" be added to the novel's cover. Ellison's endorsement was a score for the book, of course. But it was also a score for Morrison since she was the editor publishing Forrest's first book and, relatedly, the editor who could identify talent compelling enough to make Ralph Ellison take notice.

Early reviews of the novel were consistently admiring of its language. *Publishers Weekly*'s short review announced it as a "brilliant, beautiful, striking first novel" that "defies brief description." "The torrential flow of his language assaults the senses as well as the heart," the reviewer wrote. "The novel is rich, unique in its ability to skyrocket from reality into furious imagination." While Forrest was called "a Black Dylan Thomas," no doubt because of his extraordinary command of language, in a review that appeared in *The New Leader*, he was most frequently compared to other Black writers. The *Library Journal* review, for example, compared *There Is a Tree More Ancient Than Eden* to other "post–World War II U.S. experimental novels" written by Ellison, William Melvin Kelley, and Ishmael Reed. Even as *The New Leader* reviewer found Forrest's bouquets of words "astounding," the reviewer did not feel that the novel worked well in terms of shape and form.[13] The *Kirkus* and *Choice* reviews found it similarly unreadable and unsuccessful. But Morrison's postproduction editorial work, as the book's promoter, coupled with an endorsement from Ellison, garnered critical attention for the novel that would have been otherwise far less likely. This promotional work was rewarded when the novel scored a review in *The New York Times* and *The Washington Post*'s *Book World* in June 1973.

While Anatole Broyard did not mention Ellison until the third paragraph of the review for his *New York Times* "Book of the

Times," Ellison's artistry was alluded to in the review's first two lines: "Leon Forrest is one of the few authors I've read who have made an art form out of being Black. His voice quavers between praying and playing the dozens, a game that uses the tongue like a switchblade."[14] Ellison, "Black literature's magic Old Man of the Mountain," is then called upon to offer up bona fides for the novel. And while Broyard outlines in brief all that Forrest did well and all the places he faltered ("Mr. Forrest is too important . . . to risk overpraising him"), the thing most striking about the review was its subtle restatement of Forrest's transcendence of the limits of the 1960s' Black aesthetic. Quoting Ellison, Broyard noted: "Having rejected the stance of cultural self-segregation," Forrest took breathless risks in terms of form. In other words, the novel dwelled in Blackness without reducing Blackness to an object of racism. Rather, it used all literary forms available to interrogate and exalt Black history, life, and culture.

For Houston A. Baker Jr., one of the few academic critics who dared to review the book, the complexity of this experimental Blackness was the novel's strength. Lamenting the clout of the "angry positivistic crowd" that "has been allowed to lead mockingly-simplistic works into the world with great acclaim," Baker, in one of two reviews of the novel that appeared in the January 1974 issue of *Black World*, made the case for those writers, Forrest among them, who broke with these conformists and opted, instead, to represent a multifaceted Black experience "in a rich, poetical style." "*There Is a Tree More Ancient Than Eden* is a welcome addition to the rich garners of our library store," Baker wrote, "and an occasion to assert once more that the cornucopia of talent that resides in Black American cultre [*sic*] must not be fettered by the hysterical fiats of literary hustlers."[15] Baker went on to offer one of the most coherent and informed analyses of the novel and carefully charted each section of the novel and its difficult plot.

In the second *Black World* review, Zack Gilbert was less convinced that Forrest avoided compromising "authentic" Black culture in the novel. Despite finding its poetic flow moving and forceful, Gilbert questioned whether or not "Forrest was writing only for a white literary establishment and a few pseudo Black intellectuals." He closed the review with a similar question: "Is Forrest only a verbal manipulator doing excessive gymnastics with words, or is he a deep and serious writer probing and exploring new areas in the human psyche?" Morrison's attraction to *There Is a Tree More Ancient Than Eden* was, at least in part, to Forrest's ability to navigate the very conversations that prompted *Black World*, arguably the leading journal for Black literature and culture at the time, to present two views of the novel in the same issue. She recognized that Forrest's prose would be difficult for some. But there was no question in her mind that he was exactly the deep and serious writer probing the human psyche Gilbert suspected he might be. That was the kind of writer she wanted to be and the kind of writer she wanted to edit, not exclusively but certainly intentionally.

Morrison knew when she signed Forrest up for the first book that she wanted to offer an option for a second. One of the ways to build her list of books was to plan to work with an author beyond the first book if the author-editor relationship was effective. Forrest's initial suggestion for a second book was for a collection of essays—some from among those he had published in *Muhammad Speaks* and in the Woodlawn newspaper he wrote for and some that were unpublished. The book "would run some 300 pages from interviews with Elgin Baylor to Mayor Richard G. Hatcher to reviews on theater and stories on jazz musicians and Mississippi politics and controversy over methadone."[16] At the time that he proposed the idea, he was unsure whether he would get approval from *Muhammad Speaks* to reprint any of the articles. The Nation of Islam had its own press, though it did not have its own bindery. So it would have to be financially advantageous for the Nation to approve such a book. Publishing a "hard-hitting collection of news articles and essays" after the experimental novel, they thought, could actually draw more attention to *There Is a Tree More Ancient Than Eden*. With the process of securing clearance for reprinting articles from *Muhammad Speaks* constantly in flux, Morrison and Forrest decided against that project and agreed to pursue a contract for a second novel instead. Random House had lost money in publishing *There Is a Tree More Ancient Than Eden*. While it had been a critical success, everyone understood that the next book needed to be commercially viable.

In early 1974, Forrest sent Morrison an early draft of what would become *The Bloodworth Orphans*. The novel was to be the second book in a trilogy connected by location—Forest County—and by the recurring character Nathaniel Witherspoon. A big part of Morrison's attraction to Forrest was the fact that editing his fiction sharpened her craft as a writer. They shared an interest in Black culture and in experimental forms to tell complex stories. Her examination of the manuscript was meticulous. Every word needed to be perfectly chosen and necessary. "How can geese look like scarecrow? Is the protoplasm livid and drooping? Or the charred cherubim? If the latter, how can 'charred' (meaning burnt black) cherubim be livid (white with fear?)" Such lyrical play rendered passages weak and flabby, she declared. There were places where the prose needed considerable pruning. The beginning needed both pruning and revision, for instance. The early pages should be "lean and swift." Instead, the reader was introduced to a character's stepmother on page 2. She is referred to on page 5, but her name isn't revealed until page 8. This kind of withholding was unfair to the reader, Morrison noted. It was "too calculated to be of use," and it left the reader feeling manipulated.

She also recognized the pattern she thought Forrest needed to be attentive to. His dream sequences tended to be too weighty and suffocating. His sermons and testifying monologues, contrastingly, almost never were. The sermons and monologues were "almost flawless," revealing control and skill. Contrastingly, the dream sequences, which he used effectively in *There Is a Tree More Ancient Than Eden*, in this draft, dipped over "into the old 1930s stream of consciousness which is overdone in contemporary fiction" and which relieved the writer of his responsibility. Forrest needed to avoid that alluring trap. She was determined not to let him rest on his laurels and to help him create a better book. Toward the end of her comments, she wrote:

> Chapter 10. A beautiful piece. First Rate. There is some folding in upon itself in Nathaniel's thing beginning on p. 288.
>
> And then in Chapter [11] everything built up for almost 300 pages falls apart—or rather becomes something else which may be your short cut—a way of getting out of the rigors imposed by the previous chapter. . . .
>
> But Chapter 12 is funny.
>
> Leon, you can just go on with the new stuff. And consider all this later. I find the dichotomy the only real problem. The rest is mere revision, edited [*sic*], culling etc.[17]

Forrest began to address the issues Morrison raised, while Morrison convinced Silberman to offer Forrest a contract for the book. She tried to call Forrest with the good news that she had been successful. When she was unable to reach him by phone, she jotted off a quick note to him: "The contract for your book went through. It was a little difficult because we lost money on *Tree*. Yet and still . . . I hope we have commercial as well as literary success with the new one."[18] Forrest wrote back immediately, thanking Morrison for fighting for him and for her belief in his talent. Over the next few months, they talked regularly and exchanged pages of the manuscript. This time, Forrest joked, he agreed with 95 percent of the cuts, deletions, and changes she suggested. This was a 5 percent increase over his response to her suggestions for *There Is a Tree More Ancient Than Eden*. Either he was finally learning from her careful guidance, or she had worn him down.

Morrison visited Forrest that spring in Evanston. Along with Cyrus Colter, the fiction writer and former lawyer and government official who had recently become the first Black person to hold an endowed chair at Northwestern University, Forrest had invited Morrison for an official visit to the university. She offered a reading hosted by the Department of African American Studies where Colter and Forrest held faculty appointments. Morrison enjoyed her time there and wrote to thank Forrest and to give him an update on the status of the manuscript shortly thereafter. She wrote: "Your book is still winding its way through copyedit. Your typist has a way with commas that is festive to say the least. As soon as I can, I'll send the whole of it to you. I love *The Bloodworth Orphans* as the title and have marked the change on the mss. and all references."[19] Forrest was anxious to get the bound galleys for the novel. His tenure and promotion file would be under review in the fall. And he needed this book to buttress his application. He was too old to start a new career, he joked. And university life was ideal for him as a writer.

The galleys were finally ready in October, after the copy editor painstakingly worked through the manuscript, which Morrison lamented was plagued by misspellings and unclear phrases and word usage made worse by bad typing. She decided to cast *The Bloodworth Orphans* as a creative achievement, even as she was hoping for commercial success. She ended the description on the editorial fact sheet with this line: "Literary, yes, complex, yes, but this novel is a triumph of magnificent writing." The market analysis was similarly aimed. His readership was small and growing in no small part from exposure to his work in scholarly journals and in graduate courses at highly selective places like Cornell, Yale, and Wellesley. He would "remain important and become major" in these circles and beyond. His author biography connected him to the University of Chicago (though he had only studied there briefly) and noted his faculty role at Northwestern.[20] Reviews were favorable, excepting a scathing review from Broyard in *The New York Times*. As much as he admired *There Is a Tree More Ancient Than Eden*, he hated *The Bloodworth Orphans*. Sales were similarly modest and, in that regard, disappointing. It was a small miracle that Morrison was able to get Random House to offer Forrest a third contract. Five years would pass, however, before she made any serious effort to do so.

Forrest sent the manuscript of his third novel to Morrison, and she alerted him that she would have to get Jason Epstein, who had become the firm's editorial director, to approve any offer she might propose on Forrest's behalf. When an unusual amount of time passed between his submission of the draft and any subsequent conversation about it, Forrest assumed that, even with Morrison as his editor and champion, Random House had finally resolved to cut their losses. Unable to reach Morrison by phone in her office, he wrote to her asking her to retrieve the manuscript. He assumed that she had finally run out of luck in her advocacy for him. The playful prose he typically used in his letters to Morrison was replaced by solemnity:

> Obviously Mr. Jason Epstein either has no intention of reading the manuscript; or perhaps he has read enough of it a while back and decided it wasn't marketable, and is trying to wait you out before informing you of his decision. I may be wrong too, but thats [*sic*] the way things look from here.
>
> Dearest Toni: my decision to ask that you retrieve and return my manuscript in no way reflects any bad feeling on my part concerning your efforts in all of this. . . . Indeed I would be the first to say that it is rather doubtful that Leon Forrest would not be in print if it weren't for the efforts of Toni Morrison. . . . No doubt Mr. Epstein saw my name on the bound volume of the new manuscript and decided it would not be worth another financial plunge for Random House.[21]

But what Forrest did not know was that Epstein had not seen the manuscript at all. Morrison finally sent it to him a few weeks after Forrest's letter asking that it be returned and after she had read it again. While neither of the first books earned out, she confessed to Epstein, Forrest was still a literary writer whom Random House should support. Whatever determination remained for the publisher to champion good literature over pure profit motives should be applied here. This book, Morrison argued, was much more accessible in language and style than either of the previous two novels and, therefore, Morrison argued, had great potential to sell.

Epstein approved the contract a week later, "with the same modest terms as last time." Morrison passed the good news on to Forrest with a call. She was disappointed that she could not offer more for the advance, she confessed, but there was no way around that. Forrest was excitedly surprised and shrugged off the fact that the advance was low. He was clear that Random House spent more money making his novels than they earned in selling them. The advance, as small as it was, would boost the down payment he needed to buy a condo in Evanston. Morrison had already told him that she was working at Random House far less now that her career as a writer had blossomed fully. But she agreed to work with him on the novel, which they were calling *The Light of the Body Is of the Eye*. Her responses would be slower, but he would not lose his editor.

Forrest sent the latest version of the novel—he had worked on it during the period of silence—in May 1982. Morrison warned that there was no way she would get to it that summer. She would aim for August, but there was no rush since it was already too late to get the book ready for spring. What she could offer now was a phone conversation about her initial impressions. It was mid-December, however, before she sent him the copy of the draft she marked on and the attending notes she made following her characteristic editorial read of the draft. Part of the delay, she claimed, was that she needed to do careful line editing because the copy editor who had worked miracles on his first two novels was no longer at Random House. And only someone familiar with his prose could do the draft justice. "Also," she noted, "I don't have the help in this regard I once had when I was fulltime at Random House. Therefore my way of indulging authors vis a vis the condition of the manuscript is a bygone thing."[22]

She limited her notes to those observations that needed immediate attention. Some typical problems returned—the monochromatic sound among different characters, passages where the reader's attention flagged, and overdependence on favored words. A new problem area, however, was Forrest's weird use of phonetic spellings during certain characters' dialogue. Was it an effort to distinguish the level of education of some characters or what? She chided: "In any case, when I see white writers do this I scream 'racism'—so I am embarrassed to find here 'smok' for 'smoke' where there is no other way to pronounce it: 'ah' for 'I' when chances are everyone pronounced it the same way. . . . I recommend the distinctions be in diction not in orthography."[23] Beyond this, he needed to revise with pace in mind to avoid sections that were dangerously slow.

Forrest had a revised draft on Morrison's desk at the beginning of the year. First, he changed the title. He suspected that *The Light of the Body Is of the Eye* was too obtuse. And this book needed all the help it could get to entice the reader. *Two Wings to Veil My Face*, he noted, polled well with those he talked to over the holidays. Morrison agreed that the title was perfect. She was pleased with the revisions Forrest made in his January draft, once she finally found the time to read them. By June, with the draft in good shape, she accepted the fact that she needed help with the remaining prepublication steps. She wrote to Forrest.

> The simplest way to say this is that I can't keep up the pace *and* keep up the writing. So, since I have begun a new manuscript I am leaving Random House. Several problems prevented me from making that decision—one of which was your work. But two happy things have been arranged—so you need feel no alarm. One is that Lynn Strong who copedited [*sic*] your last [novel] and who was not here any longer is copyediting it as a freelancer. She is very good as you will remember. The other happy thing is I believe the editor who will handle the book is really first rate. Errol McDonald. I believe I told you about him some time ago—with a lot of enthusiasm in my voice because

I was so happy a brilliant young black editor had been hired here. . . . I am here through June and part of July.[24]

Twelve years after taking Forrest on as the first novelist she would edit, it was fitting that his novel would be among the last novels she would work on. She had become a better writer by being his editor. And she had done the hard work of challenging Random House to be faithful to its roots of promoting literary art over commercialism. Her work with Forrest—a shared achievement—was done.

CHAPTER 9

The Extraordinariness of Ordinary Black Womanhood

Dear Barbara,
I astounded myself by getting some overwhelming support for your book at [the] sales presentation yesterday. I went in hoping for a 1,500 print run and well—I was brilliant! Now I have a very severe problem—how to get all those thousands to actually buy your book. If it comes back after we advance it, I will slit my throat.[1]

Morrison's boldness in convincing Random House to print five thousand copies of Barbara Chase-Riboud's *From Memphis & Peking* (1974) was a sign of her growing influence as an editor at Random House. While the firm maintained elements of publishing culture that claimed to use literary merit as a core guide for decision-making about which books to publish, Random House was not at all interested in publishing books that caused them to lose money. Even a book that was a critical success and thereby likely to burnish the firm's reputation needed, at minimum, to earn out. Poetry collections created an especial challenge in this regard. Pitches by editors to acquire a debut collection by an unknown author exasperated sales teams, and yet Morrison prevailed upon her colleagues to trust her instincts that she could sell thousands of copies of a book of poems by a well-known sculptor who was, conversely, completely unknown as a Black woman poet.

The fact that Morrison's second novel, *Sula* (1973), was set for wide release in a few days no doubt emboldened her. Based on early reviews of the novel, it would be a critical success, affirming her position as a first-rate writer. Whatever clout she achieved as a novelist could only accrue to her benefit as an editor.

By the time she signed Chase-Riboud up for *From Memphis & Peking* in 1973, Morrison had learned a lot about the many steps of the publishing process—from acquisition, editing, and design to proofing, pre-promoting, and printing to sales, marketing, and publicity. She had also published books in a range of genres—a literature anthology, a medical handbook, a legal textbook, two collections of essays, a collection of short stories, and a novel. She had not, however, published a book of poetry. This changed quickly when, all in a matter of months, rather serendipitously, Morrison began to work with three Black women poets. In the early months of 1973, she met Chase-Riboud through a mutual friend. By fall, she was in conversation with Lucille Clifton, who was already a Random House author. A few months later, she and June Jordan began to conspire to have Jordan secure a contract with the publisher. At the same time, Morrison was working to recruit other authors and publish other books. What these three women had in common, however, was an editor whose fame as a writer was on the rise and who was willing to use whatever cachet this gathered to publish poetry by Black women writers at a time when Random House was less than enthusiastic about publishing slim volumes of poetry that were as likely as not to end up on the wrong side of the profit sheet.

The first volume of poetry Morrison published as an editor was Chase-Riboud's *From Memphis & Peking*. The volume was also Chase-Riboud's first book as an author. Like so many relationships in the art world, theirs was a function of having a mutual friend or acquaintance. Lynn Nesbit, who was Morrison's literary agent at the time, hosted a party in New York where Morrison and Chase-Riboud were both guests. A friend who knew Nesbit and Chase-Riboud incredulously remarked to everyone within earshot: "You'll never guess what Barbara has done. She's written a collection of poems."[2] By then, Chase-Riboud was gaining a reputation as a sculptor of note, but she had no formal training as a writer. She had not even taken a literature class in college. In an act of casual bravado, Chase-Riboud shared some of the poems with Nesbit, who, in turn, invited Morrison to read them. Having a client who was also an editor had its benefits. Morrison liked the poems right away. As she was apt to do for manuscripts she admired, she wasted no time proposing and getting approval to acquire the book. She had a contract drawn up and sent it to Nesbit, who logically became Chase-Riboud's literary agent. The financial terms were beyond modest—$500 on signing and $500 on delivery of the manuscript. If the firm was going to reluctantly embrace the prospect of successfully publishing an unknown, first-time poet, at least it would minimize its liability by offering a negligible advance.

Born in Philadelphia, Pennsylvania, Chase-Riboud was educated at Temple University's Tyler School of Fine Arts and Yale's School of Art, where she earned an MFA in design and architecture in 1960, becoming one of the first women of color to earn an MFA from there. Shortly after graduate school, she moved to France, where she earned international acclaim as a sculptor whose work was influenced by classical European artists and African artistic practices. By the time she and Morrison met, Chase-Riboud had exhibited her work in major galleries in Paris, Boston, New York, Berkeley, Philadelphia, Germany, and Belgium, both in solo shows and among public collections. Her photographic essays had appeared in *Harper's*, *Vogue*, and *Essence*, and her sculptures had been reviewed in *The New York Times*, *ARTnews*, and *The-Art-Form*. Logically, Morrison leaned into Chase-Riboud's success as an artist instead of trying to situate her exclusively as a poet in her own right. Part of the "brilliance" at the sales conference Morrison wrote to Chase-Riboud about was Morrison's decision to describe Chase-Riboud as "an extraordinarily beautiful black sculptress" who is "an exciting, highly promotable personality." Even before she had a robust body of work to exhibit, for instance, Chase-Riboud gained some notoriety in 1958, donning the cover of *Ebony* magazine as the young Black teenager who was studying art at the American Academy in Rome. By the time she and Morrison met, Chase-Riboud was enjoying the attention she was receiving in response to gallery exhibitions where her work was on display, especially the *Malcolm X* steles, from New York to Berkeley. The book, Morrison contended, consisted of "tough, fibrous poetry reflecting Mrs. Riboud's world and her extraordinary perceptions."[3]

While the collection was inspired by Chase-Riboud's travels abroad, *From Memphis & Peking* explored historical themes beyond places she had visited and connected personal, familial, and communal experiences with world history. The book opens with thirteen poems in the section titled "Memphis." Though she plays on the geographic ambiguity (invoking the blues refrain that alludes to Memphis, Tennessee), the Memphis Chase-Riboud refers to is the city in Egypt, where she was first exposed to a wealth of African art. The poems vary in length, style, and theme. They share a richness in allusions, however, and they reveal a heightened awareness about African ancestry. The last two poems in the section—"On Hearing of a Death in Prison (for George Jackson Blois, August 21, 1971)" and "Going to Memphis"—situate African American experiences amid world mythology, which she redirects, in terms of point of origin, from Europe to North Africa.

The next section of the book, "Anna," is an extended poem that continues the quest for connection she initiated in the "Memphis" section, by beginning with her grandmother and moving backward to Zanzibar and the Indian Ocean before connecting these histories to famous Black women and to herself and her mother. "Letters," the third section in the collection, invokes the assumptions of the epistolary form to explore personal themes of love and inquiry. In these poems, Chase-Riboud shows just how unmoved she is by feminist assertions of the day about the limitations of heteronormative love. In "To Gloria," for example (a poem rhetorically addressed to Gloria Steinem), Chase-Riboud declares her affinity to love and beauty and argues that she is no less liberated because of it: "I have / A / Problem / I / Am / Female / And / I / Am / Lib- / Erated / But / I would rather be / Beau- / Tiful / Than / Not / I / Would rather be / Made love to / Than / Not. . . . I / Am / A / Backsliding / Man-loving / Crotch-gazing / Phallus-adoring / Counter-revolutionary / Renegade."[4] As bold as the poem was, she and Morrison both underestimated how the poem would alienate Chase-Riboud from the white women who might have otherwise championed the collection.

The final two sections—"Peking" and "White Porcelains"—

continue her use of sensual language and remind us that her first art form is visual. These sections also connected her to the larger artistic vision of herself as one interested in and committed to exploring ambivalence and complexities. Morrison thought the literary merit of the poems, combined with their creative exploration of familiar themes, was evidence of the ways poetry done well—with attention to craft—could aptly hold Black experiences and poetic value at once.

From Memphis & Peking was published rather quickly by most standards. Morrison and Chase-Riboud finalized the poems and their arrangement in the volume during the summer of 1973 when Chase-Riboud hosted Morrison and her boys for two weeks in France—a bonus trip to their planned vacation in Spain. When she returned to the US with the manuscript in hand, Morrison sent it to the production team and began to focus on publicity for the book. First on the list of promotional work was an event to celebrate the book's launch. Anxious to collaborate with Random's publicity associate Caroline Harkleroad on this, Morrison soon encountered resistance from an unlikely source. Chase-Riboud was reluctant to participate in a book party and said so immediately, and she was completely resistant to reading alone at a party. They tossed around ideas about having others read with Chase-Riboud, having her record her readings in advance to play in different rooms if they were able to secure a museum as the venue, or having singer Roberta Flack accompany Chase-Riboud as she read if Flack was available and willing to do so.

While Morrison had counted on Chase-Riboud's personality to help sell the book, Chase-Riboud belatedly declared that she wanted the book to sell exclusively on its merits. She desperately wanted to avoid the fate of artists who "tap dance for prizes and coverage." When she lamented that "even coveted things like the

Yale poetry prize has [*sic*] no meaning because its value is blurred because of its commercial value,"[5] Morrison shot back:

> I don't understand what you are saying about holding a firm line between the work and the publicity. I hope you are right that people who like the work will "do things" for it without being asked—that would relieve us entirely of doing anything at all other than manufacturing it—but it is probably not a good idea for us to take that risk. We have to think of all sorts of anonymous people walking into a book store and wanting to buy the book for some reason—one reason I can give them is that they have heard or read about it. . . . I must also try to get booksellers to put in [*sic*] on their shelves and they will do that for one of two reasons: Random [House] says so or they *too* have heard about it. So. What is that but publicity? . . . This is a commercial house historically unenchanted with 500 slim volumes of profound poetry that languish in stockrooms.[6]

Morrison had fought hard to get Random House to agree to underwrite a book party, so she was quite frustrated by what she thought was Chase-Riboud's unwarranted and surprising hesitancy. She went from frustrated to annoyed when Chase-Riboud suggested that Morrison ask two of Chase-Riboud's friends who were "experts about such things," as if Morrison and the publicity team at Random House were not. The compromise, in the end, was that Nesbit and her husband Richard Gilman would host a party at the couples' Central Park West apartment on May 23, 1974.

Part of Chase-Riboud's anxiety, she ultimately admitted, was her husband's disdain for self-promotion. "Marc . . . is pathologically against personal publicity," Chase-Riboud wrote to Morrison. "He thinks one should become 'famous' like he did by sitting on a sand dune in the Sahara or in a rice paddy in North Vietnam. So, I'm fighting on two fronts: first my own natural tendency to shy away and his fuss about the whole thing."[7] Chase-Riboud's husband, Marc Riboud, was a celebrated French photojournalist best known for photographing ordinary people doing ordinary things. Two of his most famous photographs (one of a workman posed like an angel while painting the Eiffel Tower and another of a woman presenting a flower to armed national guardsmen during an anti-war protest at the Pentagon) were published in *Life* magazine. Fortunately, Morrison and Chase-Riboud had gotten to know each other well quickly, during their two weeks together in France. The rapport they developed helped them withstand the many conflicts that arose as production of the book unfolded. Instead of tension, there was wit. "Your insanity is so interesting," Morrison wrote, "not at all like most madness."

To assuage Chase-Riboud's fears about reading alone (she continued to insist that her voice was too soft, low, and timid), Morrison agreed to read with her.

Be assured that your editor will attend giving you moral support and I am not totally turned off by the idea of reading with you—as a sort of anonymous editor (who admittedly has worked intimately with the work). It would complement—not distract from—the poetry. Also, I do it well. If, however, by that time I am truly famous, as the consequence of my new book's [*Sula*'s] publication in January, then you may as well have Ms. Flack. . . . So. Go ahead and ask Lynn and hope Roberta is free.[8]

She closed the letter with sentimentality and snark: "Love, girl and fuck the sand dunes," no doubt in response to Marc's sentiment about publicity and the way he left Chase-Riboud feeling unsure.

The prepublication tussles were not limited to publicity and the book party. They also had ruminating exchanges about the book's design. In early fall, Morrison sent Chase-Riboud a copy of the preliminary design, noting that they were using Electra for the text type and Weiss initials for the titles. The copyedit team also had questions about turnover lines, but Morrison agreed to wait until the manuscript was in galleys to address the problem. In response, Chase-Riboud had a list of things she thought needed to be changed.

> My feeling is the following: That the designer didn't read the book and thought: a classy French lady who writes love poetry. Don't you think so? So, although I really wanted to keep out of it, I first spent seven hours looking at at least 3,000 book covers in the three American books [*sic*] stores in Paris. The poetry covers are the worse. I found two covers I liked: one *Fire in the Lake* and the other *The Savage God*. . . . After about thirty tries (and I did try to work without the framework of the designer's layout)—(it didn't work) I have come up with the enclosed layout which I think is superb. I didn't think I would come up with something I like as much. If you like it, fight for it.[9]

Additionally, Chase-Riboud wanted the fleur-de-lis motif changed, arguing that it was "too complicated and too floral." She wanted a new type, one that was sexier and stronger, "more American and more mysterious than the original." The word *and* needed to be dropped from the title and replaced with an ampersand to highlight the relationship and juxtaposition between the words *Peking* and *Memphis*. In her view, very little about the design in draft worked. After all, Chase-Riboud noted, she was a "fallen" graphic designer. So, the Random House designer would understand, she mused.

Morrison's response was canny. Chase-Riboud had gone to such great lengths to have the cover adjusted according to her design when the copy Morrison sent was for the title page, not the cover at all. Still, Morrison took the opportunity to address Chase-Riboud's assumption that the designer did not "know" the book.

> We talked about every detail of your book. I never worked with a designer who was such a perfectionist. . . . I think he can switch ornaments—but he chose the one he did from a Chinese silk screen pattern—which he showed me because I thought it was not "Eastern" enough. So much for Sino-French artistic sources. . . . After I have spoken to the designer (and tell him that you belonged to his guild) I'll watch for the convulsions, wait for his recovery, then propose the title page change.[10]

In response to Chase-Riboud's query about how they might handle front matter, the people she wanted to thank especially, Morrison queried:

> Will you want a dedication page . . . as well [as an acknowledg-ments page]? Sometimes both are included—the latter being a "To Honeypot without whose encouragement this book was certainly done" kind of thing. Your "Thanks to" is unusual at the end—but O.K. if we have a page that does, in fact, announce the end of the book.[11]

Morrison's artful "To Honeypot" remark was, of course, another dig at Marc, who, in Morrison's estimation, seemed less than en-thusiastic about his wife's latest adventure. At one point, the ten-sion about Marc's and their so-called friends' interventions was so thick that Morrison asked Chase-Riboud if it ever occurred to her that all the people advising her against Morrison's professional suggestions wanted her book to fail.

When Morrison sent Chase-Riboud the jacket proofs for the book, the passive-aggressive exchanges finally came to a head. Morrison chose a picture of Chase-Riboud holding a piece of her sculpture for the front of the book and another picture of Chase-Riboud for the back. The silver and black color scheme, along with the images, were meant to convey an aesthetic sense of elegance. But Chase-Riboud saw the choice differently. "I find the dust jacket slick and overmerchandised and for no good reason and to the detriment of the poems," she wrote.

> I especially object in the strongest way to Two, repeat Two phtos [*sic*] back and front. This is unheard of and really too much. The reaction here . . . is negative in that it becomes another "black book" which is not the case and "look a black girl." The whole feeling is vaguely sexist, Hollywood racist and exploitive.[12]

To put a fine point on her objection, she also accused Morrison of being trapped in the "mentality of white publishing" and of failing to take advantage of an opportunity to consult with Chase-Riboud to style the book in a way that could have benefited them both. Morrison's response was measured and matter-of-fact.

> I don't understand you. Why did you send us 36 pictures if we weren't supposed to use them—on the jacket or wherever? What did you think we were going to do with them? . . . Seven calls and two telegrams have been placed to you with no response. But the urgency regarding publicity—not judgment about jacket covers. . . . No author tells me what to do in that area. . . . If you wanted an anonymous, plain, uneventful recessive jacket

you should never have come to this publisher. The only time that works is when the poet is very well known—as a poet. You are not. The purpose of the jacket is to make people pick it up, fondle it and hopefully open the book. The acid test is on the pages. . . . Remove it [the jacket] and your book will die in every book store in this country. You have the opportunity to transfer to some people some beauty and sensibility—take a chance.[13]

Morrison did not bother to respond to the insinuation that her imagination had been overtaken by the white publishing world she had learned to maneuver so well. Her commitment to making the publishing industry bend toward her intentions as a Black writer and editor, at least as she saw it, was beyond dispute.

Their evolving disagreement notwithstanding, Morrison continued to try to get attention for the book. She made promotional pushes for it, but it received minimum reviews, even in places like *Choice*, *Library Journal*, *Kirkus*, and *Booklist*. Poet Alvin Aubert found the poems "impressive in their thematic range and complexity." The *Kirkus* review noted that the poems had a "rare combination of strength, grace and ambition" and called the book "a tough-minded, soft-hearted, often touching and always interesting book." The most national attention for the book came with a *Washington Post* article by Angela Terrell, who introduced the reading audience to Chase-Riboud as a poet and world traveler whose poetry was connected to her movement within and across cultures. "Her poems (like) her sculpture," Terrell wrote, "are a lucid reflection of their creator . . . a trip from a three-dimensional world to another."[14]

Limited though they were, all the reviews were favorable. But it did not seem to matter. In the end, the book did not sell well and got too little critical attention from the people and places that mattered. When Chase-Riboud made the appeal for a second push of publicity, as though she had cooperated with the first one, Morrison would not entertain it. Instead, she noted that advertising and promotion money, perhaps counterintuitively, was reserved for books where sales were encouraging. "Had my own better judgment been executed," she confessed, "we would have printed less the first time around. The obstacles I anticipated in sales . . . proved to be too strong."[15] In Morrison's opinion, there were three paths to success for the book. The first was the general poetry market. But Chase-Riboud was not an established name, so access to that market was limited. The second was the woman writer angle, which was not available to Chase-Riboud either.

I know how you hate these little slots and niches but the fact is, women exert an enormous amount of influence these days in publishing. There are several magazines; there are . . . feminist book clubs; and they do make up an enormous amount of the book buying public. In addition, when they take to something, they agitate for review space. I never believed that was going to happen . . . mostly because of the Gloria Steinem poem and the heavy and frequent theme of women as love objects that runs through some of your poetry.[16]

In the Steinem poem, the persona rejects Steinem's brand of feminism that correlates being female and liberated with a rejection of beauty standards and an affinity for heterosexual love. The lines that follow also make clear the persona's acceptance of the comforts of capitalism. Juxtaposing her self-parody as a "Good nigger / Southern white folks / Haul out to / Prove / Their niggers / Are / Happy / Niggers" with mentions of her donning high-end brands like Gucci, Louis Vuitton, Piaget, Tiffany, Hermès, and Givenchy, the persona confesses that she loves men. To some, this would warrant her being called a "handkerchief head / *Sexist / Slave*."[17] The beauty and integrity of the poems—especially in the poem's critique of white women's feminism and Black women's identification with it—Morrison suggested, were of less consequence than were their ideological and sexual politics, which turned the influential women's audience off.

The third path for the book was the market for Black readers. Morrison chided:

> In that area, which, like the women's movement, is an influential market and an easily identifiable one, similar marketing problems existed. Your [*sic*] were quite rightly not interested in doing a "black thing." But that meant I could not "pitch" you to that area either.[18]

With these three paths closed, along with the lack of reviews in key places and the complete dissolution of the shows the publicity team tried desperately to arrange, Morrison's hopes for the book had been dashed. In spring 1975, Morrison asked her colleague Tony Wimpfheimer to have one thousand copies of the volume held since Chase-Riboud was about to begin an international tour for her sculpture. Since there were no bids for the book's remainders, he noted, the whole quantity could be held. Morrison's experience working with Chase-Riboud was instructive. Morrison knew that having a publicity and promotion plan was an important aspect of how well a book sold. But never again would she assume an author would cooperate with her plans without explicitly saying so. She also sharpened her thinking around identifying a primary and secondary market for books she would acquire. Chase-Riboud's social capital among white cultural and artistic aficionados did not translate into a book-buying public. And alternative paths to the book's success were unavailable for different reasons. Authors needed champions beyond their editors and publishers. If they were not lucky enough to enlist influential supporters, they certainly had to avoid making powerful enemies. The same politics that yielded enthusiastic endorsements could result in quiet condemnation, which could be worse than loud and damning disapproval. The latter might at least get the book some attention.

Morrison was proud of *From Memphis & Peking* but disappointed that avoidable missteps kept a well-done book out of readers' hands. While she had no problem remaining friends with Chase-Riboud, Morrison had run out of patience when it came to the editor-author relationship. So when Chase-Riboud pitched to Morrison an idea about an epic poem on Sally Hemings, Thomas Jefferson's enslaved Black mistress, Morrison quickly declined the project but not before warning Chase-Riboud that neither the epic poem nor the diary format, both of which Chase-Riboud was considering, was the right genre for a book about such a complex woman. Years later, it was former first lady Jacqueline Kennedy Onassis at Viking, not Morrison at Random House, who would bring Chase-Riboud's *Sally Hemings: A Novel* (1979) to life. To everyone's delight, *Sally Hemings*, unlike *From Memphis & Peking*, sold well and received the 1979 Janet Heidinger Kafka Prize for best fiction by an American woman.

—

The same year *From Memphis & Peking* was released, Morrison published Lucille Clifton's *An Ordinary Woman*. Random House had previously published Clifton's *Good Times* and *Good News*

About the Earth, and both books had done well. While Morrison had been in touch with Clifton before (to provide promotional commentary for Toni Cade Bambara's *Gorilla, My Love*), Natalie Lehmann-Haupt, Alice Mayhew, and Nan Talese had been Clifton's editors for the first two collections. When Mayhew left the firm in 1971 and moved to Simon and Schuster, Talese took over as Clifton's editor. Then, when Talese left, Morrison became Clifton's editor. Morrison admired Clifton's poetry, so their working together seemed like a logical and natural fit. The two had known each other briefly as students at Howard University, too, with Morrison graduating the year Clifton arrived.[19] They had enough people and places in common that their editor-author relationship became cordial much faster than it might otherwise. Clifton's reputation and experience as a well-regarded published poet and her levelheadedness offered a welcome change from Morrison's work with Chase-Riboud.

In fall 1973, Morrison and Clifton met in New York to get acquainted and to talk through Clifton's ideas about the project she wanted to work on next. Following their meeting, Morrison wrote to Clifton to express excitement about the work Clifton's agent, Marilyn Harlow of the Curtis Brown Agency, had recently sent.

> I have read all of the new poems Marilyn sent, and they are so good—very different (the feel of the collection) from the other two. . . . It's not just content—it's the what? Fabric, I guess, or tone. Mellow. Less of the acid in *Good Times* or the outrage in *Earth*. Mind you, you cover that acid in comfort—but it was there anyway.[20]

For Morrison, the exploration of the ordinariness of Black women, individually and as a group, was a venture into the extraordinary. The need for acid and outrage was indisputable, yes; but universalizing Black women's discrete experiences was uniquely appealing and necessary.

Clifton was ambivalent about what to call the collection. Morrison's first recommendation was *In My Own Season*, because the book finished with what she described as a very strong coming of age thread. She also offered phrases from poems in the collection as alternatives, *The Woman Jar* or *Thawed Places*. In the end, they decided on *An Ordinary Woman*, lines taken from the collection's final poem.

With few exceptions, Morrison's editing of the poems in the volume was light. Clifton had titled a poem "I Am a Black Woman," for instance. "There must be 800 of these," meaning poems with that title, Morrison wrote. So she suggested calling it "And I Am Not Done Yet," which was the first line of the poem in draft. In its published version, Clifton shifted the first line to the title, dropped the conjunction *and*, and began the poem with the line "as possible as yeast / as imminent as bread."[21] The poem "To Ms. Ann," Morrison noted, worked "marvelously."

> But please delete the fourth verse. You don't need it—the three other images are thunderous and should not lead up to "Little Rock spit." . . . The other verbs are watched/walked/handed— very civilized, very poisonous. Spit—well—no.[22]

Clifton did publish the poem with a fourth stanza but without the vitriol of the original one. In the poem, Ms. Ann is a stand-in for white women who, through the years, have taken full advantage of their mismatched relationship with Black women.

For Morrison, and Clifton evidently agreed, the first three stanzas did the work of being righteously dismissive, poisonous in fact, without reducing the poem's speaker to the incivility of white women who spat at children in Little Rock. "Little Rock pulls the poem out of the ages into the newspapers," Morrison argued. The new stanza, in contrast, added the final blow, making clear that the reality of a shared humanity remained unacknowledged by the least humane ones.

The difference between Clifton's success and Chase-Riboud's, in terms of their both being Black women who published slim volumes of poetry in 1974, can be explained in at least two ways. Clifton was an established poet, for one thing. The other related benefit she had was an established Black reading audience. Accordingly, she did not need white women's book clubs to sell books, which also meant she could be critical of the ways white women upheld racism without fear of being shut out.

After publishing three books of poetry at Random House, Clifton finally completed the book of prose she had begun years earlier, *Generations: A Memoir* (1976). She had signed a contract for the book in April 1969, and she and Morrison talked about it when they first met. But they decided to publish *An Ordinary Woman* first in large part because Clifton did not feel ready to publish the memoir. She had tried to explain the concept of the book to her then-editor, Alice Mayhew. "It will take . . . months," she had confessed,

> because the bringing of one's insides out, especially for somebody who has made a life of holding very carefully her insides, is some hard. Also I think that after I bring them I shall trot them back in to hold again. That's hard. . . . I shall take me apart and then put me back together; but you know, I can do that . . . if I just would.[23]

It took five years and a new editor for Clifton to accept her own challenge. She appreciated having Morrison, another Black woman, as a sounding board for *Generations*. Morrison's enthusiasm for the book was immediate. Subsequently, they talked at length by phone about it. A few days after their conversation, Morrison wrote: "*Generations* is *so* good. I do love it. What a good time I'm going to have publishing it."[24] With Morrison on board as the editor, Clifton dedicated herself to finishing the book finally. The narrative was still sketchy in places, Morrison told her—more information was needed on Caroline's walk to Virginia, on Lucy's killing of her lover, and on Gene Sayle's withered arm—for instance. But, by and large, Morrison assured Clifton that the core of a fascinating story was there. The matter of writing the book was also complicated by the backlash Clifton experienced at the hands of her family after publishing an essay, "The Magic Mama," in *Redbook* in November 1969. Her brother and her relatives were upset by it, and this blocked her ability to write more about her family without feeling guilty. But with all six of her children in school finally, she committed to focusing her attention on completing the book.

Generations told the story of Clifton's family, tracing their lineage as far back as 1777. She dedicated the book to her father, Samuel Louis Sayles Sr., "who is somewhere, being a Man." The book exalted Dahomey women and their African American progeny. Clifton took some care to trouble her ancestor's characterization of most men as weak: "We be strong women and weak men," they would say.[25] Contrarily, the men in the ancestor's lineage, she argued, could be strong by virtue of their being descendants of strong Dahomey women, who were known to be fierce warriors in West Africa.

The reader learns about the first Samuel Lewis Sale, who was born in 1777 and legally married to the woman called Caroline Donald, born in West Africa in 1822. Clifton takes care to note that Caroline is *so-called* by the white man who is her owner, not *so-named* since she was named otherwise by her family. This nuance about naming resonated with Morrison, who understood how fiercely Black people resisted being named by anyone who did not love them deeply. Caroline, along with members of her family, was stolen from her homeland at the age of eight, and no one ever learned her African name. More important than her name, it seemed, was her lineage of being Dahomey. "Get what you want," Caroline would say, "you from Dahomey women."[26]

Caroline endured the Middle Passage and a walk from New Orleans to Virginia and became a midwife who earned the respect of the community—Black and white alike. Her daughter Lucy had a child, Genie, with a married white carpetbagger named Harvey Nichols. We are told that it must have been her choice to do so because "she was mean and didn't do nothing she didn't want to do and nobody could force her because she was Mammy Ca'line's child and everybody round there respected Mammy Ca'line so much."[27] For reasons that are never disclosed, Lucy kills Harvey and, rather than flee, she waits for the mob to come for her. Because the white community respected Caroline so much, they took Lucy to jail and gave her a trial before hanging her. Legend had it, then, that Clifton was a descendant of an openly rebellious Black woman.

Clifton's return home to Buffalo, New York, for her father's funeral and her need to meet the challenge of being orphaned frames the telling of *Generations*. She flips through the memories about ancestors who precede her and her father. Three lines serve as refrains in the text to remind her that she is the daughter of survivors. Caroline's declaration of their Dahomey heritage is one. The second is the voice of her father as he names "the Generations of Caroline Donald, born free among the Dahomey people in 1822 and died free in Bedford Virginia in 1910 . . . and Sam Louis Sale, born a slave in America in 1777 and died a slave in the same place in around 1860."[28] Slavery was a horror, her father declared, repeating the stories he had heard over the years: "Even the good parts was awful"; "but we fooled them old people. We come out of it better than they did."[29] The third line, an ending to the ancestral roll call, was similarly optimistic and channeled his great-grandmother Caroline, who would often say, "Don't worry, mister, don't you worry."[30]

Morrison was conflicted about how to market *Generations*. Was it a nonfiction novel or a memoir? Because it was short, it would not work as a family history book or an autobiography. The first set of galleys had the book titled *Generations: A Celebration in Prose*, evidencing the fact that it did not fit any category neatly really. This was part of the book's appeal, at least to Morrison. As she was with all the books on her list, Morrison was particular about *Generation*'s overall presentation. In a note to the design team, she requested that the type "be generous and graceful with the feeling of poetry but the toughness of prose."[31] It was to look like Lizelle Reymond's *Shakti*, Morrison noted, and the layout was to follow the specifications prescribed in the manuscript: "Each chapter is identified by a number. . . . Each Part is identified by a quotation. . . . In each Part, the chapter numbers begin with the number 1." Morrison considered every detail and then specified each one. As she knew and explained to her authors, the design of a book jacket mattered greatly. The cover could easily be the thing that prompted the reader to pick the book up and look inside.

The way a book is promoted is also an opportunity to engage the reader. For this book, Morrison responded to the challenge of describing a transgenre book by comparing it to a more familiar one. On the editorial fact sheet, she described *Generations* as a miniature *Pentimento*—Lillian Hellman's 1973 memoir (subtitled *A Book of Portraits* to connote that it was not a pure autobiography and an ironic foreshadowing of the impending controversy about the book's veracity). Like the Hellman memoir, *Generations* was a recollection of figures who influenced the author. Clifton's "portraits" were of family members whose stories could not be captured in a straight genre. "Without sentimentality, or granulated sugar," the fact sheet noted, "Ms. Clifton combines the simplicity and power of her poetry with the drama of a novel. . . . Funny and triumphant, Lucille Clifton's book proves her a major prose writer."[32]

Reviews of the book were plentiful and mainly positive. The sixty-nine copies Morrison sent to Random House's regular press list and the twenty copies she sent to the poetry and "Black interest" list yielded some fruit. The book scored a short mention in *The New Yorker*, which had a unique readership. And Morrison was hopeful that Reynolds Price's long review in *The New York Times Book Review* would be helpful to sales. Unfortunately, it was not. *Generations* went out of print eight months after publication. At one point, Morrison lamented to the sales team that Clifton was making appearances at locations where the book was not available. Finding the source of disconnect was a challenging one. Was the bookseller ordering enough copies of the book or not any at all? Were the people coming to hear her read reliable purchasers? It made no sense for a bookstore or event space to invite a writer without having the writer's books available for purchase. Such neglect, Morrison argued, was enough to outrage an established author, which Clifton was by then. Clifton had already begun to publish books with Holt, Rinehart and Winston and with Dutton. Morrison suspected that Clifton submitted *Generations* to Random House only because it had been contracted years earlier with the lure of a paltry advance. Morrison's fear that Clifton would move to another publisher for good came to fruition, and, to both women's dismay, they never worked together again. Clifton went on to be one of the most beloved contemporary African American poets, and Morrison, though not as her editor, continued to be one of her greatest admirers.

—

Either by design or coincidentally, Morrison and June Jordan began discussing publication of a collection of Jordan's poems a few months after Morrison brought out Chase-Riboud's *From Memphis & Peking* and Clifton's *An Ordinary Woman*. Jordan had already published several books and was, by all accounts, a popular poet who did the hard work of promoting her writing to the full range of audiences.[33] She was well connected in Black poetry circles and supported by the best-known critics. She commanded standing-room-only crowds at most of her readings, while also managing to publish in poetry magazines and journals—a nexus that highlighted her versatility. Morrison was enthusiastic about working with Jordan and committed to fighting to get Random House to publish her work. If she had any chance at publishing poetry she admired and that could have commercial success, Morrison was convinced it would be with Jordan.

"I want very much to publish a book of poetry by June Jordan," Morrison wrote to Silberman in June 1975. "Aside from the quality of her work, the attached sales information should remove the obvious reluctance I would have about taking poetry on."[34] Silberman appreciated Morrison's advocacy and supported offering Jordan a contract, in principle. But the only way the firm could take her on, he told Morrison, was if Random House became her only publisher. Because Jordan was under contract for a novel at Simon and Schuster, the initial contract negotiations were stalled. And Morrison and Jordan's new and untested relationship began to fray before it could even unfurl.

What began as an exchange between writers with mutual respect devolved rather quickly into a series of miscommunications. Initially, Morrison suggested to Jordan that she could get a contract rather quickly, in a matter of days. Weeks went by, however, with no word from Morrison. What Jordan did not know was that Morrison needed to find a way to respond to Silberman's concerns about how well Jordan could perform as a novelist. There was, still, the matter of the Simon and Schuster contract; and Silberman was scheduled for a monthlong vacation. Hearing nothing and having grown impatient, Jordan had her attorney reach out to Morrison, first, for an update and, subsequently, to return the manuscript. Morrison returned the manuscript as requested but also took a moment to write to Jordan directly.

> Last Thursday I returned your material to your lawyer at her request. I didn't want to call you with if-y information—only with a yes or no. . . . I can't figure out why you didn't trust me; I know you wanted things settled but, had no idea there was a time crisis involved; . . . I would have felt so much better if you had given me the deadline and the ultimatum yourself. Keep doing the work though. I love it.[35]

Jordan's response was immediate. It was also alternately complimentary and incredulous. She led with admiration.

> Of all the people remotely able to publish my poems, you are the one I have been hoping to interest, and work with; I would

hope that you know this is because you are the beautiful writer who has given all of us the works you have created. . . . In addition, what you have done, as editor, for Black letters, per se, seems to me altogether wonderful, and essential.[36]

She then pointed out that after their meeting in May (and a phone call the next day), Morrison suggested that the contract would come quickly. "Well, during the interim five or six weeks that have passed since that call," Jordan wrote, "I heard nothing from you—no phone call, note, letter, contract: nothing at all. The unexpected silence was most uncomfortably reminiscent of the silence my previous publisher interposed between us."[37] She read Morrison's silence as disinterest in the project, even if that disinterest was confounding. So she directed her attorney to inquire on her behalf—not so much because she wanted to apply pressure but because she had been out of town, and her attorney was based in New York City. She ended the letter on an apologetic and hopeful note: "I am sorry that because we don't know each other well enough to accurately assess the import of an exchange or, on the other hand, of unexpected silence, things have come to their current resolution that I am seeking, with this letter, to obviate, and move beyond, positively."[38]

Perhaps to eliminate confusion and to make her point explicitly, Morrison laid out the facts as she saw them over four pages. Her first point was that she, not Random House, was interested in publishing Jordan's poetry. In other words, no executive had prodded Morrison to sign Jordan up for a book. Rather, Morrison had sought her out personally and would have to convince the firm to offer Jordan a contract. That reality was attended by major challenges—the difficulty of placing poetry, the difference between selling juvenile and young adult books (which Jordan had done with some success) and adult trade books, and the publisher's near exclusive interest these days in making a profit.

Morrison also took the opportunity to answer specific questions Jordan had posed about the contract. There would be no guarantees of promotion or of a publication date. And Random House was indeed interested in a multibook contract—a book of poems, an adult book on Bessie Smith, and Jordan's novel, for which the publisher would have to pay Simon and Schuster since Jordan had received an advance for the book. "A strict profit-making sequence would be 1st Bessie, 2nd novel, & 3rd poetry," Morrison wrote. "Your preference is just the reverse—and I can accommodate you, although it would be harder, since you are the determiner of the way you work. And I wouldn't meddle with that."[39] The back-and-forth about the contract continued until they finally reached an agreement but not without first battling each other rhetorically in letters, signifying along the way.

Morrison claimed that her four-page letter was an attempt to be clear. Jordan took offense to its forthrightness. Morrison, for instance, was blunt in saying "Random House (the people whom I must persuade to issue a contract) are not at all interested in publishing your poetry. I am." Even if Morrison wanted to make the point that it was her advocacy alone that would make a contract possible, she did so by highlighting the publisher's complete disinterest in publishing Jordan's poetry. The tone of the letter also took Jordan aback. Jordan was confident in her ability to sell books and quite proud of her track record in doing so. But Morrison reminded Jordan that her best success in selling books was limited mainly to juvenile books, which relied on institutional sales to libraries and schools and largely as paperbacks. Adult trade, conversely, made its money in sales of hardbacks in bookstores, mass paperback reprint sales, and first serial rights. And there were no first serial rights in poetry.

Jordan claimed to be so shocked by Morrison's letter that she had to read it repeatedly with time between readings to be sure she understood what Morrison had "elected" to write. Morrison wrote back that Jordan's letter "befuddled" her, so when she received it, she tried to call Jordan repeatedly. But she kept getting a busy signal. So she wrote the letter and opted to dispense with "the normal language of [the] industry (euphemisms)" and to write, instead, the way she talked. She thought Jordan's precise questions deserved very precise responses. After noting that the duo had now had two huge misunderstandings, Morrison closed the letter with a bit of sarcasm and a quip. Since something must be wrong with the way she communicates when she does so forthrightly, her recourse must be to communicate "in the sly manner that most people use when they talk or write about business." And that was a pity, she wrote. Then, in the final line of the letter, she inquired about how Jordan was feeling: "How's your neck? Are you still taking the medicine?"[40] Jordan wrote back that she was better but still confined and did a wellness check of her own— "How are you? Less harried, I hope?"[41]

After months of back-and-forth, the contract for a book of poems and a book on Bessie Smith was finally executed and signed in May 1976, and Morrison and Jordan began the work of selecting the poems, giving them titles, and arranging their order in preparation for publication. Jordan had published three collections—*Who Look at Me* (1969), *Some Changes* (1971), and *New Days: Poems of Exile and Return* (1974)—and contributed her poems to edited collections. So they had plenty of poems from which to choose.

Jordan warned Morrison, however, that she did not yet own the copyright for the poems in *Some Changes*, so her preference was to focus mainly on the poems in *New Days* and to use poems from *Who Look at Me* if needed. This was in addition to twenty new poems she completed for the new collection. Jordan's biggest concern was making sure her growth as a poet was foreground in the arrangement rather than choosing poems that suggested a coherent vision. She wrote to Morrison:

> When you begin with *Who Look at Me*, and you work through all the poems . . . you do see that there have been serious changes of rhythm, emphasis, structure, purpose, and concern. . . .
>
> If you look at the love poetry of *Some Changes* you will have to conclude that, by the time there were *New Days*, I had been rescued from some rather serious albeit contemporary problems of fear, self-doubt, and trembling uncertainty. In *New Days*, the love poetry is alternately casual, sexual, mocking, kidding around, direct, and so forth, as well as serious.[42]

Jordan was also concerned about the similarities readers might observe between her work and Ntozake Shange's. "Shange's poetry derives much from her study of my work," Jordan noted; "this is clear if you know my work . . . but if you don't know when and who, it's the kind of problem I would really rather not have to cope with, at this point in my life."[43] Dating the poems individually was one way to address all the concerns.

Morrison was concerned that a thematic organization might do some poems a disservice. With a series of love poems in sequence, for instance, the power of one poem or another could too easily be deflected simply because of where it falls in the grouping. Organizing this collection according to the books the poems were published in would likely cause copyright problems, since that would essentially be a reprint of each collection. A combination of theme, tone, and chronology seemed to be one way to solve the problem. And while it was not a perfect solution, it did at least create a strong editorial position on which they could build. The key would be to select only the finest poems for inclusion. Morrison left the task of choosing which poems were among the best to Jordan, at least for the first pass. "My own ideas lean toward the successful poems which are not always the 'important' ones," Morrison wrote. "So I'd like your list first. . . . Once I have your list, we can argue."[44] There were minor glitches, too, that would need to be addressed. The beginning lines of two poems were identical, so one would need to be changed. Another poem had two copyright dates, so the correct one needed to be determined. Two poems had titles that were too closely related and would need to be differentiated somehow. And a poem with one title had a page and a half of the same lines from a poem with a different title. This would need to be corrected.

Jordan made the adjustments quickly, but then, in July, Simon and Schuster contacted Random House about what they argued was a violation of Jordan's contract with them. Jordan had a two-book deal with the firm—the novel, which Random House was aware of, and an untitled young adult book, which they argued Jordan had verbally agreed would be about the life of Bessie Smith. Random House was unwilling to pay for the novel she was obliged to deliver to Simon and Schuster, so that novel was intentionally eliminated from the final contract Random House offered her. But now, Simon and Schuster claimed that Jordan knowingly violated the deal with the firm by signing up with Random House for a book on Bessie Smith. The matter was further complicated by the fact that Jordan's agent at the time the Simon and Schuster contract was signed—Wendy Weil at Julian Bach Literary Agency—had withdrawn from her work with Jordan. She was now represented by Joan Daves, who argued that a novel based on Bessie Smith's life and a biography of Smith were aimed at different markets and could not be considered the same book. There was also the matter of Simon and Schuster's failure to pay Jordan the $1,250 advance for the book. The legal team at Random House agreed that the two books were different but also expressed concern about her failure to deliver manuscripts for which she had received advances.

Random House's counsel Gerald Hollingsworth wrote to Morrison:

> It is my opinion that we are not legally impeded by her agreements with Simon & Schuster from going ahead with our April 1, 1976 two-book contract with Ms. Jordan. . . .
>
> It does seem to me that Ms. Jordan should agree in fairness to allow us to set off the debt to Knopf against sums payable under your two-book contract. If she will not agree to such an arrangement, I would be concerned about paying her the first two $1,500 installments on Work #2 (the Bessie Smith novel) in view of her past performance record with Knopf and S&S.[45]

As it turned out, Jordan had also agreed to have Simon and Schuster prepay Knopf the $2,250 she owed that firm with earnings from her Simon and Schuster contract. Jordan agreed to allow Random House to withhold 25 percent of her earnings, after the advance she received as earnings, until the Knopf balance was repaid. Once she signed the agreement, the legal department gave

Morrison the green light to initiate publication of the book of poetry, which they agreed would be titled *Things That I Do in the Dark: Selected Poems of June Jordan 1966–1976.*

Morrison had the editorial fact sheet submitted immediately—announcing the latest book by June Jordan, a New Yorker who graduated from Barnard and the University of Chicago; whose poems appeared in no fewer than thirty-one magazines, journals, and newspapers and in nineteen anthologies; and who had won a Prix de Rome prize and a Rockefeller grant in creative writing. Morrison also included Jordan's teaching credentials, noting that she had taught at Yale, City College of New York, and Sarah Lawrence and had lectured at the Guggenheim Museum and the Donnell Library. With the fact sheet the sales and publicity team needed complete, Morrison turned her attention to copyedit and design tasks. The permissions team was in a mad scramble to secure written confirmation that Jordan had rights of publication or held the copyright for all the poetry included in the volume. With all the prepublication problems with the contract, the firm was unwilling to release the book without clearing all permissions, even if it meant delaying a publication date that might weaken sales. *Things That I Do in the Dark* was scheduled for release in June 1977. A few days before Christmas 1976, Morrison made the case for an earlier release. A summer release date, she told Jason Epstein, would be a "certain death" for the book.

Ms. Jordan enjoys huge sales, but they are dependent on a college market which 1) buys much earlier and 2) which she lectures to extensively in April and May.

We very much need bound books in April—it is absolutely crucial. Would you have production effect some change?[46]

If need be, Morrison was willing to move the publication date for the book of another of her authors—Leon Forrest—to make sure the team could give Jordan's book the attention needed to have it released earlier. Morrison's plea worked. The publication date was moved up to March, and review copies were available at the beginning of the year.

At the same time Random House was sending review copies of *Things That I Do in the Dark*, Jordan was embroiled in a public denunciation of the most widely circulated poetry magazine at the time, *American Poetry Review*. Jordan, along with poet Adrienne Rich, charged the magazine with racism, even though Jordan's poems were to be included there in a special folio of Black poets in the January 1977 issue, the same month Jordan and Rich released their manifesto. *American Poetry Review* was buttressed by its library subscriptions, newsstand distribution, and the highest reputation among other magazines and journals. The *Review* claimed to be representative of the best of American poetry, but it hardly was in the view of those who signed the statement of protest. They declared that it had biases against women and minority poets, against young poets, and against poets who use new forms. These biases were inevitable, they argued, because the editorial board was all white and predominately conservative. The recommendation followed the critique—that the magazine make itself responsible to the small-press community to democratize its influence, that a revolving editor from the female and/or minority community be assigned to each issue to ensure that one-third of the space in the magazine involve minority and women poets, that the magazine seek out young, unknown writers to publish and review, and that the magazine publish and review the work of innovative poets who challenge how American poetry can sound and look and what it can mean.

The letter of protest received significant attention, and though it was signed by several writers—David Ignatow, the *Review*'s editor at large who resigned and issued a separate statement to define his position, among them—Jordan and Rich were rightly viewed as spokeswomen for the charge. The call to end unchecked racism at a highly influential poetry magazine inevitably drew attention to Jordan's work, priming the pump for the release of her latest book. In February, Jordan's essay "Second Thoughts of a Black Feminist" was published in *Ms.* magazine, giving her more publicity still for the forthcoming release. In many ways, Jordan was a publicity department's dream author. She was well connected and regarded in a variety of circles. She could command audiences at universities and community centers and museums alike. She was deliberate about planning her itinerary and making as many appearances in an area or region as possible, and she was extremely organized in terms of documenting her professional activity and supporters.

Having overcome the rocky start, Jordan and Morrison managed to publish *Things That I Do in the Dark* with only minor difficulties in the end. But the friendship that could have been never was, despite their attempts to support each other outside of their editor-author relationship.[47] When Jordan gathered a group of fellow artists, who called themselves "The Sisterhood," she included Morrison in that number. Jordan and Alice Walker had the idea to create a space for Black women artists and writers who could build community with each other as serious friends and who would honor each other without being in competition with one another.

Morrison joined Jordan, Walker, Lori Sharpe, Ntozake Shange, Vertamae Grosvenor, Nana Maynard, and Audreen Ballard on a frigid first Sunday in February for what the invitation announced as a "chitlins and champagne dinner for a kind of Black sisterhood of the Spirit."[48] Later that week, on Thursday, Morrison met with Abike (Patricia Murray) and Ballard for lunch to consider the ways she might contribute to the group's publishing agenda. Morrison attended only one additional meeting of the Sisterhood before withdrawing her attention. She supported the group in spirit and provided salient advice about how Black women writers could improve their publishing odds. But the reality was she was focused on her own writing more than anything else. *Song of Solomon*, her third novel, would be released by Knopf in August. And having never established the ideal working relationship with Jordan, Morrison handed Jordan off to fellow editor Anne Freedgood to work on the Bessie Smith book that was a part of the two-book contract Morrison had arranged. When Jordan never delivered the second book, Morrison was forced to admit to the subsidiary rights team that Jordan was, once again, "either in or near litigation concerning publishers' efforts to get advances returned."[49]

Despite her best efforts to work with Black women authors to publish commercially viable volumes of poetry, Morrison's work with Chase-Riboud, Clifton, and Jordan did more to convince the determined editor that the firm's reluctance to publish poetry was well-founded than it did to convince her that she could beat the odds. Fortunately, between 1974 and 1977 when she pursued this fiscally imprudent endeavor, she also had books like *The Black Book*, Angela Davis's *Angela Davis: An Autobiography*, and Muhammad Ali's *The Greatest* on her list. These had all sold well. It would seem impossible otherwise that she could take on a little-known, deceased writer named Henry Dumas. After spending a few uninterrupted hours reading his work and being smitten by his artistry, Morrison was certain that she had no other choice but to try.

CHAPTER 10

Will the Circle Be Unbroken?

A few hours before her friends Margaret and Quincy Troupe were scheduled to return to their Central Park West apartment with her eight- and twelve-year-old sons, Slade and Ford, Morrison rather casually flipped through the Southern Illinois University Press (SIUP) editions of two collections by Henry Dumas. As she moved through the pages of *Ark of Bones and Other Stories* and *Poetry for My People*, it was as if she were spellbound. "His variety was astounding," Morrison remarked.[1] Two other factors captured her imagination. He was well situated in the culture—there was no question that he understood Black culture of the South especially. And his writing reflected new possibilities for enacting a Sankofa approach in a literary text, something she experienced in life but not in literature. "He was also the only writer I had read who had a future look and a backward look in the same text," she noted. The other writers were in a particular time per text.[2] She was sure Dumas was the kind of writer who needed a national audience, and Random House was the publisher that could offer it.

Like most of the literary authors whose work Morrison admired, Dumas was one of those writers who defied neat categorization. He wrote across genres effortlessly. He produced an abundance of poems that revealed a command of poetic craft, and his choice short stories were peerless. Morrison was also struck by his willingness to write against or beyond accepted literary conventions. This was the work she was trying to do in her own fiction, of course. Dumas was a kindred spirit in this way. He felt comfortable playing with narrative and form and completely ignored the supposition that every good story had a beginning, middle, and end.[3]

Dumas grew up in Sweet Home, Arkansas, a small, rural town south of the state capital of Little Rock. Sweet Home had a population of less than three hundred people in the six-mile stretch that comprised the town. Growing up without radio or TV, he spent a lot of time outside observing nature. He also acquired a penchant for storytelling early on in life. After visiting his aunt for the summer in 1944, Dumas moved to Harlem to live with her for a short time before his parents joined the many who left the South for the north in the Great Migration to try to make a better life for themselves. He was a student at the famed Frederick Douglass Junior High School in Harlem and wrote for the school newspaper at the High School of Commerce, where he declared in his yearbook that he intended to become a writer. He attended City College for one semester before enlisting in the United States Air Force, in part to help pay for college. Sometime after receiving an honorable discharge, he moved back to the East Coast, this time to New Jersey to attend Rutgers University. For years, he continued to write without publishing, until he became a contributing staff member of Rutgers' literary magazine, *Anthologist*. His first publication in this journal was a short story titled "A City Game," which won first prize for fiction in the magazine's 1960–61 volume. By 1964, he had published three poems and three short stories, all in the *Anthologist*. But the voluminous output from his around-the-clock productivity, by and large, went unpublished.

During his time at Rutgers, Dumas gained a reputation of being somewhat enigmatic. He admired classical music but rejected most of European culture. While stationed in Saudi Arabia, he began to study Muslim culture closely. As he observed Muslims being devout to Islam, he committed to being as devout to Christianity. Those who knew him well speculated for years that he might become a preacher. But Dumas eventually dismissed religion and focused more on philosophical understandings of the world. Around this time, too, he became involved with white literary types who encouraged his affinity with interracial exchanges. This trend, which was happening on college campuses all over the country, did not escape Rutgers. Dumas grappled with the challenge of feeling at home in the interracial literary space and being drawn to the struggle for Black civil rights. At the same time his fascination with white male American writers like Walt Whitman and Ralph Waldo Emerson began to grow, Dumas joined the NAACP and became publicity chairman of the New Brunswick chapter in 1961. As a person from the South, he could not ignore the pull toward Blackness as tensions grew during the Civil Rights Movement and the promise of Black writers grew beyond a coveted few. Gone were the days when a single Black author like Ralph Ellison, who had ignored Dumas's overtures of engagement while they shared time at Rutgers, could command the attention of mainstream publishers as the lone voice of Black America.

In 1966, Dumas accepted an invitation from his former classmate at Rutgers, Hale Chatfield, to become assistant director for the Upward Bound program at Hiram College in Ohio. Not long after, he moved from Hiram to East St. Louis to take a job as a writer in residence with the Experiment in Higher Education at Southern Illinois University, where he met Black Arts Movement poet Eugene Redmond. While he was there, Dumas's ideological position shifted from efforts to create interracial solidarity to a belief in the primacy and uniqueness of Black culture. Dumas was not alone, of course, in his layered journey toward ideological and artistic clarity. Nor was he alone in his involvement in interracial relationships, his frequent abandonment of his family to explore his artistic pursuits and other relationships, his return to the Black community in the wake of the Civil Rights Movement, or his experimentation with drugs. He was somewhat anomalous, however, in terms of how prolific he was as a writer, even though most of his work went largely unpublished until after his death. In 1970, not quite two years after Dumas's untimely death, Chatfield and Redmond collaborated to coedit the SIUP editions. Troupe knew Redmond as a fellow poet and happily put Morrison in touch with him.

In her initial pitch to Silberman to republish Dumas's work, Morrison proclaimed that Dumas "was certainly the most powerful black writer of the sixties."[4] No doubt she knew this was an exaggeration at most and debatable at least. Still, she used the superlative without reservation, even if she was alone in her characterization of Dumas's magnificence. Publishing Dumas's work at Random House, while gratifying, was not without controversy. For one thing, it involved an estate and not an author who could navigate the process of publishing a book smoothly. SIUP had published *Ark of Bones and Other Stories* and *Poetry for My People* in 1970 with Chatfield and Redmond as coeditors. Amiri Baraka— cited on the edition as Imamu Ameer Baraka (LeRoi Jones), the name he was using at the time—wrote the preface to *Poetry for*

My People, and Dumas's friend and Rutgers classmate, the poet Jay Wright, wrote the introduction. For the Random House editions, however, Redmond emerged as the sole editor of both books.

Morrison wrote to Vernon Sternberg at SIUP, indicating Random House's interest in republishing the books. Frances Walker, who worked in the rights and permissions unit of SIUP, informed Morrison that the press did not control rights to the books, that his widow, Loretta Dumas, did. Morrison proceeded to work with Redmond and Loretta on the trade editions, limiting her interaction with Chatfield to one conversation where she informed him of Random House's intent to bring Dumas's work back into print. Once Loretta agreed to sell the rights for the two books to Random House, Morrison began to craft a narrative about Dumas as a legendary martyr with a hungry following. In her memo to Silberman, for instance, she noted that he had been "killed by a cop for no reason at all," an act that only intensified readers' love for him and his writing.

In truth, Morrison knew only a few people who had read Dumas closely. But she needed a selling point, and an awaiting Black audience unable to acquire books that were out of print by a beloved, deceased author was as good as any. On the one hand, the posthumous publication of his work would create a challenge. There would be no author to do the hard work of getting attention for the book. On the other, because the books had been published already, the work of preparing the manuscript, largely as a reprint, was already done. What was left for her to do was to create an informed persona. Relying on Redmond's recollection and interpretation of Dumas, Morrison portrayed him as a mild-mannered man with a reputation for "spiritual beauty [that] was legend in the Black community."[5] Whether or not she was aware of his struggle with alcohol and drug use and his alleged volatile behavior during his Rutgers days is unclear. No one who knew him would have disagreed that he was warmhearted, but none who knew him well would have denied that he was also tormented. The gone-too-soon beautiful spirit was a sentiment she knew she could sell.

The letter of invitation Morrison sent to announce the book party for *Ark of Bones* and *Play Ebony, Play Ivory* was unambiguous in its celebration of Dumas as an affirmatively Black writer who wrote for Black readers.

> It is very difficult to do publicity for [a] no longer living writer. But we are determined to bring to the large community of Black artists and Black people in general this man's work. . . . Already several people have agreed to come and read from his work: Angela Davis will read, I will read, Jane Cortez will read, Eugene Redmond will read—and Melvin Van Peebles, John Williams and many, many others have offered their support.[6]

In early September, Redmond sent Morrison a list of people (and their addresses) he thought should be invited to the party, which was held October 13 at the Center for Inter-American Relations on Park Avenue in New York. It was well attended by a list of "Who's Who" in Black literature and culture and covered by the press as such. Chatfield had been one of very few white people on the list. He sent regrets. "Dear Ms. Morrison," he wrote. "I decline with thanks your kind invitation to be on hand for the Henry Dumas commemorative book party to be held on October 13. I do this largely in deference to your expressed interest in emphasizing Henry's importance to the black community—a matter which I can both understand and commend."[7] He mentioned that he and Dumas had been close for years, since their days at Rutgers in fact, and that he was pleased that new editions of Dumas's work would be available for growing interest in "Hank's" writing.

Shortly after Random House published the books, Chatfield wrote to Albert Erskine, then vice president and editorial director of the firm, to express his distress about having his editorial efforts erased and then represented as Redmond's. The books were essentially the same, Chatfield argued, the biggest difference being the title change for *Poetry for My People* to *Play Ebony, Play Ivory*.

According to Chatfield, he had made the selections of poems, grouped and ordered them, titled the sections in the collection, edited the textual problems, composed the notes, and obtained reprint permissions for the SIUP editions. Redmond, in Chatfield's estimation, was merely "an advance man" and "a valuable source of advice."[8] The Random House editions were not new editions, Chatfield fumed. Rather, they "eliminate[d] only the original prefaces and, from the poetry volume, an index of titles and first lines." The new title for *Play Ebony, Play Ivory* (which Redmond made to distinguish it from Margaret Walker's poetry volume *For My People*) was not original either, Chatfield noted. It was the title he "had assigned to the first group of poems in the book" and, therefore, was "not a remarkable adjustment."[9] In other words, the books could hardly be called "revised" editions.

When Erskine directed the concern to Morrison, she insisted that the assumption that the Random House editions would be revised was Chatfield's, that he had mistaken her comment about the intent to publish a trade edition as her intent to publish a revised edition. And since the rights to the material belonged to Loretta Dumas, Morrison contended, the dispute about editorship seemed to be between Chatfield and Redmond, not between him and Random House. In Morrison's view, Chatfield needed to address any conflict that needed to be resolved to Redmond.

Chatfield rightly assumed that there were racial politics at play. Morrison had constructed Dumas as a definitively Black writer. Redmond, a Black poet and scholar-activist with clear ties to Black people, could be Dumas's champion among the target readership. Chatfield, a lesser-known regional white poet could not.

In Chatfield's next letter to Morrison, the cordial tone of the first letter was gone. It was clear that the books were largely reprints of the editions he had completed and that he had been displaced as coeditor. He wrote:

> It may well be, as you say, that I should perceive myself as having "differences" with Mr. Redmond, yet permit me to make a few observations—by way of getting some feelings expressed, and thus hopefully putting them as much to rest as their restlessness will allow. . . .
>
> It does not suffice to lay these injuries at the door of Eugene Redmond alone, for it is conspicuous that the Random House editions were set (with minor adjustments) directly from the S.I.U. Press volumes, or from photocopies of them. Thus it is not possible that the Random House editorial staff could have failed to notice that there were *people* behind these books. . . . That nothing Random House has as yet said or done in this matter even hints at apology seems to me graceless and mean-spirited. So. Enough.[10]

Morrison could not disagree. But she refused an apology with her silence. She did agree to include Chatfield's name on the second printing of the books, pending approval from Loretta Dumas and Redmond. But even here the disrespect prevailed. Redmond would need to approve; and, as Morrison presented the offer, the coeditors would be listed as Eugene Redmond and Hale Chatfield, instead of as Hale Chatfield and Eugene Redmond, in keeping with the SIUP editions. Not surprisingly, Chatfield declined this compromise. It would not matter in the end because no second printing was ever warranted.

Chatfield's claim of disregard (not just of him but also of Wright and Baraka) was not the only indignity Morrison encountered. While she was fighting to have Dumas positioned as a champion of Black writing, she alienated the staff of one of the leading Black publications, *Negro Digest / Black World*, when she neglected to cite the magazine as the place where Dumas was first published nationally to a Black audience. Hoyt Fuller, *Black World*'s editor, quickly and quietly expressed his displeasure about the way Random House, and Morrison by association, seemed to belittle *Black World*. Part of the argument was frivolous. The books were printed in hardcover and paperback. *Black World* received paperback instead of hardcover copies of the books to review. But coupled with omitted acknowledgment that Dumas was first published nationally in *Negro Digest / Black World*, the claim that Morrison and Random House were impertinent to a fault toward the magazine was certain.

Carole Parks, *Black World*'s associate editor with whom Morrison was personally acquainted, took the matter rather personally and made it a point to say so. She wrote to Morrison directly:

> I first spoke to someone in your permissions department about the deletion of BLACK WORLD credits from bound galleys of the Dumas volumes. You, however, put the matter on a more personal level when you called to say that you were the editor and would try to have the proper credit included. I think you felt we would not make an issue if we knew you, a competent

Black editor, were involved. And you were right. I, on the other hand, was wrong in assuming that, after you found it was "too late" to make the addition, you would acknowledge the magazine in *some* way, at some time, somewhere.

Parks interpreted the omission of *Black World* as the home of Dumas's first national publication as fodder for the wrong-headed notion that he might have otherwise languished "unappreciated were it not for some white liberal or far-sighted *individual*" like Morrison.[11]

Ironically, Parks's argument that Dumas "*chose* to write for NEGRO DIGEST, to speak to a Black audience whenever he could" and that he was, in turn, "honored and *nourished* by those people" was the very contentious, hard-line position that Morrison had taken in promoting his work. Only two non-Black journals—*New York Age* and *Rolling Stone*—were on Redmond's list of places to send advance copies of the book for review. They were leaning into Dumas's Blackness, some thought, to a fault. But Parks had no way of knowing this. She also took offense to Morrison's use of words like "cult" and "legend" in reference to Dumas's readers and his legacy in the promotional materials. The words were dangerous in her view, in the same way that Morrison had contended the nationalism of the Black Arts Movement could be. Finally, she accused Morrison of using Black culture to her personal advantage.

I see a rather ugly pattern developing around your "event" books. One could infer that you are not just interested in advancing your already prestigious career, but in singlehandedly (perhaps even unconsciously) advancing your own version of Black "history."

Here, Parks was referencing the publicity for *The Black Book*, a lot of which featured Morrison. Morrison shot back:

> Hoyt's letter bothered me. Yours hurt me very deeply. I didn't "discover". Dumas. I only agreed, at the suggestion of Quincy Troupe and Eugene Redmond, to try to publish him commercially, and I cannot claim, as *Black World* seems to, to "own" him.
>
> It was Gene who provided me with the manuscript. . . . The term "cult" is his also. I deferred to his judgment as the editor of both collections and as a friend of Dumas. But the omission of the credit was *my* error.

Morrison assured Parks that credit lines would appear in the second printing and returned to a defense of the personal attack she felt. Publishing Dumas would not advance her career, she noted. It was not even a sound financial venture. But she was determined to keep Dumas's work in print and to introduce him to a broader audience. "I cannot imagine how that 'advanced' my *career*," she wrote. "Such a funny word. I don't have a career, you know. I just work."[12] Morrison owned the error, which she had already done in a letter to Fuller, but not without first injecting a characteristic sardonic tone when she felt wrongly accused. Publishing Black books, for her, was an event. Should it not be? she queried: "Perhaps they should be done quietly? Secretly? . . . Perhaps I should leave 'nourishment' to *Black World*." She expressed her disdain for Parks's accusation more directly. "I have always respected your work and your honesty," she wrote. "And I am sorry that you cannot return the compliment. More, than that, I will miss your friendship. I thought you knew me."

Morrison felt she was being attacked on all sides for not handling the reprinting of Dumas's work with more care. Yes, she was ecstatic about publishing Dumas's poetry and fiction. But the missteps were costly, this one especially since losing the confidence of the editors at *Black World* could have been ruinous to her reputation as being committed to Black culture. The possibility of earning a reputation as a Black editor willing to facilitate the exploitation of Black culture for gain at a white firm most Black authors and publishers were already suspicious of would have been detrimental to her standing in the community. Her push for Black engagement with the books was so strong that she could have easily been accused of leaning in to Dumas's Blackness too much, perhaps even to a fault. Defending herself to a Black publisher, she told Fuller, was tiresome.

> I neither have nor take the time or energy to issue an order [for review copies], run down to the mail room, tell the (Black) staff there to send paperback books to one set of people and hardcover to another. In Dumas's case, they had more paper than hard. . . .
> There were no ugly implications—only ugly inferences.[13]

Haste and inefficiency, hers and Redmond's, were to blame for the failure to acknowledge *Negro Digest* in the reprint, not malice. While she never repaired her friendship with Parks—Parks did introduce Morrison on a panel at the Black Writers Conference at Howard University a few years later—Morrison did feel some relief when *Black World* had her close friend and former Howard University colleague Clyde Taylor review the books for the magazine.

In a short but favorable review of *Ark of Bones*, John Deck of *The New York Times* declared that nothing about Dumas's fiction "will tolerate comparison to its predecessor. . . . Dumas had a rich and varied talent, and he was foremost original."[14]

Not long after publishing *Ark of Bones and Other Stories* and *Play Ebony, Play Ivory*, Morrison read the draft of a novel by Dumas that Redmond suggested could "be salvaged and edited into a work of substance."[15] Silberman agreed to a two-book contract, for a novel and a collection of short stories, with Redmond as editor of both. The total payout for the contract was less than Morrison hoped for, but the limited sales of the first two books meant that Silberman could not be persuaded to agree to more than $5,000—$2,500 at signing, $1,250 upon submission of acceptable drafts, and another $1,250 once the books were published. This meager sum was to be shared by Redmond and Loretta Dumas. By summer, Redmond had sent a copy of the manuscript of the novel they were calling *Visible Man* but published as *Jonoah and the Green Stone* to Morrison for review. A month later, he sent the manuscript for what would become *Rope of Wind and Other Stories*.

Because she wanted the novel to be released as quickly as possible to build on what little momentum they had with the release of the other two volumes, Morrison made it a point to read and edit *Jonoah* before heading to Europe that summer. But she did not correspond with Redmond about it until early fall. Her schedule for the book's preproduction work was disrupted even more when her father became ill and died unexpectedly. She was out of the office for a little over a month but continued to work on the book intently. The organization of the book was perhaps the greatest challenge. She noted:

I first moved several Chapters around because they seemed so very much out of sequence: "Fear, Mirror & Memory" is so clearly the first chapter in Part Two and "The Color Puzzle" should follow "Naked." But to do it would require genuine rewriting. So I returned to the order you had settled on in the first place.[16]

Similarly challenging was how to deal with repetitious passages that were likely rewrites of sections. Some parts of the repeated material read better than its source material, while other inserts added little value.

Reading the whole mss. through the insert of "Up from Msippi" pp. 91–93 is all wrong. It looks like and reads like a patch. Nor is it needed—since it says nothing that hasn't already been said in the book. Unlike Jubal's Song—which *does* belong and the final song of p. 170.[17]

They would need to strike a balance between rewriting and taking small liberties with the text.

Dumas's notes suggested that the novel was to be written in three parts, but he had only completed two at the time of his death. It still held together well and took important risks with magic—the Green Stone of the novel's title; a conjure lady (so named); and a witch doctor, who tells Jonoah about the Green Stone that carries him to safety in a dream where he flees a mob of white men. Reviews of the novel celebrated Dumas's "mystical vision." Troupe, one of the critics most familiar with Dumas's aesthetic and who, in no small way, was responsible for bringing Dumas to Morrison's attention, described Dumas's achievement in the novel this way:

Transformation is what we are dealing with here; the idea or notion that art—in Dumas' case, a sort of Coltrane beyond the blues, but still of it, sort of thing—and when that same art has grown out of the collective memory of a people, or a shared idea or concept, and if that art is articulated well, then that art can reach the magic level of epiphany, and carry whomever it touches to heights of spiritual ecstasy. Dumas . . . has always been able to do this, and in *Jonoah and the Green Stone*, he does it once again.[18]

Even with all the problems that obviously attend an unfinished work, the novel, in Troupe's estimation, is no less "a beautiful, haunting and great piece of writing. It is the work of an American genius, one of the finest to come along in many a year." The short *Kirkus* review concurred: "There are many rough spots and unanswered questions but even as fragments these scenes are affecting, and the mythical nature of the work allows you to project much of the author's intentions. A special talent, curtailed."[19]

Jonoah did well enough critically to ensure that Random House honored the final manuscript Morrison contracted with Loretta Dumas and Redmond for the collection of writings titled *Rope of Wind*. By now Morrison knew that very little about the circumstances of Dumas's death had been verified. Early on, she repeated the story that Dumas had jumped the turnstile and been shot by a transit cop. Another account, she later learned, was that it was a case of mistaken identity. And the story that appeared in the *Amsterdam News* suggested that he was shot after slashing the face of a transit authority policeman who intervened in a fight between Dumas and an unidentified man.[20] In any event, he had been killed by police at a young age, and Redmond's characterization of him as a martyr had the dramatic effect Morrison needed to promote a deceased author.

While Morrison never wanted to be viewed as a hero who saved

Dumas from relative obscurity, her willingness to push Random House to publish not one but four books posthumously affirmed her commitment to publishing Black literature that took artistic risks, not simply Black literature that would sell. For her, Dumas was a writer who managed to capture the depth and fullness of Black life with an artistry she had not seen among his peers. At his best, he had command of literal and figurative language, of myths and biblical allusions. He had imagination around theme and the literary skill needed to represent Black consciousness and Black perspective with a forward, backward, and present look.

Part of what attracted Morrison to Dumas was how his work was, at once, reflective of and divergent from the aesthetic thrust of the Black Arts Movement. As meaningful as the period was, she also found it limiting in some ways. Dumas seemed to keep these challenges at the forefront of his artistic vision. Another artful storyteller who tried to negotiate that tension was John McCluskey. Morrison and McCluskey first met in 1970 at a reception following a dinner talk Morrison gave to the Metro Writers Workshop in Cleveland. The workshop was a collective of local parents, teachers, librarians, and writers who organized themselves following a conference titled "Books That Don't Exist: Literature for Inner-City Children" sponsored by Case Western Reserve University. McCluskey was on the faculty at Case Western and an editor for the workshop's publishing arm, New Day Press, which developed written materials by Black authors about Black subjects for Black audiences. Morrison was in high spirits when they met that night, McCluskey recalled, perhaps because she was so close to her hometown of Lorain and in the company of her sister, Lois. When he told her about a novel he was working on, Morrison encouraged him to send her the manuscript when it was complete.[21] Three years later, he did.

Her enthusiasm for the draft was immediate. "It was a quieter kind of book for the time," Morrison noted.[22] By "quieter" she meant that it did not have the rage characteristic of so much of the work produced by male writers during the Black Arts Movement. McCluskey understood this distinction— between his novel and much of the literature of the Black Arts Movement—well. In the late 1960s, he had begun attending OBAC (Organization of Black American Culture) meetings in Chicago, where editor, teacher, and writer Hoyt Fuller convened a collective of writers, artists, historians, intellectuals, and community organizers to support the belief that the arts can help create and support a cultural revolution. McCluskey found these meetings enlivening, but he also found them limiting since the Black Arts Movement tended to give far less attention to fiction than to poetry and theater. Another thing about the movement that challenged him was his admiration of writers who were dedicated as much to craft as they were to culture—writers like Robert Hayden and Ralph Ellison, both of whom he had met. McCluskey heard from Hayden firsthand, at a Fisk Writers Conference, what it meant to be perceived as not Black enough and, as a result, to be excluded from a literary movement. McCluskey and Morrison agreed that Black writers who troubled the so-called Black aesthetic could appreciate the energy and dynamics of the Black Arts Movement without being subsumed by it or uncritically adopting what they perceived as its worrying limitations.

Like Morrison, McCluskey was born in Ohio. He grew up in Middletown, where he was a star football player and a saxophonist. He went on to attend Harvard University, where he became the first African American to start at the position of quarterback for an Ivy League team. Though he had always been an avid reader, it was not until his junior year at Harvard, when he enrolled in an introductory creative writing class, that he began to consider writing seriously. During his senior year, he took an advanced creative writing course and completed his honors thesis on the sociology of literature, where he focused on literature by Ralph Ellison, Chester Himes, James Baldwin, and Richard Wright. After earning his BA in social relations from Harvard in 1966, McCluskey entered the MA program in English and creative writing at Stanford. He left after three quarters, though he eventually returned to complete the degree in 1972.

Before the release of his first novel, McCluskey had published one short story, "Nairobi Nights," in *Black World*, the leading Black magazine at the time, for which Fuller was editor and McCluskey a regular contributor.[23] He had also published a chapter of a work in progress, which would become *Look What They Done to My Song*, in Orde Coombs's 1971 anthology *What We Must See: Young Black Storytellers*. When McCluskey sent the draft to Morrison in 1973, she felt it was good enough to warrant a contract. But she also thought it could use more work. There were moments of excessive preachiness, she noted, and some scenes needed to be cut. Others needed to be sharpened to connect moods, images, and characters. When Morrison sent the manuscript to Pat Fogarty, an internal reader, for a second opinion, Fogarty agreed that the draft had "enough strength to stand as is now, but could be made better without much trouble." Fogarty wrote: "This man is a really good writer, especially in writing dialog and building individual scenes. . . . This is very impressive writing: rich, mobile."[24]

With Fogarty's endorsement of her assessment of the novel, Morrison invited McCluskey to New York to discuss the manuscript. The meeting lasted around an hour, but it did not take Morrison much longer than that to make two critical points—

characters alone could not carry the novel (it had to have a driving idea), and the novel needed to be three-dimensional in every way. Readers needed to see how the author presented the story, the characters, and the place from every angle. "You need to walk around and look up at it from below, to look down at it from above," McCluskey recalled Morrison saying.[25] A novel could create the feeling of 360 degrees in several ways, most deliberately with careful attention to the characters and the world they lived in. As their meeting ended and Morrison prepared to walk McCluskey downstairs to greet his wife and son, who had made the drive with him from Cleveland to New York, the two affirmed their excitement about the book, and McCluskey began to mull over ways he might envision the novel more like a globe than a disk.

Part of the challenge was finding the best way to tell Mack's story with sufficient depth and clarity but without overwriting it. McCluskey tried to explain what he was after to Morrison, as she suggested revisions for a section she thought was too wordy:

> I want to be clear that Mack is not indulging in some exotic spiritual trip and that the last act is not a detached high. The religion or spiritualism suggested in his conversation with Rev. Fuller and Antar (ch 13) is a new-time religion, not imported from the East, but a home-grown variety with one foot in Georgia and the other in Harlem. So the pain and isolation in his seemingly random movements reflect a doubt (can music offer a social good?) that is blown away with the communion of the last chapter. He has brought a large range of folk together and has touched them.[26]

Morrison also insisted that Rev. Fuller's sermon at the end of the novel was too long. McCluskey argued that it helped clarify

Mack's journey and that it was needed to create "the drama of the preacher-audience conversation (call-and-response?)." Morrison disagreed and held no punches in her response: "You are dead wrong about the sermon. It's going to be the part everybody skips over. It's simply impossible to catch the oral power of such a delivery in print. It is really wooden and deadening to read it."[27] Ultimately, the back-and-forth with Morrison helped him refine Mack's character, even as the novel was, in no small part, about Mack's inability to clarify his life's purpose in relation to community. Even so, Morrison argued, the portrayal of the novel's protagonist could not be ambiguous, even if he was still becoming. He needed full development.

As a complement to the male characters who emerged in fiction during the Black Arts Movement, Mack is more internally focused than driven by external motivations. He is a product of a movement but intently reflective about its impact on his understanding of himself as a Black man in relation to his community. As he travels from Sante Fe, New Mexico, to Boston, he encounters a range of characters who help move the novel along and give some shape to its musical style since there is no traditional plot. Along the way, we meet Ubangi, a pseudo-hustler; Reba and Dupree Sledge, the couple who takes Mack in temporarily; Antar and Omowale, the rhetorical revolutionaries; Novella, Mack's lover; and Rev. Fuller, Novella's pastor. Mack's adventures, as he attempts to fulfill his desire to be a successful tenor saxophone player, inform the novel's actions, but what the novel is really about is his spiritual journey toward self-definition and emotional maturity, ultimately, in service of the Black community. Mack's "song" is a metaphor for his journey on the one hand and his belief that his music has liberating potential on the other.

Morrison and McCluskey worked together to find a way to

"indicate the nature of the odyssey right off" instead of at the end of the novel and through another character.[28] The title was one way, Morrison suggested. "I read the final version of the manuscript some weeks ago and have been thrashing about for a handle," she wrote. "Usually getting a title isn't so important at this stage, but because the book needs a title that will really pull it together in the reader's mind before he opens it I am desperate. . . . I think we need a sentence-title like 'Been down so long looks like up to me.'"[29] After fits and starts with a range of options (including *Pilgrims*, *I Have My Own Song to Sing*, and *Like a Ship Out to Sea*), they settled on the title they thought best from the beginning—*Look What They Done to My Song*. It captured Mack's disappointment that music could not create the unity he hoped for after all.[30] That tension, McCluskey told Morrison, was at the core of the novel.

Reviewers gleaned McCluskey's vision for the novel, even if they saw that vision (of music as a path to redemption) as problematic at times. There was consistent agreement about how deft McCluskey's use of language, especially Black vernacular and idioms, was. And comments about his command of craft were consistent. More challenging, they noted, was the limitation of the jazz novel as genre. For Larry McMurtry, who reviewed the novel for *The Washington Post*, this made the book's parts more successful than the whole. But, by all accounts, *Look What They Done to My Song* was a successful first novel that suggested much promise from the thirty-year-old writer who managed to avoid all the trappings that attended the path of a post–Black Arts Movement novel. "McCluskey has memorably captured the failure of monologues spoken in vacuums," Alicia Metcalf Miller argued in the *Cleveland Plain Dealer*, "the agony of choosing to grow up and the ongoing battle between weariness and spiritedness that is not only Black but human." Russell Atkins was similarly congratulatory in a long review for the *Cleveland Magazine,* noting that McCluskey explored Blackness's ethnic definition both within and beyond the fixed and accepted prescriptions. While Atkins lamented the novel's use of Black books' staple diet of cuss words, understandings of music as soul, petty crimes, pimping and prostituting, Black militancy, and rousing church services, he argued that McCluskey revealed an awareness of these limitations and attempted to lift the novel (and Mack's song) "out of prescriptive cliché."[31] Atkins continued: "John McCluskey places himself squarely in the center of the problem, which is: keeping the recognizable ethnic identity of a work while being fresh and original." In Atkins's view, McCluskey did as good a job as any playing familiar tunes with a sufficiently unique sound.

After *Look What They Done to My Song* was published, Morrison had to assure McCluskey that Random House was doing all it could to promote and sell the book. Her response to his query about how marketing and publicity were unfolding for the novel proved to be a lesson in postproduction realities that were predictably daunting to first-time authors. She had sent 182 copies of the book out for reviews—to magazines, newspapers, columnists, colleges, book clubs, paperback houses, and to specific Black reviewers with whom she had personal relationships. In the latter case, sending copies to anyone willing to write a review was useful only if the person could secure a venue to publish it. "If there was a magic formula for selling everything we printed, we would know it by now," she told McCluskey. "The only sure shot (and it is not 'sure') is a huge campaign costing some $20,000. . . . And unless the book is selling, we would spend $20,000 to earn $15,000."[32] She also explained to him bookstores will only buy what they wanted to buy (and what they think they can sell) and that everyone was competing for the same shelf, counter, and window space.

The people who really want the book should not be deterred when a store did not have the book in stock but should ask the bookseller to order a copy.

In Morrison's view, the book had done relatively well for a first novel. "You could have written a lousy, sensational, sexy book and you'd probably not have this problem," she remarked. "(Except some other editor would have to publish it.) But you wrote a good one and it is slowly but surely finding its readership (almost 2,000 people!)."[33] Her first novel, she often repeated to the authors she worked with, sold a mere three thousand copies before gaining traction. Great reviews of a first novel could set the stage for more sales for a second novel. But *Look What They Done to My Song*—the quiet, little book she loved—was the only book they would publish together.

Four years later, Morrison was drawn to another book by a Black male author that picked up the themes of music and self-discovery McCluskey pursued in his novel. Ted Solotaroff, a senior editor at Bantam Books, shared with her a copy of Wesley Brown's *Tragic Magic*. Bantam was ready to publish the novel in paperback, but Solotaroff needed to secure a publisher for the hardcover edition. Morrison read it and agreed that Random House should be that publisher. The novel was essentially complete when Morrison received it. Brown had worked closely with Solotaroff on the technical and structural aspects. So Brown and Morrison focused their energy on sharpening the language and storytelling in the novel.

Tragic Magic told the story of Melvin Ellington (aka Mouth), a Queens, New York, native who had just been released from prison. Like his protagonist, Brown was arrested as a conscientious objector to the Vietnam War and served an eighteen-month sentence in jail. Even as he was deliberate about using autobiographical elements in *Tragic Magic*, Brown was reluctant to probe certain aspects of his life, especially some of the prison stories that ended up in the novel. Morrison convinced him that these stories could help ground and enhance it. The things writers were most resistant to telling were often the very things they should write about, she told Brown. Similarly, she argued, so much of the best writing happened when writers moved toward and not away from the source of historical hurt that was also personal, even when it was painful for the writer to do so.[34]

Brown used stream of consciousness and a series of flashbacks to structure the novel, which critiques racism, capitalism, the limitations of sociopolitical revolution, and masculinity. Following his parole, Mouth encounters old friends and family and memories that help him interrogate his past and his path forward. At every turn, he explores what it means to be a man—to a girlfriend who does not need him to protect her from other men, to his prison mates, and to the men in the community who feel the need to prove their masculinity. Like so many of the novels Morrison published, *Tragic Magic* situates the reader in a well-crafted fictional world that allows us to see the main character's interior life. The narration holds the reader so closely that we cannot help but to see what Mouth sees—that the cost of preserving an exacting masculinity is high. It is impossible for any of the men in the novel to establish and maintain intimate relationships with women or anyone because they are so guarded on the one hand and disappointed in their ability to live up to the impossible standard on the other. The thing Morrison appreciated most about the novel was not its critique, however, but its determination to find new language and new ways to open up the possibilities for Mouth and the reader's ever-changing self-discovery.

Once the manuscript was complete, Morrison turned her attention to the novel's design. She instructed the design and copyediting team to design the novel "openly with generous margins and nice ornament to accompany the folio." The section at the beginning, called "A Few Words Before," was to be treated as an introduction, with "deep sink on that page and another on page 6 where the story actually begins."[35] As important as the look of the book were the endorsements it carried on the jacket. The right commendation for a book, especially a first novel, Morrison had long been aware, was one of the best ways to build anticipation for a book and to get visibility for an author. When she received James Baldwin's comments about *Tragic Magic*, she had those included as the book's back ad. Baldwin's lengthy remarks opened with an anecdote that imaginatively situated Brown among Muhammad Ali, Miles Davis, and Duke Ellington.

> The way I heard the story, Muhammad Ali and Miles Davis were yodelling in Duke Ellington's dressing room, and they yodelled so loud that their voices shattered the mirror into many mirrors. The Duke was understandably irritated and wanted to get the mirrors put together right away. But none of them could get to it right away. Miles had a flight scheduled, and Ali had a poetry reading, and the people had already filled the hall, waiting for the Duke and then somebody said, well, let's get Wesley Brown. They knew that he could do it, because of his skill and patience and love.
>
> So, Wesley Brown got his hands on the mirror, and here it is. . . . In other words, Brown is one hell of a writer, arriving on the scene not a moment too soon, and with power.[36]

Baldwin's endorsement heightened the novel's appeal to critics and did some of the hard work of explaining its cinematic structure to readers. It was not enough, unfortunately, to garner significant attention for the novel, which went out of print until it was reissued in 2021 with far more acclaim and with consistent reference to Morrison as the book's editor.

Author by author, book by book, Morrison was determined to build an editorial identity that mirrored her belief that the cultural terrain was best traversed when every kind of author was given meaningful opportunities for storytelling. While Black women writers were being published in record numbers, Morrison looked beyond the trend and acquired novels by Black male writers as well. No doubt she was interested and invested in celebrating the success women writers were experiencing. She was among these writers, after all. But her ability to edit all kinds of fiction challenged the simplistic notion that affinity with one group had to come at the expense of another. There was more than enough room across the rich literary landscape for all. Publishing Gayl Jones's fiction would certainly prove this.

CHAPTER 11

Green with Envy

When Morrison met Gayl Jones in October 1973, a Black women writers' renaissance was already underway. Toni Cade's *The Black Woman: An Anthology*, Maya Angelou's *I Know Why the Caged Bird Sings*, Mari Evans's *I Am a Black Woman*, Nikki Giovanni's *Re:Creation*, Audre Lorde's *Cables to Rage*, Louise Meriwether's *Daddy Was a Number Runner*, Sonia Sanchez's *We a BaddDDD People*, Alice Walker's *The Third Life of Grange Copeland*, Margaret Walker's *For My People*, and Morrison's *The Bluest Eye* were among the books that made 1970 a watershed year for Black women writers. As much as these writers made Gayl Jones possible, she was clearly in a league of her own. Without hesitation, even if with hyperbole, Morrison announced *Corregidora*, Jones's first novel, an outright game changer. "No novel about any black woman can ever be the same after this," Morrison boldly declared in the May 1975 issue of *Mademoiselle*.

Morrison first read Jones's work after being introduced to it through poet Michael Harper. For years, Morrison invited her friends who also taught creative writing to send her manuscripts they thought were good. Harper, who taught at Brown University, took Morrison up on the offer and sent her a box of manuscripts by one of the students he thought was among the most talented. Overwhelmed by the sheer volume of pages of material she received, Morrison put off reading until she could find time to sort through the work. She recalled: "There were hundreds and hundreds of pages in the box."

> So formidable a package could not be tackled lightly or quickly. Every time I looked at it, my heart sank. . . . I kept putting it off. The presence of this box intimidated me and finally it threatened me. If I didn't read it, I would never get rid of that presence.
>
> One Saturday morning I had two hours before I had to take the children somewhere. I went into the bedroom and opened the box. . . . Two and a half hours later, the children came banging in wanting to know when I was going to get ready. . . . I had been helplessly caught in the work of a twenty-four-year-old girl named Gayl Jones. A short novel she had written called *Corregidora*. . . . So deeply impressed was I that I hadn't time to be offended by the fact that she . . . had no "right" to know so much so well. She had written a story that thought the unthinkable.[1]

Almost incidentally, through the insightfulness of a friend, Morrison stumbled upon a writer who was, in many ways, an ideal. "This girl," Morrison suggested, "had changed the terms, the definitions of the whole enterprise" of storytelling and of the novel.

Jones was not completely unknown, since she had published short stories in impressive venues: "The Welfare Check" in *Essence* magazine, "The Roundhouse" in *Panache*, and "The Return" in Random House's *Amistad II*. But she was without a publisher, which meant Random House would not have to compete with other firms to publish her work. Jones had plenty of manuscripts completed, too, so Morrison was also relieved of the worry of too long of a delay between Jones's first and subsequent books. Such delays not only compromised any momentum, in terms of critical attention, a new writer gained with the publication of a first book, but unreasonable delays could also undermine Morrison's argument to her editor in chief that Jones was worth pursuing as a long-term talent for the firm. Contrastingly, Morrison had the good problem of deciding which manuscripts of Jones's to ready for publication first. Importantly, too, Jones was a Black woman novelist. Before publishing *Corregidora*, all the novels Morrison had brought out—Bryan Woolley's *Some Sweet Day*, Michael Moorcock's *Breakfast in the Ruins*, John McCluskey's *Look What They Done to My Song*, and Leon Forrest's *There Is a Tree More Ancient Than Eden*—were by men.

Morrison wasted no time arranging a meeting with Jones. As interested as she was in Jones's drafts, Morrison also wanted to meet the writer in person to discuss the different manuscripts she had reviewed. Morrison wanted to work on *Corregidora* first, the story of Ursa Corregidora, a blues singer who must learn to move beyond a legacy of sexual abuse she inherits from the women in her family. After the Brazilian coffee plantation owner, whom the novel refers to as "old-man Corregidora," burns the records that document enslavement and sexual abuse on his plantation, the Corregidora women—Ursa's great-grandmother Great-gram and her grandmother Gram—create an oral history to ensure that their story is told. Ursa's mother marries her father and gives birth to Ursa, not out of love but out of an obligation to "make generations," to ensure that the story is passed on. When Ursa loses her ability to reproduce (after a brute-force miscarriage and hysterectomy), she must find a new way to give voice to old man Corregidora's violence and acts of erasure. As the last of the Corregidora women, she must create an identity that transcends a family history of abuse. By the end of the story, she seems poised to break the cycle finally.

In its earliest draft, the "Corregidora" manuscript was too short to be a novel but far too long to be a short story. Morrison suggested that Jones extend the manuscript to novel length, which she did immediately. What Morrison found most compelling about the story was that Jones had managed to capture the full weight of an important but less talked about aspect of history—the sexual exploitation of women during slavery and the psychological and spiritual toll it took on those trapped in its legacy. Lodged in their family history was the horror of enslavement on a deeply personal and familial level and the impact of that horror and its legacy more than a hundred years later.

Morrison's early comments on the longer draft were direct and instructive. "First of all," she wrote to Jones, "get Ursa's language range defined. She moves from things like 'I seen the way' and 'I'ma walk out' to 'We've too much anger for each other' and 'What have I engendered?' . . . Second," Morrison noted, "sexual activity does not have the same function in literature as it has in life. In the former it must reveal something. Otherwise it runs the risk of being simply titillating or at worst boring."[2] Part of the challenge had to do with the fact that Corregidora women were at once frigid and sexually free. Morrison thought too many of the narrated scenes ran toward the scatological, so she suggested that Jones carefully reread all the passages that included sex scenes with an eye toward deleting the "gratuitous obscenity."

A few other matters also needed attention. The paradox of

Gram and Great-gram's hatred and lust for old man Corregidora needed to come across more deliberately. This is where Morrison was most helpful—in pushing Jones to use the novel to interrogate that paradox. It was "important to note," Morrison pointed out, "somehow that although Corregidora's women hated him, they were very attracted to him too. Their guilt (a combination of this hate and lust) is part of their remembering and a good part of their determination to keep him alive."[3] This impulse to "make generations" was as much about keeping him alive as it was about resisting his attempt to erase the record of what he had done to them. Morrison also prompted Jones to go back to the pages that had been drafted and revised in haste: "For example, Ursa's song ought to be a straight narrative of childhood sexual fears or whatever. May Alice and the boys—the fragments are really a cop out. You know—being too tired or impatient to write it out." Calling the writer out on those places in a draft that are weak was the work of a good editor, in Morrison's view. And a good writer, she argued, knew exactly where those sections were and either hoped they might go unnoticed or conceded that it was the best the writer could do at the time.

At Morrison's prompting, Jones added pertinent new material about Ursa's mother. In the new additions, we learn that she married Ursa's father, Martin, for the exclusive purpose of having a daughter to pass on her family's story. Her mission of making a new generation accomplished, she leaves Martin, returns to her maiden name, and takes a vow of celibacy. When Martin realizes that reproduction was her only motivation for marrying him, he publicly declares her a concubine. To round out this new material added to the manuscript, Morrison suggested that Jones create for the reader an atmosphere at her mother's house in Blacktown, the city the story is set in. "What is the house like, what kind of current life does the mother have?" Morrison queried. Adding this would help us know Ursa's mother and, by extension, know Ursa. And we had to know Ursa better by the end of the novel. That was the point—to know how she got from one place to the other and that she was "doing to Mutt what her grandmother did to Corregidora and for the same reasons." This last point, Morrison noted, was extremely important. She concluded the letter to Jones with encouragement and enthusiasm: "When these things are done, Gayl, you will have a truly powerful novel—really one of the best."[4]

Jones's response was immediate. She wrote back to Morrison, expressing gratitude for the direction and noting how the suggested changes had been handled.

> I've tried to keep Ursa's language consistent in all speech parts and vocabulary, but at times I wanted certain changes in the narrative parts. I hope the narrative parts I left work—and then near the end she assumes more the oral-storytelling present-tense type telling.
>
> I wasn't really sure about the gratuitous obscenity. I've given a reason for her language changes and some of the language she uses.
>
> I tried to bring out all the points you mention . . . giving background to the mother's life, and not copping out on Ursa's past and relationship with Mutt.[5]

Morrison was satisfied with the changes and sent off a quick note to Jim Silberman, the editor in chief. Jones was a born writer, Morrison contended. Silberman must have been immediately curious, since Morrison was not prone to excessive aggrandizement about writers she edited. But here was Morrison referring to Jones as an "incredible, incredible" writer before confessing that Jones's writing turned her "green with envy."[6]

Despite Morrison's assurance that the novel was fantastic and that Jones had other manuscripts in draft that could quickly follow the first novel's publication—two things Morrison thought warranted a higher than normal advance—Silberman reduced the proposed advance from $4,000 to $2,500, with $1,000 due on signing and $1,500 due on delivery. Jones accepted the offer but was concerned enough about it, no doubt through the provocation of others, that she reached out to literary agent Cyrilly Abels about possibly representing her in the future. Morrison had previously told Jones that she did not need an agent right away. The hard work of getting a contract for her first book was done, after all. Getting an agent once the book was out would not be a problem.

It was also clear that Jones often looked to those she trusted to guide her choices. Only two days after hearing from Abels, Jones sent Morrison a copy of Abels's letter and asked Morrison what she should do. Jones's inquiry about Abels was likely Morrison's first indication of Jones's malleability, a problem that would plague Jones her entire career. Morrison reiterated the point that Random House could handle postpublication matters (sales to magazines and foreign publishers and the like) as effectively as an agent could and that Jones should wait until after *Corregidora* was published to revisit the matter. Of more consequence now was the need to get quotes about the book from established writers.

Morrison was convinced that readers would be as enthusiastic about *Corregidora* as she was, but she was still determined to secure quotes for the jacket from reputable writers to get the book the kind of attention needed to make the reader pick up the novel, get a handle on its story, and read a few pages before being compelled to buy it. Her first big score was a comment from James Baldwin, who read the novel in the galleys Morrison had sent him. "*Corregidora* is the most brutally honest and painful revelation of what has occurred, and is occurring, in the souls of black men and women," Baldwin wrote; "it dares to confront the absolute terror which lives at the heart of love."[7] For a relatively unknown writer like Jones and her first novel, an endorsement from any established author would be helpful. A glowing endorsement from Baldwin, then, was a golden ticket. It would make all the difference in terms of getting the attention of reviewers, critics, and readers alike. Morrison was prepared to delay the book's publication for months if needed, in fact, to avoid sending it out naked—that is, without the right quotes from the right people announcing the book's achievement.

The draft of the book jacket for *Corregidora*, which was designed by the same person who had designed the jacket for Morrison's second novel, *Sula*, had met Morrison's approval. She had Baldwin's quote added to the back of the jacket immediately, and she added the endorsement to the editorial fact sheet's keynote. The keynote announced Jones as a writer "with a staggering gift" and described the novel as a "profound book as full of meaning as it is of horror, with characters so vivid you can hear their footsteps. Certain to chill and impossible to put down."[8]

The likelihood of the book's critical success became apparent almost immediately. It had its first serial sale to *Ms.* magazine and another section placed with *Fiction* magazine. Alice Walker joined Baldwin in providing commentary on the book, though Walker's was less complimentary and vague. *Corregidora* impressed Walker with its exploration of "the amazing variety, complexity and richness of the human condition as it has been experienced by Black people in America," and Jones's understated and eloquent style in the novel did the work of interrogating "a scarcely explored area of historical fact."[9] Morrison did not find Walker's statement particularly compelling. It could have been about any book and any writer. But Walker's willingness to provide a statement did signal the likelihood that she was willing to use her influence to bring attention to Jones and the novel. Walker had published *The Third Life of Grange Copeland* and *In Love and Trouble* by then, but her more important role was perhaps as an editor at *Ms.*, a magazine with a significant readership of women who bought books.

Morrison was so determined to make the first novel she would bring out by a Black woman a success that when she agreed to write an essay for *Mademoiselle* about a reading experience that moved her, she chose to write about *Corregidora*. This novel created delight, stripped away her editorial expertise, and reduced her to a hungry rather than a professional reader. Such a reading experience was rare, she noted. But reading about Ursa Corregidora had that effect.

> Ursa Corregidora, the last of the line, is legend, phoenix, ghost, sister-love. A kind of combination Billie Holiday and Fannie Lou Hamer. Poignant, frail and knee-buckling. She was every wilted gardenia, and every plate of butterbeans. She was lye cooked in hominy. . . .
>
> Ursa Corregidora is not possible. Neither is Gayl Jones. But they exist.[10]

In the final prelaunch push, the publicity team sent galleys and first copy versions of the novel to the usual review venues like *Kirkus*, *Library Journal*, and *Publishers Weekly*; to national newspapers with influential book critics like *The Washington Post*'s *Book World*, *The New York Times Book Review*, and the *Chicago Tribune Book World*; and to magazines with relevant readerships like *The Atlantic*, *Harper's*, *The New Republic*, *Ms.*, *Cosmopolitan*, *Esquire*, *Mademoiselle*, *Glamour*, *Vogue*, and *Playboy*.

Within months of its release, *Corregidora* was reviewed in all the right places to garner the kind of critical attention they hoped for. Two reviews appeared in *The New York Times*, one on May 25, 1975, and another on April 21 that same year. In the former review, Raymond Sokolov wrote, "Gayl Jones . . . proves that literature does progress and that there can come a time when you look around at your culture and conclude that, well, we've learned how to do a few new numbers." In his review of *Corregidora* and Rosalyn Drexler's *The Cosmopolitan Girl* for the "Books of the Times" column in *The New York Times Review*, Christopher Lehmann-Haupt described *Corregidora* as "a powerful slice of life, written in a perfect idiomatic pitch" and declared: "Miss Jones has posed an existential dilemma of the American black woman, if not all American women—namely, how to disentangle love from anger, and whether to give in to one or the other."[11] Maya Angelou's front-page review of the novel for the June 1 issue of the *LA Times Book Review* celebrated Jones's discipline and achievement:

> Ms. Jones eschews sentimentality . . . and becomes one of few writers I've read who is able to employ just the right amount of discipline to hold her flamboyant characters in check as they live in the vortex of melodrama. . . . There is not one word too many, no superfluidity of emotion and no dearth of stark beauty. *Corregidora* is a poem to black women and black men.[12]

Without saying so, Angelou nodded as much to Morrison as editor as to Jones as writer in her recognition of the discipline on display in the novel. Mentions in *The New Yorker*, *Time*, *The New Republic*, *Playboy*, and *The Village Voice* also helped created buzz about the novel.

As the reviews came out, requests for interviews came in. And the challenge of promoting a shy author became frighteningly apparent to the publicity team. Jones refused to do television interviews, much to the team's chagrin, and had limited availability for other interviews since she was still a graduate student. The reality was Jones had very little interest in doing any promotional work for the book. She preferred not to talk at all, in fact, especially not to strangers. Even after she realized her shyness would impact the amount of money she could earn on the advance for her next books, she confessed to Morrison that she had no idea that publishing her writing would involve so much public-facing work. Her shyness was also accompanied by a tendency to be easily manipulated, a reality that created another challenge when it was time to sign her second contract, this time for two books.

Since Jones had multiple fully drafted manuscripts on hand, Morrison had a contract proposal for two new books drawn up even before *Corregidora* was released. She and Jones had already agreed that the second novel they were calling *The Trial of a Man and a Woman* should immediately follow *Corregidora*, and a collection of short stories would follow the second novel. The sentiment seemed to be that a second novel about a woman who castrates her lover would create a reputation for Jones as a writer willing to deal with the dangerous tension between men and women that had its legacy in slavery. Morrison knew that the preemptive contract could work to Jones's advantage on the one hand but could shortchange her on the other. If *Corregidora* sold only modestly, the two-book contract for $5,000 might be viewed as generous. If *Corregidora* did well, however, a contract for two books, even if one was a collection of short stories (which tended to be less profitable) for the same amount per book as Jones's first book might seem unfair.

The uncertainty of the matter was enough for Jones to reach out to Liz Darhansoff, one of the literary agents Morrison had suggested Jones consider after Jones declined Abels's representation, to determine if she should sign the contract. Jones's confidence in her decision to approach Darhansoff waned almost immediately. She wrote to Morrison apologetically:

> I hope you aren't angry with me . . . When I got the contract, although it did seem strange to me that I wasn't getting more money . . . my first impulse was to sign the contract. . . . The reason I got in touch with Liz Darhansoff was that I had previously spoken with her on the telephone. . . . But the main reason was because you had recommended her. I guess I thought that you might not be *so* angry with me if someone you recommended were "talking for me."[13]

Jones went on to say repeatedly how sorry she was and that it was all because she was afraid to talk. Of all the people she talked to, fellow writer Quincy Troupe appeared to be the person who provided the most clarity. Jones was one of the writers, in fact, who contributed to *Giant Talk*, the anthology Troupe and Rainer Schulte published under Morrison's editorship at Random House the same year *Corregidora* was published. His connection to both women helped navigate the situation. Troupe suggested to Jones that Morrison had likely pushed for a higher advance but had been unable to secure one, in part, no doubt, because the "businessman upstairs" had no idea how well the first novel would do and because Jones's shyness severely limited any advantage an author's publicity might otherwise give.

Even as she had some sense of how shy Jones was, Morrison was taken aback by the timidity Jones expressed in the letter. This same writer who wrote the unimaginable seemed uncertain about everything and uncomfortable with anything other than writing.

> I don't know what an agent-writer relationship should be. . . . I feel like I'm in this really strange situation when all I really want to do is to be writing. I wouldn't even think about contracts. . . . Everything else seems scary and I am really unsure about myself and what I should be doing/saying. I hope that you will forgive me if in all the things coming at me for me to do and say, I have chosen the wrong thing(s) to do or say.[14]

After the two had a conversation to clear the air, Morrison wrote to Darhansoff, at Jones's request, to alert Darhansoff that Jones had changed her mind about wanting an agent. Ironically, Morrison had talked to Jones before about getting an agent. But when Jones learned that she would have to send her work to the agent, not directly to Morrison, Jones declined the offer. The "Grand Opera," as Morrison referred to the matter, was a function of Jones's "emotional tic" and of the undue influence and interference of the so-called friends who were all laying claim to her as "their" writer. Jones's friends' concern was likely well-meaning. Without an agent, it would be easy to take advantage of the writer. But by all accounts, Morrison was Jones's strongest advocate at Random House and beyond.

As Morrison prepared for the publication of *Eva's Man*, Jones earned a special award of merit from the George A. and Eliza Gardner Howard Foundation, Bantam bought the paperback rights to *Corregidora*, and Motown expressed interest in buying the film rights to the novel. Early interest in making the novel a motion picture certainly strengthened Jones's position with the firm as they prepared to publish *Eva's Man* in 1976 and *White Rat* the following year.

The one major change Morrison suggested for the draft was that Jones try her hand at another ending for the novel, one that made the closing act more explicit. Jones reverted to an earlier ending of the manuscript, which had been much shorter before using the questions Morrison posed to give the story and the characters additional layers and texture. They agreed that the new ending was better and began to focus on language inconsistencies. Morrison thought the inconsistencies were a distraction. Jones had a more nuanced view. "I agree with what you tell me," she wrote.

> For some reason though I like inconsistencies in language. No, my reason is because in oral storytelling and dialogue they are there. . . . Sometimes I hear people who would generally say Naw saying no for emphasis or prolongation. . . . But I will look at everything and also try to find other names besides E-a.[15]

Morrison thought the protagonist needed a name, and it could not be *E-a*. *Eva* was a logical choice, especially since the omission of a letter in the name had no clear function. The character simply had not yet revealed her name to Jones.

In general, Jones turned revisions around quickly. But this time, she was explicit in her determination to do so because she was moving to Ann Arbor to begin teaching at the University of Michigan. By now, she was far more confident in her writing, including her personal correspondence. She was comfortable with Morrison especially. "I'd like to try to get it done within the next two weeks before I go. . . . I'll call you if I have any problems with revisions or if I need more time," she wrote rather casually, unlike in earlier letters where she was deferential and apologetic almost to a fault.[16] By November, she noted, too, that she was now more relaxed in terms of her teaching. And she liked Ann Arbor and the university. Her biggest lament was that teaching took a tremendous amount of time away from writing. But, by and large, the second novel was done; and she and Morrison were satisfied with the draft.

With the manuscript ready to move to preproduction, Morrison resolved to settle on a title for the book. Neither of the titles they had been toying with—first *The Trial of a Man and a Woman* and later *Deep Song*—had the appeal the book would need to tempt the potential reader to pick it up. Morrison suggested *Eva's Man*, "since the thing happens when all those men merge into one and she is full up."[17] Jones agreed and appreciated Morrison's feedback.

> The new title seems right. I was unsure at first, because I had been with the other title so long.
>
> I'm pleased by the editing of the ending as it works now. The additional part had seemed awkward to me. Now it comes together.[18]

Then, there was the matter of how best to market the book—a book that finds its protagonist in jail after years of sexual abuse culminates in the castration and murder of David, the man with whom Eva spent five days in a rented room before turning violent.

The editorial fact sheet for *Eva's Man* described the book as having "the same eerie power that excited reviewers of *Corregidora*" and as "another sensual, brooding and magnificent novel" by the writer Gayl Jones.[19] Building on *Corregidora*'s success had benefits.

The novel had sold 5,300 copies—a good number for a first novel by a largely unknown writer—and interests in the novel's film rights (including a request from actress Cicely Tyson) continued to grow before fizzling out years later. But a second novel that pit Black women and Black men against each other was also controversial, all the more so since it erupted in deadly violence. What message was Jones communicating exactly with Eva, a protagonist who sees castration and murder as the preferred recourse and who comes to realize too late from her prison cell that the violence she enacts does not soothe the weariness years of sexual contempt and sexual assault created. And what are readers to make of the fabled Queen Bee, the woman Eva's mother and Miss Billie, her mother's friend, recall mysteriously outlives her many lovers? How much of Eva's tragic story is true, and how much is imagined? When and how do the stories about different experiences bleed and blend together?

Alice Walker's response to the novel, which Morrison had sent to her in galleys hoping for something she could use for a promotional blurb, was telling. She wrote:

> I have never before read a book that made my heart ache with such despair and fear and grief. . . . Its insight into the terrors of our lives is so acute it almost sends me screaming, like a madwoman, into the night. Gayl Jones is a miracle because she can bear to relate this incredible pain of her own vision. She does this in exquisite language; though blood seems to come from her fingertips.[20]

Walker was shocked and depressed by the book, she confessed to Morrison. But what's more, *Ms.* had just bought a short story, "The Collector of Treasures," by the South African writer Bessie

Head about women who changed from docile to violent after unrelenting sexual abuse. The women in the story drugged their men and castrated them while they slept. Like Eva, the women in Head's story are imprisoned. "It strikes me as incredible," Walker wrote, "that out of two such different cultures this one vision emerges. We must be doing worse than even I thought, and I was never that optimistic."[21]

Eva's Man was controversial, and Morrison knew it. It struck a nerve among Black readers and beyond. The writer and critic Jean Stafford called it "pustalant" and threatened never to read a book bearing the Random House colophon again. No stranger to censorship threats, Selma Shapiro, the firm's vice president for publicity and public relations, defended Jones as a talented writer and the novel as a work the firm respected. She belted back at Stafford: "I cannot believe that you, as an author and critic, wish to interfere with the rights of other writers to be heard."[22]

Jones was similarly defensive of her right to write Eva as a character. Even as she disagreed with Eva's actions, Jones felt her disapproval of Eva's choice had no place in the novel. Her job was to allow Eva to tell as much of the story as she was willing to tell, however scandalous its telling might be. In Jones's view, Eva is problematic in *Eva's Man* the same way Trueblood is problematic in *Invisible Man*. Easily, Jones could have added *The Bluest Eye*'s Cholly Breedlove to this list. The question was whether the Black writer should ignore such characters and avoid such territory for fear of portraying a negative image of Black people. Instead of the latter, Jones felt compelled to try to reclaim complex Black characters who are riddled with contradictions but who are making an effort to achieve their version of wholeness. For Jones, that quest for wholeness is what mattered for the ideal of heroism or the heroic image in a novel, not a quaint story about a modest or ordinary Black protagonist.[23]

As was the case with *Corregidora*, Jones was reluctant to do a lot of publicity for *Eva's Man*. Morrison had the team send out a bevy of copies—109 to newspapers, 81 to magazines, 19 to columnists, 21 to college adoptions, and 52 to the "Black list," which included critics, reviewers, and outlets with known interests in books by Black authors. Despite the challenges Jones's reluctance to make appearances to promote the book presented, the publicity team championed the novel. Morrison knew, too, that they made a tremendous difference. She assisted when she could by joining Jones for interviews.

D. Keith Mano's *Esquire* article about Jones and her first two novels captured the author-editor dynamic adequately. First, Morrison admitted that she knew the implications of publishing *Corregidora* and *Eva's Man* back-to-back. The risk of two novels that "tear up men," in her view, was worth the desired effect—to capture "that element of carnal, raw, economic, sinister sensuality."[24] Then Mano, who referred to Morrison as Jones's "Svengali editor," remarked on how self-erasing Jones was, while Morrison assumed the "I" pronoun when referring to Jones's work. "*I* published *Corregidora*," he quoted Morrison as saying. Tongue in cheek, Mano wrote: "I suspect the title page of *Corregidora* should read, 'by Gayl Jones, as told to Toni Morrison.'" He was wrong there, but he made his point. What he did get right, however, was the role the publicity team played in helping to build a readership for Jones. In fact, Harriet Algrant, head of publicity at Random House at the time, was also included in the interview. As Algrant and Morrison remarked, having in-house support, especially in the publicity department, kept *Corregidora* from getting the minimal treatment first novels usually get. It was worth noting, as Mano did, that the publicity team was all women. Women were becoming a force in publishing—from agents, editors, and writers to salespeople and readers. Morrison and Jones found themselves happily at the center of this watershed period, even though, ironically, neither Morrison nor Jones identified squarely with feminism or with the notion of Black women writers being in vogue. That had a short shelf life. They were looking for lasting change.

Determined to keep the rhythm of steady publications for Jones, Morrison suggested that they prepare select short stories to follow *Eva's Man*. The collection, *White Rat*, needed minimal work, especially since some of the stories had been previously published. Jones was also readying a draft of a novel she was calling *The Melrose Woman*, intending to have it published after *White Rat*. And she expressed interest in publishing poetry. "I'm glad that you are interested in a collection of narrative poems," Morrison wrote to Jones. "I don't know how striking the sale of such a collection would be, but it might be a dazzling publishing venture."[25] With Jones, Morrison was willing to test her limits as an editor by publishing a collection of poems, even if she was doubtful about the financial feasibility of such a project.

In early March 1977, Morrison decided which of the stories to include and shared with Jones a proposed table of contents to show how the stories might be ordered. Jones preferred the stories that were more experimental. Morrison resisted that impulse, however, and persuaded Jones to include those that were more traditional. With this third book, it was important to reflect some variety in Jones's style rather than risk having all her work have the same tone. "Sameness," Morrison chided, was "not quite the same thing as a distinctive style." Achieving subtlety and discovery in traditional or semi-traditional modes was harder to do. "But when it works," she added, "it does magnificent."[26]

Morrison also suggested title changes. A story Jones called "Friends" would be changed to "A Quiet Place for the Summer"—because "Friends" sounded too much like "Persona," the title of another story. She also thought they should send "Persona" and "Your Poems Have Too Much Color in Them" to Charles McGrath at *The New Yorker* for possible use in an issue. These stories were readable and written well. And exposure to *The New Yorker*'s readership could help both in sales and with critical reception.

Logically, Morrison used the success of *Corregidora* and *Eva's Man* to promote *White Rat*. The editorial fact sheet for the collection of twelve stories boasted that *Corregidora* had sold five thousand copies to date and its paperback rights to Bantam, while *Eva's Man* had sold 3,590 copies, first serial rights to *Ms.*, and paperback rights to Bantam as well. Importantly, though, *White Rat* would give readers a better sense of Jones's depth as a writer. The stories' subjects ranged from an aging mulatto with identity problems to a young graduate student trying to make sense of faculty drama at a department party. Then, there were the stories about a young woman visiting the country and learning about love and about a bridge personified to recall the man murdered under its arch.

Reviews of the collection were mixed. Jones was complimented for her range, dialogue, points of view, and overall giftedness as a writer. But most reviewers had grown weary of her characters' insanity and sexual exploitation and noted that, even as the stories were less avant-garde in terms of style than the first two novels, they still demanded too much of the average reader. Mel Watkins's review for *The New York Times* followed this sentiment.

Gayl Jones, a young novelist of the first rank, demonstrates in these tales that her talent and disposition may not easily lend itself to shorter fiction. Although her prose here is starkly arresting and indelible as in her novels, except for the longer stories such as "Jeveta" and "The Women," these tales are simply doleful vignettes—slices of life so bedeviled that they seem distorted.[27]

The other unspoken challenge for the success of *White Rat*, unspoken at least until Diane Johnson's review in the November 10, 1977, issue of *The New York Review of Books*, was the competition factor. Morrison's third novel, *Song of Solomon*, was also published in 1977. The advantage of this was that Morrison could talk about *White Rat* (and the other books she edited around that time) anytime she was interviewed to promote *Song of Solomon*, which won the National Book Critics Circle Award that year and which was Morrison's breakout novel, in terms of sales. The disadvantage of sharing a publication season with Morrison, however, was that, among critics, there did not seem to be room for more than one highly successful Black writer, let alone more than one successful Black woman writer.

Morrison lamented this errancy explicitly. In an interview with Judith Wilson for *Essence* magazine, where Morrison admitted to feeling dissatisfied with the commercial success of the books she edited, she noted:

When I publish Toni Cade Bambara, when I publish Gayl Jones, if they would do what my own books have done [in sales], then I would feel really fantastic about it. But the market can only receive one or two [Black women writers.] Dealing with five Toni Morrisons would be problematic. I'm not talking about quality of work—who writes better than I do and stuff. I'm just talking about the fact that, in terms of new kinds of writing, the marketplace receives only one or two Blacks in days when it's not fashionable. That's true of literature in general, but it's particularly true for Black writing.[28]

Similarly, when Zia Jaffrey asked Morrison about the intelligence of the criticism of her books, Morrison noted:

Once I was reviewed in the *New York Review of Books*, with two other black writers. The three of us, who don't write anything alike, were lumped together by color, and the reviewer ended by deciding which of the three books was the best. And she chose one, which could have been [the best], but the reason it was the best was because it was more like "real" black people.[29]

Here, Morrison was referring to Johnson's "The Oppressor in the Next Room," which reviewed *Song of Solomon*, *White Rat*, and James Alan McPherson's *Elbow Room*, books that had nothing in common except the authors' race. Morrison rightly described that kind of reduction as absurd. That Johnson thought *Song of Solomon* was the "best" was beside the point.

Johnson's review revealed two problems. One, that Black books that ventured beyond realism were likely to have their authenticity questioned. And, two, that books by Black authors, no matter how different they are one from another, were negligently pitted against each other, with one of them being designated as "the best." Since she was aware of this tendency, Morrison tried to avoid releasing more than one book in the same season for fear that critics could put them in competition with each other rather than give them individualized attention. The more books she edited, however, the more difficult this became. In addition to publishing *White Rat* that year, for instance, she also released Bambara's second short story collection, *The Sea Birds Are Still Alive*; Leon Forrest's second novel, *The Bloodworth Orphans*; James Haskins's *The Cotton Club*; and June Jordan's poetry collection, *Things That I Do in the Dark*.

As soon as *White Rat* was ready for publication, Morrison proposed to Jason Epstein a two-book contract for Jones's next two novels. Epstein had agreed to pay Jones $5,000 for the next book, but Jones wanted a contract for two novels instead of one. Morrison knew Jones had more than enough work in draft to get the next two novels out as quickly as they had released the first three books. So Morrison suggested to Epstein that they offer Jones a contract for $10,000—$1,500 would be due upon signing, $3,500 upon receipt of the first book, and $5,000 upon receipt of the second. Epstein was reluctant, however, and would not agree to offering the same amount for both novels. Morrison's advocacy for Jones was admirable. "I think you are making a mistake by not signing her up for two books," Morrison wrote. "I don't see how I can pay less for the second one. . . . I have arranged the contract so that we are not out of any money in any large degree but how can I tell her that . . . the second one is worth less. The only alternative I can suggest is perhaps buying an option on the second one."[30]

Morrison also noted that Jones was considering getting an agent, suggesting that they needed to sign her up for the two books before that happened. The strategic mention of an impending agent was meant to remind Epstein that an agent would mean competition for the firm if the agent felt Jones was not getting the best deal at Random House. She also provided him with the profit and loss statements for Jones. Before she and Epstein sorted the matter out, Morrison wrote to Jones to explain why the contract that was sent was for one book instead of two. Rather than admit that she was not able to convince Epstein to give Jones a fair contract, Morrison maintained that the contract had been drafted before they agreed to sign Jones up for two books. The editor in chief was away, Morrison claimed, and redoing the contract would cause more delays.

> We can do one of two things now: you can sign this contract for the second novel; or you can return this one unsigned and wait until I have renegotiated the original terms in view of a two book contract or I can renegotiate the contract and buy the first novel (whichever one you prefer to work on first) and offer an option on the second payable upon receipt of the complete and acceptable mss. for the first.[31]

Morrison offered Jones alternatives to the two-book contract, quite probably to save face and to buy some time, even as she claimed that Random House had no preference about which way they should proceed with the contracts. Unable to secure the contract she knew Jones deserved, Morrison hoped Jones would sign the contract for one book instead of agree to an unfair one for two books.

In that same letter, Morrison also raised the issue of Jones taking on an agent. "I would like you very much to consider taking Peter Matson as your agent," Morrison wrote. Matson was a successful agent, "as well as a very low key and gentle man," in Morrison's view. She suspected that he and Jones would work well together. And Morrison was convinced that having a respected agent was the only way to force Epstein's hand. Jones accepted Morrison's recommendation, though her time working with Matson was brief. He counseled Jones not to sign the option letter but to focus on readying *The Melrose Woman* manuscript for publication. Matson also recognized that Jones's artistic life was remarkably layered. She wrote fiction and poetry in volumes. "There are so many facets of her career that it is a little bit like stepping into a three-ring circus, with all the acts going on at the same time," he wrote to Morrison.[32] Matson quickly realized what Morrison had managed with seeming ease was actually quite complicated.

By February 1978, Morrison and Jones's editor-author relationship changed, subtly at first and then dramatically and unexpectedly. All of a sudden, Jones was dissatisfied with the manuscript of *The Melrose Woman*. In her view, the kind of work the book needed was not the kind of work she could do easily at that time. Morrison was clear that Jones should work on whichever manuscript she felt most passionate about, be it *The Queen Bee*, *Almeyda*, *The Melrose Woman*, or something altogether new. In October, Jones sent the early pages of a manuscript she called *Palmares* to Morrison, noting that the full manuscript was one thousand pages total. Two weeks later, Morrison asked for the remaining pages right away.

> I am on page 327 and so far it is marvelous. There is no question in my mind but that this is the book we should substitute for the novel we signed up. . . . I want my reading of it to be fairly uninterrupted, first because it is so incredibly well done, and second because I want to see how well it is sustained. I am extremely excited about it.[33]

Her excitement about the book notwithstanding, Morrison realized almost immediately after sending off her letter to Jones that something was awry.

This was the first time in their years of working together that Jones had gone silent for months at a time. Startlingly, too, Jones had discarded Matson as her agent and was now working with an unknown one, Bob Higgins. Morrison knew Jones well enough to recognize Higgins as trouble. She warned Jones that Higgins had written to Random House in August that year, inquiring of the publisher's interest in investing in his publishing projects. No doubt full of regret for encouraging Jones to get an agent finally, Morrison implored Jones to consider whether Higgins was acting in her best interest. She did not say it outright, but Morrison certainly meant to imply that Higgins was more self-interested than he was committed to Jones's work.

Jones and Higgins first connected when she was an assistant professor at the University of Michigan, where he studied philosophy. Before his arrival in Ann Arbor, Higgins had already evidenced problematic behavior. After initiating a police standoff on Staten Island, he jumped out of a window, falling six floors but surviving and proclaiming himself the new messiah. Once he became involved with Jones, he opened two investment businesses and took over from Matson as Jones's agent. Higgins, whom Jones later married, demanded that all correspondence about his client be sent directly to him.

The first difficulty arose after Random House sent Higgins a subagency license agreement on *Eva's Man*. Not long after receiving the agreement, Higgins expressed concern about being able to sell the book. His next letter expressed his intent to conclude a film deal for *Corregidora*. Morrison had already notified Jones that the deal with Motown for the film rights was not one Jones could endure, and it had fallen through. Motown wanted full exploitation rights (which would allow them to use Jones's life story for promotional purposes), and Motown had rejected several of the guarantees Random House required, a number of them at Morrison's prompting. Jones was more than an author on her list. She was a delicate person Morrison felt compelled to protect as best she could. There was no way they could accept the offer, Morrison argued, even more so considering Jones's desire for privacy. Inquiries from other places might be more flexible in their negotiation for the film rights, Morrison suggested.

Higgins's exchanges with Robin Straus, who worked with film and performance rights at Random House, raised another red flag and prompted Straus to express her concern to Morrison. Higgins lambasted Straus about the delays in correspondence and refused to provide a phone number where he could be reached. He insisted that he would do business only by written correspondence. While Straus agreed with Higgins's complaint about the firm's efficiency, it was idiocy, she lamented to Morrison, for an agent to try to sell performance rights by mail: "Have you ever known a Hollywood producer who reads? Who doesn't require a three word handle on a book and a dramatic presentation of the plot?" Straus continued:

> As you know, we wanted to have Higgins call so that we could discuss returning performance rights to Gayl Jones with the provision that we receive 5% of performance income (what in effect we would get if we hired a subagent) and that we be sent the license agreements to make sure nothing violated our contractual rights. At this point, however, I don't think we should deal with this man and therefore if Gayl Jones wants Higgins to represent her, I feel very strongly that Gayl must insist in writing that her rights be returned to her.[34]

Knowing that Morrison cared deeply about Jones's career and that she was excited about her early read of *Palmares*, Straus turned to Morrison for advice about how to proceed in a way that would not compromise Jones's working relationship with Morrison and the firm.

Morrison decided to write to Jones directly rather than have Straus try to negotiate with Higgins. She sent Jones all the correspondence Random House had received from Higgins and a brief letter noting that she was "alarmed by the contents of some of this correspondence" and by the way Higgins described her work. "In any case," Morrison wrote, "the decision about whether he is operating in your best interests is yours to make."[35] If, indeed, Higgins was to continue negotiating on her behalf, Jones would need to write directly to Morrison asking that the performance rights be returned to her, after which point, Jones could assign the rights to anyone she chose.

The tone of Jones's letters to Morrison shifted aggressively immediately thereafter. Morrison found it hard to believe that it was Jones who wrote the letters demanding that all future correspondence be sent to Higgins. Jones's timidity was well established and evidenced by years of cooperation on the one hand and apologetic articulations of uncertainty on the other. As Higgins's letters continued, tension mounted. Higgins began to refer to unnamed legal counsel while arguing that *Palmares* was not under contract, only manuscripts Jones referred to as *The Melrose Woman* and *Queen Bee*. Morrison reminded Jones that they had agreed that *Almeyda* could substitute for *The Melrose Woman*. Since *Palmares* was a revision of *Almeyda*, *Palmares* was, in fact, one of two books under contract with Random House, not an option book as Higgins suggested. Annoyed by Higgins's attempts to manipulate the situation, she referred him to Random House's lead counsel, Gerald Hollingsworth.

Higgins held no punches in expressing his distaste for Morrison and Straus and their roles in publishing Jones's work and selling film rights to her books. "Since Morrison's and Straus' understanding is that Ms. Jones is their ward," he wrote, "it is only to be expected that Straus, turning matters over to her heavy, Morrison, to do the dirty work, would find my position, as proper, plain and straight forward as it is, offensive."[36] Their alarm was unfounded, he claimed. Rather it was informed by their belief that "they have the bag of doughnuts, to dispense on a basis of favors and obsequiousness" and by their history of dealing with "Harlem junkies, opportunists and perverts" rather than with serious men like Higgins.

Over the next few months, Morrison and Higgins debated about Jones's contractual obligations, and Morrison ultimately had Random House release *Palmares* after Higgins outlined the manner in which Morrison was to edit the novel. She found the demand insulting, obviously, since she had nothing to prove in the way of being a competent editor. Regrettably, Morrison declared, Jones would have to find another editor and another publisher for her work because Random House wanted nothing to do with Higgins, who, to them, was unreasonable and unpredictable.

Jones eventually found a home at Naomi Long Madgett's Lotus Press. Rather than risk any potential breach of contract with Random House, Jones opted not to release *Palmares* as a novel and adapted it for verse instead, publishing it as *Song for Anninho* in 1981. She refused to do any readings or to support any publicity efforts for the book or for *The Hermit-Woman*, which she published two years later. Her reticence to promote her books was well known, since she did little in the way of publicity for the novels she published at Random House. But without Morrison as her surrogate and advocate, the books (including *Liberating Voices: Oral Tradition in African American Literature*, which she published with Harvard University Press in 1991) went largely unremarked on. When Higgins was arrested in 1983 for felonious assault against an activist at a gay rights parade, the couple fled to Paris, where they remained for years before returning to Jones's hometown in Kentucky to care for her ailing mother. Sadly, Morrison and her protégé never reconciled, and Higgins continued to exercise control over Jones's life until he killed himself during a police raid, shortly after Jones published her first novel in twenty years, *The Healing* (1998). Jones survived the raid and went on to publish a fourth novel, *Mosquito*, the following year.

In 2021, Jones finally published *Palmares*, the last novel she worked on with Morrison. Jones had submitted the manuscript to Morrison early in the year in 1979. But Morrison warned Epstein that Random House should only publish the book if he was in love with it. After years of supporting Jones's career, Morrison was unwilling to deal with Higgins. It was one thing to promote a shy author who preferred to stay out of the public eye. It was quite another to do so for an author whose surrogate hurled insults at her greatest champion. Following the publication of *Palmares*, in the tradition of old where she published books in rapid succession, in 2022, Jones released *The Birdcatcher* and reissued *Song for Anninho* in a two-volume collection of narrative poems titled *Song for Almeyda and Song for Anninho*. Then, in 2023, she published *Butter: Novellas, Stories, and Fragments*, all with Beacon Press. Not surprisingly, the one constant in the promotion of Jones's new books and in all the stories about her reemergence as a writer was her connection to Morrison, her one-time editor and friend, who had wondered all along how the magic of Gayl Jones was possible. As it turned out, in some ways, it was not.

CHAPTER 12

Boxing the Champ In

O n the crisp Tuesday morning of January 6, 1970, a lively crowd of nearly one hundred radio and television reporters, accompanied by still photographers and camera crews, converged on the twelfth floor of Random House's editorial offices in anticipation of one of the largest press conferences the company had ever hosted. The space, which had been reconfigured for the occasion, buzzed with anticipation as representatives from all corners of the media landscape—television, radio, syndicates, newspapers, and magazines—filled the room. All eyes were fixed on the stage as they awaited the announcement that brought them there—a groundbreaking book deal with former heavyweight boxing champion Muhammad Ali.

Ali arrived at the press conference impeccably dressed and in a jovial mood. One look at the cameras that were trained on him, and he performed for the audience in the way that only he could. As was his custom, he was full of bravado and predictions. "I believe that this book will outdo all of them that's been written," he bragged. There to present Ali with the ceremonial check, reflecting the $60,000 advance he received upon signing the contract, was Random House president Robert L. Bernstein, who sat next to Ali and appeared to enjoy the fanfare as much as the camera-friendly Ali did. Ali chided the audience on the one hand, noting that they did not really know anything about him, and teased them on the other, suggesting that the book would be a tell-all that set the record straight. Even if he had to tell the story from jail, he boasted he would divulge all the details about the seedy proposals government officials made to him, about the shady side of the boxing business, and so much more.

Not all the reporters in attendance were friendly admirers of the deposed champion. One asked, for instance, how Ali reconciled his well-known affinity with the Nation of Islam and its Black separatist views with his decision to publish his memoir with a white publishing house. Unfazed and unwilling to acknowledge the primacy of the question, Ali responded in a way that suggested that white people could not be completely avoided. "How could I fly if I wouldn't go on a white airline? . . . I would have to take off these white-made shoes or ride on camels or elephants," he offered, full of animation. "We don't have nothing—we don't make toothpicks, we don't make zippers to zip our pants. Every dollar I accept is a free dollar. I never do anything against my belief."[1] Part of what Ali needed to reconcile for that reporter and others was the Nation of Islam's belief (especially its leader Elijah Muhammad) that Black people needed to be self-sufficient and Ali's willingness to do business with a white publisher. Ali's point that every dollar he accepted was a free dollar, presumably, was that he chose to publish with Random House on his terms.

While Ali did not disclose it, one thing that appealed to him was that the firm had a Black senior editor, Charles F. Harris. Upon meeting Harris, Ali acknowledged his surprise that there was a

Black man among the group of white men trying to convince him that he should publish his book with Random House and not with Simon and Schuster. Harris had, in fact, used his connections with the Nation of Islam and with friends in the Black community in Chicago to get Ali to come to Random House for a meeting in the first place. Harris had worked with the Nation in New York over the years and was a trusted ally. And he was well connected with writers and publishers in Chicago, who helped put him in touch with Richard Durham, the journalist who was helping Ali tell his story. The greatest fighter in the world needed the greatest writer. So no one was surprised by Ali's declaration that Durham, too, was among the best of the best.

Ali was not the only one who had to explain the partnership. A different reporter asked Bernstein what he thought might be the implications of signing up a convicted felon, which Ali was at that point, for a book deal with such a high payout. Having anticipated the question, Bernstein pulled his pipe from his mouth, leaned across the table toward the microphone, and replied that the day publishers refused to publish controversial books would be a bad day for democracy. Random House was no stranger to controversial authors. Still, Bernstein deflected potential ire by playing up the company's determination not to be outdone. They had recently lost out to McGraw Hill on the opportunity to publish popular Black Panther Eldridge Cleaver's *Soul on Ice*, Bernstein noted, because McGraw Hill was seen as the "more radical publisher."

The truth was public sentiment about Ali was still mixed. He might have been a sympathetic hero when he refused to enlist in the army in the spring of 1967 if he had done so simply as a conscientious objector. But Ali's decision not to step forward when his name was called at the army induction ceremony in Houston was also informed by his conversion to Islam three years earlier.

Ali's public affiliation with "Black Muslims," as members of the Nation of Islam were sometimes errantly called, unsettled some of his most ardent supporters. Even when Elijah Muhammad suspended Ali from the Nation—supposedly because of Ali's intent to continue boxing to make more money, which contradicted the Nation's beliefs about sports—Ali defended the leader's decision, noting that punishment was the appropriate response to wrongdoing. Ali would not, however, accept one white female reporter's claim that as a Muslim, he ascribed to feelings of hate for all white people. "Can you show where I've ever said I hate any white person?" he insisted. "I'm a victim of hate. I have a right to hate evil." Any calm he evoked with that comment was likely compromised by the pronouncement that he would not only play himself in a film about his life but that he was also considering a role in a film about insurrectionist Nat Turner. What Ali managed to do at the press conference without ever putting pen to paper was to make defiance a novel curiosity. Whenever he was asked to clarify an enticement, he gave the response every publisher hoped for—you would have to buy the book to find out. "Six dollars and fifty cents will tell you," he teased.

All the events leading up to the press conference and in the weeks immediately thereafter suggested that the book would be a windfall for both Random House and Ali. In November 1969, Durham mentioned the project to Verne Moberg at Pantheon while discussing another project Durham had pitched about the Port Chicago disaster that occurred July 17, 1944, when munitions exploded aboard the SS *E. A. Bryan*, killing 320 men on duty, 202 of them Black. Durham casually commented that Simon and Schuster was prepared to make Ali an offer for a book Durham was to help him write. Ali had an offer, Durham claimed, but he was confident that Ali would consider additional offers from other publishers that saw "some business advantage in publishing the official Muhammad Ali autobiography."[2] As soon as he heard the rumor that Ali's camp was shopping his project around, editor in chief Jim Silberman asked Harris what he knew of the enterprise. At that point, Harris had not heard about the project. But, through the historian Lerone Bennett Jr., Harris knew how to get in touch with Durham. The two had never met, but Harris quickly became acquainted with Durham, who shared with Harris that the key players on the Ali book project would be in New York soon to meet with Simon and Schuster. They were willing to come to Random House because Studs Terkel had told Durham that André Schiffrin, the editor at Pantheon (which Random House owned) who had conceived and edited Terkel's *Hard Times: An Illustrated Oral History of the Great Depression*, was "the greatest in the country, perhaps the greatest the country has ever produced."[3] Determined to intercept the meeting, Harris arranged for a limousine to pick Durham up from the airport and to take him to the Sheraton Americana on 7th Avenue and 52nd Street on the condition that he would bring Ali by Random House the day before he was to meet with any other publishers. Durham agreed.

In tacit agreement, Harris and Silberman managed to keep the appointment quiet. When Ali arrived at Random House with his attorney Chauncey Eskridge, the five men—Harris, Silberman, Ali, Eskridge, and Durham—met in a conference room where the atmosphere remained subdued until Ali began to bait his audience with animated anticipation of the book's revelations. At one point, Bennett Cerf, who owned the firm, conveniently made a casual appearance, greeting "the Champ" as a fellow celebrity. Renowned for his wit and TV appearances on *What's My Line?*, Cerf added a bit of levity to the room as soon as Ali recognized him. The two jostled humorously with each other for a short time before

Cerf excused himself, pulled Harris and Silberman aside, and, with characteristic directness, stated that he wanted Random House to publish Ali's book. Harris and Silberman knew, at that point, what needed to happen.

Harris's strategy was simple—stay within the limits of what they were approved to offer to make a deal, in terms of money and royalties, and avoid a bidding war with other publishers. Ali was due at Simon and Schuster the next morning, and Harris and Silberman wanted to do everything they could to close the deal. They convinced Ali's team to come back to the Random House offices the next morning before taking the planned meeting. Harris held no punches about what he had been able to accomplish with the writers he worked with. He informed Ali's team that he had been the editor for football sensation Jim Brown's *Off My Chest*. Importantly, too, Harris had helped the Harlem mosque get credit to purchase books when they could not get credit elsewhere. In other words, he had undeniable credibility, not just with these two experiences but because he was relatively well known among the Nation, especially in New York, through his work in Black cultural circles. Contrastingly, they knew no one at Simon and Schuster.

Even though the threat of a prison sentence for Ali was real and even as Ali was indeed a controversial figure, the Random House team was confident that they could help him produce a book that would do well financially, for the firm and for Ali. The initial offer was for $100,000. Ali's team rejected it outright immediately. When Silberman made a second offer, this time for $175,000, Ali's team asked Harris and Silberman to leave the room so they could caucus. Ali's manager, Herbert Muhammad, who was also the son of the Nation's leader Elijah Muhammad, had not made the trip. But presumably, Eskridge had been in touch with Herbert Muhammad during the break they all took for lunch and then again when Eskridge returned to the room to say that, with an offer of $225,000, they could close the deal. Silberman had only been cleared to offer $200,000, but when he took the number to Bernstein and Cerf, they approved it and returned to the room with Silberman to celebrate.[4]

Once the deal was brokered, the goal was to have the draft written in a year and the book published not long thereafter. The actual timeline was far more prolonged, however, and a change in editors happened along the way. While Harris had been instrumental in securing the contract, he was not on the best of terms with Random House's leadership. When he finally left the firm, the message he communicated to the authors on his list was that he and Random House had different ideas about the work he wanted to do. Beyond this, it was unclear what the critical differences were. Harris had been successful at Doubleday and at Wiley before joining Random House. His success was due in no small part to the way he understood publishing from a business perspective. Before becoming an editor, he learned the ins and outs of the financial aspects of book publishing. He would take this expertise with him to Howard University to establish a university press there. After Harris's departure, Silberman worked directly with Durham before eventually handing the project over to Morrison.

The layers of complexity that attended the book project revealed themselves early on. Durham struggled to get enough time with Ali to prepare and review drafts. Interference from the Nation and the Louisville boxing group was ongoing. Durham was fighting on multiple fronts. One of his early messages to Silberman was a warning that Eskridge had allegedly accepted a fee to allow *Sports Illustrated* to do a special biographical interview with Ali for the magazine. "This dilutes Champ's concentration on his autobiography, reduces its importance to him," Durham wrote.[5] They could not stop magazines from doing "regular stories based on casual interviews," but no special, in-depth interviews should be entertained or sanctioned. Durham knew the request had to be cleared by Random House, and he implored Silberman to deny it, more so since Ali's license to fight had been reinstated. (His lawyers argued that other boxers convicted of crimes had been allowed to fight and that denying a license to Ali was arbitrary. The judge agreed to reinstate his license to fight in September 1970.)

A year later, Durham had made only minimal progress on the book. He confided in Silberman: "I believe I've finally satisfied most Muslim officials that I won't interject anything into the book but the truth."[6] Their reluctance, Durham inferred, was a part of the stalled progress. He continued to work on the draft and eventually began to work with Morrison, who had been assigned to the project after Harris left and after Silberman's impatience grew. Morrison and Durham worked well together, even if only minimally, from the beginning. Her biggest role was encouraging him to make progress on the manuscript. When he finally sent her pages to review in May 1972, Morrison outlined for Silberman forty topics, by her organization, covered in the draft and the number of pages Durham had drafted for each.

There were details on Ali's major fights to date, on the paternity charges a prostitute brought against him, on his training after the Olympics, on incidents with celebrities (including Nat King Cole, Sam Cooke, the Beatles, and Sidney Poitier), and on his separation from his second wife, Belinda. Morrison and Silberman were excited to finally have pages to review, but the enthusiasm did not last long. Durham went quiet on them for months, prompting Morrison to schedule a meeting with Ali's manager, Herbert Muhammad. Part of the problem was that Ali had begun to fight again, and his attention was now split between training, fighting, and working with Durham on the book. His first post-reinstatement match was against Joe Frazier in Madison Square Garden on March 8, 1971. Frazier won in fifteen rounds, giving Ali the first loss of his professional career. He was reeling from his loss to Frazier and negotiating the tension between him and the Nation of Islam. He did not seem to get back on track until after a seventh-round TKO victory against Floyd Patterson on September 20, 1972.

Silberman doubled down on the pressure Morrison applied to Herbert Muhammad with a detailed letter to Muhammad expressing Random House's frustration.

First I want to thank you for the most helpful meeting with Toni Morrison. . . . Your conversation with Toni leads us to feel that you can help us extricate ourselves from a problem situation. . . .

Our major concern, of course, is that the book is neither completed nor apparently in the process of being completed. . . . Even with a generous allowance for lateness, you must agree that more than two years [*sic*] delay is excessive.

In spite of our strong admonitions to Mr. Durham to stop travelling and sit down and write, the situation has deteriorated. Of the dozens of times that Durham has promised that material was being sent, only three times did we receive any—totaling 166 pages—and these 166 pages are by no means ready to go to press. . . .

I am sure you can appreciate our feeling that what began as a plan supported by good faith and patience among all parties has reached the point of fiasco.[7]

Silberman offered reasons Durham had given for the delays—that he could only share pages after they had been approved by the

Nation and that Herbert Muhammad required Durham to travel with Ali (presumably to write and to avoid having Ali take time off to work with Durham). Durham finally offered some explanation in October, a few weeks after Morrison met with Herbert Muhammad.

No doubt influenced by Herbert Muhammad's directive, Durham first corrected the implication that Muhammad had anything to do with the delays in getting the draft in on schedule. The responsibility of drafting pages was solely Durham's. Next, Durham explained why it was important for him to travel with Ali. Durham felt he needed to work with Ali as events unfolded rather than hear about them secondhand. Most importantly, he claimed, he was now in the position where the base of the manuscript was done. All that was left to do was to stick to a schedule to complete it. He wrote: "The plan is now to devote all of the next three or four months . . . in Chicago on strictly writing and finishing the rough chapters already in process."[8]

Instead of submitting fifty pages a week as Silberman insisted, Durham proposed a "gradually escalating scale of delivery beginning with 50 pages or upward for the end of October, 150 pages or upward for November, 200 for December and 240 for January." He promised five chapters by November. He even gave the chapter titles—"Irish Jerry," "What's My Name?," "One Step Forward," "Oswald," and "The Liston Wars." Silberman and Morrison agreed to this schedule and threatened to secure another writer if the schedule was not kept. While Durham did not keep the schedule completely, he did submit enough pages for Morrison to offer significant notes on the draft in progress.

She offered her comments in three categories—organization, format, and fabric. At the time, the chapter titled "Old Friends and Dinosaurs" opened the book. Morrison thought it worked.

"The first part is very revealing," she noted; it "establishes Ali right away as candid, real, vulnerable, likeable, admirable, etc. Also the initial discussion of 'losing' has great significance for the whole Ali story as well as the Ali as a black man and a fighter dimension."[9] She had concerns about the inclusion of the Joe Frazier dialogue in this chapter, and there were a few moments where Ali's voice lapsed into a literary adaptation of it. But these were few and far between, Morrison noted, and very minor. One of the reasons they were so patient with Durham was Morrison thought the writing was good. She admitted that in the pages "the writer is superb, the subject is great, and the whole thing is authentic and full of many shades of things." In terms of format, she wondered if the guiding approach was the use of flashbacks, and if so, how it would end ("on what note and with what event?"). If flashbacks were not the mode of development, was it suspense, chronology, or loosely related sequential chapters? Without the full draft, it was hard to recommend the best approach. But these were the questions she thought they would need to consider.

Morrison spent the most space in her notes offering comments on what she called "fabric" or connective tissue. She appreciated "the Staggerlee quality of the long conversation" between Ali and Frazier, for example. Here, she noted, "The reader is in the delicious position of eavesdropping." But that conversation also needed reflective expository passages. Pages and pages of straight dialogue were too tedious, in terms of the reading experience. Her recommendation was to retain the rapid exchange quality of the section while adding breaks and reflection. Another section she lifted was the one that focused on Sonji. Morrison wrote: "There is something curiously charming about their cooperative re-telling of their lives. . . . There is an *audience*, and there is a 'tale-telling' quality that is good. The problem is how to retain these elements and still have a chapter." One suggestion was to rewrite it as a narrative scene that was just happening. But that would compromise lines Morrison thought were beautiful and honest, lines that relied on an awareness that a book was being written.

> I think what I am trying to say, is that the "book" as a part of the book would be a fantastic element to retain. Somehow it places the reader on a par with the business of writing a book, you know the book is not an alien thing. Here, I know, I am thinking of black people, and how much they would love that. Ali is not posturing . . . he is Making a Book. It is a kind of inside thing, an attitude about books that is disarming. It is though we are writing the book with him, making it all happen with him. Still, there must be some way to avoid the stark dialogue format and keep the dialogue, the honesty of rapping in order to put it in the book, the full and candid acknowledgement of what is going on.[10]

Overall, Morrison thought these latest pages were in good shape. She was struck most by the draft's address, its privateness that was also public. Ali was willing to expose himself and to expose his relationship with others. The writer was present but absent, thus giving the appearance that the reader is making the book with Ali. She concluded: "This cannot be the total format of the book, and certainly the author does not think that either. . . . But I truly love the quality of this participation, this living book idea."

Excitement about the progress of the manuscript was high but tempered. Durham had not met his deadlines consistently, but he maintained contact, which was an improvement in itself. Then, Ali stopped by Random House unexpectedly at the start of 1973 to say he was sorry the book was late and that he was one hundred percent behind the project. But in Durham's view, Random House's desire to get the work done as quickly as possible needed to be balanced against getting it done in a way that would make for the best book. Ali and Herbert Muhammad suggested that Durham join them at Ali's training camp to write there. Morrison had previously advised against it. Her position was that Durham did not need more information. Rather, he needed to spend time writing what he already had notes on and taped conversations of. But Durham convinced her that he would not spend the time "'digging up' new stuff" but allowing Ali to insert what he thought was relevant and necessary. Ali needed to feel like he was finishing the book himself, not like it was being written for him, Durham argued.

Another reason he needed to go to camp with Ali was because Ali had four fights out of the country scheduled for 1973. Morrison relented and hoped Durham would make good on his word. But he also had to convince Silberman to let him work at his own pace. "Try this my way," he wrote. "Allow me the exotic pleasure this time of calling you first with the work, rather than vice versia [*sic*]. I am highly conscious of the overhangings. But now that I've got the ball, I run faster and better when I give myself the illusion I'm in charge of it and the whistle won't blow before I wrap it up. I beat deadlines when I feel no deadlines."[11] When Silberman wrote to Morrison—"Toni, what next?"—she responded: "Give him the rein. I *know* it's working."[12] The pressure was on, but if Morrison trusted Durham, Silberman would, too.

Durham continued to work, but Ali explained the delays from his point of view. He wrote to Silberman:

The day you signed me up, my next serious appointment was supposed to be the federal pen and I then felt like looking back on life and talking about it. But suddenly they let me back in the ring.

It was [as] if you had signed up Jesus Christ to do His book just before His last Supper and then lo and behold Jesus finds out they not going to hang him after all. He would do just what I did. He wouldn't have time: to talk about his old life, he'd be too eager to get out into the world and whip some disciples back in line, let the world know who's the greatest before the Romans changed their minds.[13]

In short, it was far easier to focus on writing about his "old" life when he was unsure what his new life would be. He admitted to giving the book too little time and then to being unwilling to let it go until it was the book he wanted in the world. Add to this the fact that Durham started the year with a bout of pneumonia in both lungs, and it was clear the delays would continue. Ever the showman, Ali teased: "And don't worry about me loosing [*sic*] a fight to any of these home-made tramps (Oh, I mean champs) none are ready for this year but next time I come up I'll bring Frazier and Foreman along and let you referee while I whip both chumps—in your office . . . to show you signed up the real champ." As a final show of good faith, Ali claimed, he canceled a fight in March so he and Durham could work on the book.

At the end of February, Morrison sent Durham two copies of the manuscript with her comments. She was more than encouraging. "Ali comes through in these pages superbly," she wrote: "proud, warm, honest, courageous, intelligent and very, very real. If the balance that is due is like the enclosed, you should all be very pleased."[14] Two months later, Durham sent a telegram instead of the promised pages, however, announcing that Ali was in Louisville seeing a specialist for his jaw, which was broken during the

March 31, 1973, fight with Ken Norton in San Diego. Ali's jaw had been wired to accelerate its healing, but it needed to be tightened to prevent his compulsive talking. Ironically, Durham noted, "This broken jaw defeat was traumatic to him, but from a story view added dimensions."[15] The time alone in Louisville, "away from religion or fight schedules," Durham wrote, had proven to be highly productive.

With more pages finally in hand in July, Morrison mapped for copy editor Lynn Strong a list of things to do regarding the manuscript—replacing the "Bundini Sugar Ray" story in the "Resurrection" chapter; cutting the "Gold Dream" chapter but keeping the Joe Louis–Ali conversation and Ali's comments about his cornermen being nervous; having legal review all the material around the Frazier-Liston fights and parts of the material related to the first Quarry fight; verifying the facts of the public events told to *The Ring* magazine; making the changes suggested so far by legal; reviewing the manuscripts for consistency of facts; and listing all the queries they had for Durham. Most of these involved the use of real and fictious names and written approval (or tapes) of conversations with Sonji that she might have thought too intimate to publish or conversations with Ali's cornerman Drew "Bundini" Brown that were potentially libelous. Morrison was determined to do as much work as she could while awaiting the final pages.

When Ali fought Frazier for the heavyweight championship on January 28, 1974, Durham and Ali offered Silberman and Bernstein tickets to the fight as a consolation prize since months had passed since the latest deadline had gone unmet. Silberman and Bernstein's tickets were magnificent, Silberman admitted, but the effect of great tickets would only last so long. The goal was to put the book out in September 1974, since Ali had reclaimed the title. This meant they needed a draft by March at the latest.

In the meantime, Morrison and Silberman met with Durham to identify the topics that needed to be covered in the final draft. By April, they were clear, however, that they would not meet the goal of a September release date. Ali wanted to talk about "the unique cloak-and-dagger manner in which the $10 million purse [for a match with Foreman in October] was put together" and about how the location "shifted from the heart of New York to the heart of Africa."[16] Ali insisted that these matters be included in the book. They could only make the book better, he claimed. They would make the delay worth it.

Morrison agreed that this was the logical climax to the story. She also agreed with Durham's point that the fight was without precedence in terms of promotion, location, and prize. Whether Ali won or lost, it would all make for a wonderful story, especially if his three-year comeback ended with his winning a title match, which he, of course, fully expected to win. Morrison, Silberman and Durham agreed that all but the final chapter, which would cover the fight in Zaire, would be submitted the week of May 22. But by May 7, Morrison shifted from Durham's patient defender to his outright critic. The problem was Durham's secretary (or whomever he sent to deliver the pages) left a mere thirty-eight pages. The fact that they seemed hastily done annoyed her. The clandestine delivery to the receptionist without asking to see or speak to Morrison or Silberman infuriated her. The package was dropped off "and hurried away," as if the manuscript was a ransom note. She wrote to Durham in full candor.

> For some reason that I cannot quite explain I was ashamed. On every level—professional, personal—I felt a deep and painful embarrassment. . . . Only my vigorous and sincere agitation has kept this contract alive. . . . But the contempt for those efforts

which you displayed in last Thursday's scenario left me so melancholy and so hurt I believed I would strangle if I didn't tell you how I felt. . . .

You have never seemed to choose candor in dealing with me, a fact that has depressed me for a long time now. . . . I could manage with your patronizing me. I cannot manage with your contempt.[17]

Morrison was right—they had no coherent manuscript and had made very little progress in the past year.

Durham's silence persisted through the May 22 deadline. Ali finally weighed in at the end of June. He was preparing to fight Foreman in his "old home town Africa." He offered to buy them tickets to see his prediction come true in Zaire and suggested that they should keep the telegram to print in the book to show that he predicted his victory by knockout in twelve rounds or by unanimous decision. He promised to make good on his commitment and alerted Morrison and Silberman that Durham had been ill again and was recovering from surgery. Morrison sent a less tempered letter to him inquiring after his health and asking about the progress he had made. Durham offered no response, so all Morrison could do was wait.

In the meantime, Ali's charisma was on full display for the "Rumble in the Jungle." He embraced fans and local customs with such seeming ease that even those closest to him were amazed by his ability to connect with people across cultures. For seven rounds, Ali strategically used his rope-a-dope technique to absorb Foreman's punches. Foreman aggressively pursued Ali and landed significant blows, but in the end, Ali wore him down and scored a knockout by the eighth round.

No one from Random House took Ali up on the offer to attend

the fight, so he had to send a telegram from the Intercontinental Hotel in Kinshasa the night he won the fight.

> Remember I predicted it all in my last telegram. . . . I told you exactly what would happen and the round. I told you I wouldn [*sic*] stop until I had won my title back. This s [*sic*] the last chapter needed for my tory [*sic*] Now I feel free to finish with the ending I want.[18]

He signed it "Muhammad Ali World Heavyweight Champion." They could not have manufactured a more dramatic ending to this still unfolding saga.

Morrison began to assemble the pages they had and to chart the status based on the outline of the book as she imagined it once it was complete. She created four columns—subject area, chapters in house, pages, and status. No chapter could be marked complete. Each was labeled either *in draft*, *scattered*, *more to come*, or *no material*. Some of the sections she labeled *rough* did have transcripts from tapes that she could at least use to draft it if it came to that. And there were pages on topics that could not be neatly placed if she decided to retain them. Some pages would have to be discarded. But her in-progress assemblage could only go so far.

Though, as of January 1973, Eskridge was no longer the agent for the book, Silberman was in touch with him and Herbert Muhammad to determine how they might help get the book completed. Ali, in the meantime, was fielding offers about the movie rights to his life. One way to get Ali's attention, Silberman thought, was to remind Ali that Random House owned motion picture rights to his life story. Ali's desire to play himself in any movie or TV special depended on the book's completion. Only then could Random House pursue film and dramatic works on his behalf. Anything else would be a violation of his contract.

Durham resurfaced in late February 1975 with the Zaire chapter and the revision of the induction chapter. He and Morrison were on speaking terms again. And yet another contract addendum was signed. They had a final editorial meeting, and this time, Durham met all the deadlines Morrison set. He and Morrison agreed to spend the whole month of May working together in New York to review the entire manuscript. As quickly as Morrison suggested edits, Durham made them. They finally had a full draft. When Morrison got the news that the book had been chosen as the main selection for the Literary Guild, she announced to all that any changes to the uncorrected galleys needed to be on her desk by August 22. A version of the galleys was already with the proofreader and copy editor. Changes Durham suggested and those of the proofreader and copy editor would be made, and the type size needed to be enlarged. Otherwise, the book was ready to go. The plan was to print one hundred thousand copies—the largest first printing of the list for the year.

After years of delays, Morrison was pleased with how the book turned out. She shared her confidence and the likelihood of the book's success, financial and otherwise, with Herbert Muhammad and thanked him for the role he played. The $60,000 plus $0.59 per book royalty offer from the Literary Guild was the first indication that she was right. Even a well-done book needed heavy promotion, though. Morrison proposed the international book fair to be held October 8–12 in Frankfurt as their first engagement. There, Random House would auction the book among foreign publishers to the highest bidder. The bids were likely to be higher if Ali was present, so she insisted that he be there. For the promotional tour in the US, Morrison wanted Ali to be available November 3–26. The plan was to have him appear in several cities and to do television, press, and book signings in each location. His victory over Frazier in the Philippines, at the "Thrilla in Manila" on October 1, cemented everyone's excitement about the book, which was released days later. Finally, almost six years after Durham began to shop the book with publishers, *The Greatest* was published to much acclaim.

Among Morrison's final acts as the book's editor was to lend her credibility as an author to its merit in terms of its craft. In the book's promotional materials she admitted to being bored by sports and always a bit puzzled if not annoyed by the roar of the crowd. But Ali's autobiography was so well done, she argued, that she did more than understand the crowd's roar. She joined the crowd. In *The Greatest* was a portrayal of "one of the most interesting, perceptive, independent, humane, fresh and inventive people in the world." In this book were real people, not a book of stereotypes. This was a book "about friendship and anger and loneliness and courage and humiliation and love and ambition and vulnerability."[19] It was a story anyone could relate to, "about the things that are a part of everybody's life regardless of background, sex or age," and a book of which she was extremely proud.

Importantly, *The Greatest* was financially successful. In addition to the Literary Guild serial sale, the firm also sold serial rights to several major outlets, including *Book Digest*, *Newsweek*, *The New York Times*, *Playboy*, and *Rolling Stone*. Disappointingly though, it did not make the American bestseller lists. While it was on the large chain bookstore B. Dalton's list for several weeks, the booksellers' list was different from a general readers' list. That list was made up of sales at places like Scribner's, Brentano's, or Doubleday, the stores that reported to the bestseller list. *The Greatest* sold more than ninety-four thousand copies from its first printing but largely at places where Black people bought books, none of which were among the standard booksellers whose sales were counted. In this sense, the disconnect between the actual number of books sold and the way reporting declared books bestsellers helped Random House see how inherent biases made it impossible to rely on reported information to determine non-white groups' interests and book-buying tendencies. Morrison's point that well-done so-called "Black books" that received the right kind of marketing and promotion could sell as well as any other books had been made yet again. She did not need the validation of a bestseller list to prove it.

CHAPTER 13

Free Angela

No matter the season, Morrison's office pulsated with vitality. Amid the stacks of manuscripts clamoring for her attention and the constant ebb and flow of people traversing in and out, Morrison enjoyed the intricate rhythm necessary to be among the best in her craft as editor. Confidence had been her steady companion. And with each success gained and challenge overcome, her awareness of her ability to help an author tell a compelling story only deepened. This self-possession, buttressed no doubt by her growing success as an author, was so woven into her professional identity that she approached each task with a fearless determination.

From the moment a Marin County judge issued a warrant for Angela Davis's arrest on October 13, 1970, until the moment a jury acquitted her on June 4, 1972, the world watched closely, curious about how this radical scholar/activist would fare. Amid claims of innocence, Davis was captured and remained in jail for seventeen months before finally having a bail hearing a few days before her trial was scheduled to begin. During these months, as a "Free Angela" campaign emerged and grew exponentially, she became a symbol for social justice and revolution, especially for political prisoners. Her supporters celebrated her resistance and advocacy. Contrastingly, her detractors deemed her a dangerous threat—her open identification with the Communist Party USA was in direct opposition to so-called democratic stability. The case garnered national and international attention and tremendous support, especially from liberals and the progressive left. Rallies were held, petitions were signed, postcards were distributed, and a defense fund was established. By the time of her release, Angela Davis was a household name.

For twenty-two months, a gag rule prohibited Davis from speaking publicly. Once acquitted, she reluctantly agreed to a press conference immediately following the verdict to thank her supporters and to advocate for the release of all political prisoners, including Ruchell Magee and the San Quentin Six.

Shortly thereafter, Davis agreed to go on a speaking tour to encourage the local committees working on her behalf to continue their work. She went to Los Angeles, Chicago, Detroit, New York, Dallas, and Atlanta before going on a monthlong tour abroad to the USSR, Central Asia, the German Democratic Republic, Bulgaria, Czechoslovakia, Cuba, and Chile. Without exception, her appearances were met with large crowds and media coverage. Given the significant public interest in hearing from Davis, it was inevitable that offers for a book contract to tell her story would arise. But only one editor would persuade her that she could write the kind of book that really mattered, a book that was as much about a movement as it was about any one person's life.

Morrison wasted no time after the June 4 acquittal in trying to convince Davis to bring her next writing project to Random House. While still in prison, Davis had coedited *If They Come in the Morning: Voices of Resistance* (1971) with her longtime friend Bettina Aptheker. A compilation of texts about political prisoners, the prison system, repression of political figures, and resistance to political repression, *If They Come in the Morning*, published by Third World Press, opened with a letter from James Baldwin to Davis and included contributions by Aptheker, Julian Bond, John Clutchette, Fleeta Drumgo, Ericka Huggins, George Jackson, Ruchell Magee, Huey P. Newton, and others. Morrison could not arrange a meeting with Davis directly, but she was undeterred. Instead, she met with Aptheker for lunch before the end of the month to get a sense of Davis's interest in writing a book while the trial was still fresh in her memory and on the minds of a curious public. Immediately after their lunch meeting, Morrison wrote to Aptheker:

> As you requested, I am summing up my preliminary thoughts on the type of book Angela Davis might do—the one I believe would be the most effective and sustaining next work: A series of pieces on her recent experiences in the arms of American "justice"—subjective in approach and perception, moving . . . from the personal view to the universal judgment. . . . The book would be personal and political (there is no difference anyway) but the tone would meet the requirements of each encounter, event, or reflection.[1]

At that point, Morrison did not envision the book as an autobiography. Instead, she thought of it as a series of coherently organized essays that would culminate in a long section that situated Davis's experience amid the political history of the United States. "The book, like its author," Morrison wrote, "would be both the theory and the thing, the idea *and* its manifestation." It would also live beyond its covers, "a non-book in the truest sense." Most important of all, the book would be good: "So powerful—it boggles the mind."

At the same time that Morrison was pitching the idea to Aptheker, Davis's lawyer, Leo Branton, was in conversation with Bernard Geis, publisher of Bantam Books, about a possible Davis autobiography. Branton and Geis both had connections to celebrities, and they shared the view of Davis as a celebrity who could command attention on all fronts. Branton, a well-known Black attorney of Hollywood types, counted Nat King Cole and Dorothy Dandridge, for instance, among his clients before joining Davis's legal team. Geis was a publisher whose fame rose not long after publishing Art Linkletter's *Kids Say the Darndest Things* as an editor at Prentice Hall. Launching Bernard Geis Associates (BGA) after the success of that book, Geis began the trend of heavily promoting books in a manner reminiscent of the way Hollywood promoted movies, with marketing and publicity activities to create anticipation. With Linkletter, Groucho Marx, and television producers backing him financially and otherwise, Geis attracted celebrities to become authors on the one hand and attempted to make his authors celebrities on the other. BGA was successful until Geis fell out of favor with his associates by publishing novels based loosely on celebrities and their sexual exploits. By 1971, he had filed Chapter 11 bankruptcy, petitioning the court to give him more time to pay creditors. To compensate for these financial woes, Geis resolved to bring out his paperback books in collaboration with other publishers.

Four short months after Morrison met with Aptheker, Branton signed an agreement with Geis for a book deal on Davis's behalf. Random House executives were stung by their failure to originate the contract they had hoped for. *The New York Times* announced

the deal—"Miss Davis Signs to Write Memoir: California Radical
Accepts Bantam-Geis Book Offer."

> Angela Davis has signed an agreement with Bantam Books,
> Inc., and Bernard Geis Associates to write a book entitled *The
> Education of a Revolutionary*, Mr. Geis announced yesterday.
>
> Mr. Geis said he arranged the deal, under which Bantam
> is paying the former member of the philosophy faculty at the
> University of California a "high six figure" advance against
> royalties. . . .
>
> Asked how he had arranged the transaction, he replied,
> "charm, eloquence—and money."[2]

According to the *Times* article, Geis would help edit the one-
hundred-thousand-word book that would give Davis's life history
and a comprehensive view of her social philosophy. Conspicuously,
there was no mention of the publisher that would be responsible for the book's first release in hardcover. Weeks before Geis
resolved to get Bantam some positive publicity (and to quiet concerns about his bankruptcy) by making a splash with the Davis
book deal, Geis and Jim Silberman were already deep in negotiation to have Random House be the Bantam partner. Random
would publish the book first; and Bantam would publish it a year
later in paperback. In late September, in advance of an October 3
meeting, Geis had shared with Silberman (and Silberman, in turn,
with Morrison) a copy of the five-page narrative outline Geis had
drafted for the book.

The day after their meeting, which included Morrison, Geis
wrote to Silberman that he found their gathering "not only con-
structive but most pleasant." He assured Silberman: "I'd like
nothing better than to work with Random House in general and

with you and Toni in particular on the Angela Davis book."[3] They danced around the shape the book would take exactly, however. Geis felt strongly that it should be a straight autobiography. Morrison was less convinced about that approach, and she warned Geis that Davis would not likely be interested in writing a tell-all book. Morrison's observation worried him because he knew that it was Branton, who had Davis's power of attorney, who had signed the agreement on her behalf. At least at this point, though, Geis would not be deterred. "When Miss Davis gets back to the U.S. of A.," he wrote, "we are not only going to request that the book live up to the description of Paragraph 1 of her agreement but we're going to be very persuasive about it." The description in the paragraph he referred to was innocuous enough. The outline, on the other hand, was far more suggestive. The "bare bones of the Angela Davis story"—her childhood in Birmingham, her schooling in Greenwich Village and then in college and graduate school, her affiliation with the Communist Party, her expulsion from the faculty at UCLA, her relationship with the Soledad Brothers, and her flight and trial—would "assume intimate form and significant meaning in the telling" and "penetrate her abiding sense of privacy."[4]

A full paragraph of the outline was also dedicated to Davis's relationship with George Jackson, which was the source of much speculation. Had all of Davis's legal troubles really been about a romantic relationship between Davis and Jackson as the prosecution had claimed? The book would set the record straight once and for all. Baiting curiosity, the outline read:

> Now that George Jackson is dead, only Angela can give a true account of their unique and tender love story. The prosecuting attorney at San Jose, searching desperately for a motive, de-

scribed their relationship as "A passion that knew no bounds, had no limits and no respect for life." It was indeed a passion, but a passion of the spirit. Through the concrete of Soledad prison before Angela was indicted, in their letters and in their encounter in jail, and later across the distance between their separate cells in two separate prisons, a profoundly fulfilling relationship developed between them.

Davis's much-awaited return to the US on October 12 received media attention. The *Times* announced her arrival in New York to JFK Airport: "After a tour of 6 Red Countries." Silberman shot off a quick note to Geis: "I see by the papers that Angela Davis is back. Ought we to talk further?" Silberman and Geis were both anxious to finalize an agreement. What neither man knew at the time was that Davis was not at all convinced that she should write anything that resembled an autobiography.

With a little maneuvering, Morrison was finally able to schedule a meeting with Davis. Morrison arranged a lunch date instead of meeting in the office. The less formal meeting would give them the opportunity to get to know each other on a one-on-one level and without the distractions that were inevitable in Morrison's busy office. For many, Davis was an icon. For Morrison, she was a writer whom Morrison could help tell a powerful story. As they ate, Davis gave Morrison all the reasons she was reluctant to write an autobiography. An autobiography was individualistic, and Davis was interested in community. She was a mere twenty-eight years old, far too young to write a life story. In that sense, too, there was so little material in her life that demanded treatment by itself in the context of the genre. Add to that the fact that, by and large, the autobiography was a genre dominated by male writers, and Davis found little appealing about the notion of writing the story of her life.

Morrison heard Davis out before launching an argument of her own. In Morrison's view, Davis could write a book that was not individualistic but that could expand the reach of campaigns and movements against racism and misogyny. The book did not have to be a life story. Rather it could be a political instead of a personal autobiography. It could defy genre, really, and make an important contribution without following the genre's practice of giving advice. Morrison was clear. Davis could write exactly the kind of book she wanted to write. She should take the next few days to write down all she thought was important and wanted to share. They could give shape to its organization later. In a few short hours, Morrison's persuasive enthusiasm shifted Davis's sentiment from having no interest in writing any form of autobiography to being receptive to exploring the possibilities of doing so.

Making good on her promise to Morrison, Davis went to Cuba alone to try her hand at writing everything she wanted to say, just as Morrison had suggested. Holed up in a cabin in the eastern part of the country, in the mountains of Oriente, Davis wrote every day, stopping only to eat and sleep and, occasionally, to take long hikes. After a month, she had produced seven hundred typewritten pages, which ultimately became the book's first draft. Morrison read it quickly and knew immediately that they had the makings of an important book. It was after that first read, in fact, that she envisioned the structure of the book. They would take a cinematic approach. The book would start at the end of the story—the familiar one everyone thought they knew—and fill in the gaps through flashbacks.

When the warrant for her arrest was issued, Davis was heavily involved in the Soledad Brothers Defense Committee, a group that helped raise funds for and awareness about the case against George Jackson, Fleeta Drumgo, and John Clutchette. The three men were inmates of Soledad, a California state prison, when they were charged with the murder of one of the guards. Three days earlier, three Black prisoners had been shot and killed by another guard during a riot. Seven months later, on August 7, 1970, at 10:45 a.m., Pacific Daylight Time, seventeen-year-old Jonathan Jackson, the younger brother of George Jackson, interrupted the trial of James McClain, an inmate at San Quentin Prison who had been accused of stabbing a prison guard. Earlier that morning, McClain and other witnesses had been transferred from San Quentin, where he was serving five years to life for burglary, to the Marin County Hall of Justice, where he would stand for trial. Jonathan entered the courtroom with guns and handed them off to McClain and two witnesses for the trial, Ruchell Magee and William Christmas. They took the judge, the prosecutor, and three female jurors hostage and attempted to flee in a van. They exchanged fire with police. Judge Harold Haley, Jackson, McClain, and Christmas were killed and prosecutor Gary Thomas and Magee injured. When a grand jury investigation revealed that Davis had purchased several of the weapons, she was indicted. Davis maintained that she had bought the guns for her own security. California law allowed her to be charged, despite her not being present at the crime scene. Davis's involvement with the committee shifted quickly from advocacy for the so-called "Soledad Brothers" to federal charges against her, charges supposedly related to an attempt to negotiate their release.

From August 18, 1970—four days after a judge issued a warrant for her arrest—until October 13, 1970, when FBI agents found her at a New York City Howard Johnson's Motor Lodge, Davis was among the FBI's "Ten Most Wanted." For fifty-six days, Davis was on the run. She had every reason to be distrustful of the government and its law enforcement. Months earlier, at

Governor Ronald Reagan's behest, the University of California, Los Angeles, had dismissed her from the philosophy faculty for being affiliated with the Communist Party. When the Supreme Court of California ruled that a professor could not be banned for party affiliation, the university regents declined to renew her appointment, this time claiming that remarks she made in speeches were politically incendiary. By February 1971, the Free Angela Davis movement was well underway with more than two hundred domestic and fifty international communities protesting for her release. In addition to galvanizing support for her release, the campaign highlighted issues of racial injustice, political repression, and broader struggles for civil rights. On June 4, 1972, an all-white jury in San Jose, California, found her not guilty on the charges of murder, kidnapping, and conspiracy. This was the crux of the story. Context about her life before and during the trial would provide a deeper understanding of her experiences and perspectives. And it would be limited to what the reader needed to grasp the significance of her journey and its relation to the broader social and political landscape in which it unfolds.

Like Morrison, Silberman thought the draft was in good shape. "It does . . . need editing—particularly in those spots where the author lapses into vocabulary of the academic," he wrote to Morrison. "But she does create scenes vividly and with your help they can be even more vivid."[5] He and Morrison agreed that once Davis had revised a few chapters to her and Morrison's satisfaction, they should share a copy with Marc Jaffe, Bantam's editorial director. Silberman was clear in his suggestion that the sample pages—to see if Bantam felt the draft was on the right track—should go to Jaffe, not Geis. Geis's interest in a book filled with salacious details would get in the way. Jaffe, contrastingly, was a well-regarded, serious editor who would care more about producing a good book than a sensational one. But Morrison, following the terms of the contract, sent the chapters to Geis directly. Shortly thereafter, she warned Silberman that Geis was distressed about the pages he read. "Says its awful etc., wants a meeting," Morrison scoffed.[6] Not only did she regret sending Geis the chapters, but she also declared that she was completely unwilling to submit any of her editing to him. Instead, she shared subsequent drafts with Jaffe, who agreed that the four chapters in hand were sufficient to warrant paying Davis $25,000 of the advance (half of which Random House paid to Bantam) that was due her upon the publisher's approval of four chapters.

By December 1973, Davis had completed another draft of the manuscript. Still, they were months behind Geis's ambitious schedule. Just before Christmas, Morrison sent a copy to Random House's general counsel, Gerald Hollingsworth, for a legal review with a January 15 deadline for his findings. In the meantime, there were eight handwritten pages of queries to which Morrison needed Davis to respond as she revised the penultimate draft. By then, Morrison and Davis had developed more than a good editor-writer rapport. They had become friends. It was clear to Morrison, and Davis agreed, that the only way to complete the revisions for the book in a reasonable amount of time was to have Davis stay in New York while she worked on it.

Morrison and Davis's friendship developed naturally. Somehow they escaped the awkwardness that tended to come with the absence of a shared history. What they did have was enough common ground as Black women to build a meaningful connection, which was only strengthened over the next few months, after Morrison invited Davis to stay with her and her boys in Spring Valley. During the summer and early fall of 1973, they commuted to the Random House office on East 50th Street in Manhattan every day. The office was a haven for Davis—a vibrant space filled with books, constant foot traffic, and a palpable energy fueled by diverse creative and intellectual pursuits.[7] Living in Spring Valley also gave Davis relief from the hustle and bustle of city life and from an overwhelming schedule. Everything about the arrangement worked. There, Davis could do the things normal people did, like cook and enjoy her family, whom Morrison welcomed in her home as well. They could go for a run, which they often did, without the burden of media scrutiny. They relished each other's company, enjoying the freedom to engage one another as equals without the need to showcase their intellect for others. They could exchange serious and silly ideas alike without the pressure to impress or outsmart anyone. It was simply a joy of shared intellectual camaraderie.

Morrison and Davis worked intensely on the book from January until June, when Morrison distributed a complete copy of the uncorrected proofs internally for review. The pages of queries Morrison wanted Davis to address required her to shift her thinking and writing style from that of an academic to a compelling storyteller. Questions ranged from the simple to the emotionally probing: What did certain acronyms stand for? Where was the school she attended in New York exactly, on what cross streets? Did she mean to use the word *historic* in the second line of page 133 of the draft? Such questions, though tedious, were easy to address. Explaining why Jonathan Jackson came off as a person, while his brother George came off as a mere idea would take more time and more intellectual energy. Davis should not assume that everyone had read Jackson's *Soledad Brother*, so her portrayal of him needed to have more depth and dimension. Even as what Davis wrote about Jonathan was better than her depiction of George, the section introducing Jonathan (and there should be only one such introduction instead of two, which the draft had, Morrison noted) needed attention and revision.

The first paragraph where we meet Jonathan was too thick, Morrison indicated.

> Make him a brilliant boy with a man's job. You hint later that his attempt to free his brother is romantic (ms p. 21) wasn't it? However "right" or "moral" it was more Robin Hood than not. I assume that is why you emphasise his youth. But your description here makes him appear to be a sage. And because you hit it so hard (how smart he was) it reeks of an apology for him—which you certainly need not make. The treatment of him later in the Soledad Section—rubbing sleep out of his eyes—is much better. Most people love him and admire his act anyway.[8]

There were also words Davis used casually that needed to be unpacked.

> It would be helpful to know what you mean by eroding one's humanity. Humanity is a vague word in this context. You repeat the idea frequently throughout so it is pivotal. "Breaking will" is clear; forcing prisoners into childlike obedience is also clear; but what is erode their humanity. Their humaneness? Their natural resistance?

Then, there were the moments where an idea or question might seem obvious to the reader that Davis presented as surprising. For example, when Davis narrated her decision to move to San Diego for school, she wrote that she was surprised upon arrival by how few Black people were there. "Was [Herbert] Marcuse the only reason you went to San Diego? Why didn't you ask what the black population on campus was?" the reader would surely wonder. "Your surprise is surprising."

There were also indirect references to conversations Morrison and Davis had that needed attention. "You wanted to say something about Algerians sleeping on grilled steam exhausts," Morrison reminded Davis. In places in the manuscript where she referenced letters, Davis also needed to quote directly from them, some of which Morrison had seen. Morrison was not shy about taking certain liberties with things that needed to be added. In one instance she wrote: "Turn the ms. p over. Here I wrote something to dramatize impact of the Manifesto on you. It is a 'key' event & needs to be made stronger. Read my insert on back & see if it's OK." In another instance, she noted:

> I added a concluding sentence about your disappointment. Otherwise it's left hanging. Also I thought—at one point—this was a good place for the dog-fight recollection. It explains your compulsion to action—imperviousness to risk etc. But I know you put it elsewhere—where it is equally effective.

Certain sections just did not work, and in these instances, Morrison offered a combination of critique, instruction, and intervention.

> p. 380–383. The Cuba section is disappointing. It is a *very important* section. But it reads like a brochure. I can re-do it to remove its tendency to jargon. The tone is too unlike the earthiness, the liveliness, the reality of the people themselves.
> p. 386. Delete re-cap of Invasion.

p. 389. Delete ref. to criticism of Chinese Socialism or explain them.

p. 396. What parallels did you notice? What did you see that proved that Socialism erased racism?

There were no signs of the fact that this was the first autobiography book Morrison edited. Quite the contrary—Morrison gently guided Davis to help bring her story to life on paper as though Morrison knew exactly what the book needed to be. In some ways, she did, in part because she had seen what it should not be. In a *New York Times* review of Regina Nadelson's *Who Is Angela Davis? The Biography of a Revolutionary*, which had been published in September 1972, Morrison was mercilessly critical of the book's failure in her view. As she would later do in her fiction, Morrison began the review in medias res. Playing on the title *Who Is Angela Davis*, Morrison opined: "On the other hand, who is Regina Nadelson and why is she behaving like Harriet Beecher Stowe, another simpatico white girl who felt she was privy to the secret of how black revolutionaries got that way?"[9] Morrison's biggest critique of Nadelson's biography was its insinuation that Davis's courage was a function of her exposure to white culture and her militancy a result of her "white teachers, white boyfriends, white psychoanalysts, and a special brand of white terror perpetuated on some respectable colored folks." Nadelson, whom Morrison referred to sardonically as *Regina* and *Miss Regina* alternately, had gone to Elisabeth Irwin High School with Davis and naively tried to defend her by labeling her an American. In Nadelson's view, Davis was a Black leader and a liberated woman, yes; but she was also an American who "is kind and funny." Morrison's signifying was pitiless. "Yessum, Miss Regina. We all are," she wrote. All in all, the book was "a Cyclopean view of Angela Davis that leaves the reader with a wholly useless biography, somehow offensive in its one-eyed stare. Maybe because the other thing about Cyclops was that he too had a taste for human flesh."

Nadelson was not alone in experiencing the wrath of Morrison's indignance about what she viewed as a gross misread of Davis (though Morrison did ignore J. A. Parker's *Angela Davis: The Making of a Revolutionary*, which was published after Nadelson's book). Once a solid draft of Davis's manuscript was complete, Morrison sent a copy to Bantam, in keeping with the contract for the joint publication. The Bantam editorial team sent a report, almost surely penned by Geis, about their view of the draft. After reading the report, Morrison fired off a four-page response to Silberman that expressed her frustration with the reviewer's seeming need to use Davis's life for personal reasons. Morrison wrote:

> I mention this not to carp but only to indicate that I have found the requirement of Angela to meet somebody else's need (be it personal, sexual, political or whatever) to be overwhelming. The fantasy moves between two poles. One is "give me some of what you have." The other is the "Come on now aren't you really a sweet charming girl?" . . . I think both these poles operate in many responses to this work particularly when the reviewer is persistent in her comparison of her own life to Angela's.[10]

Another problem was the reviewer's repeated refrain about the need to see more of Davis's "humanness" in the draft. Morrison was unsure of what the reader meant exactly by this, but she suspected that it was chauvinistic. *Humanness*, Morrison noted, was "a word white people use when they want to alter an 'uppity' or 'fearless' nigger."

The report also seemed to suggest that Davis could not be as political as her self-portrait intimated, that there had to be some element of her life where politics were not involved. Morrison was quick to dispute this: "Believe me she is an almost totally political person. She does not think the way most people do nor respond the way most people do to ordinary events." To make her point, she gave an example of a time in the airport when Davis confronted a white man who spoke unkindly to a Black woman Davis did not know. "She walked some distance," Morrison wrote, "to get into the battle before I could bat an eye. The brawl stopped not when the police were called but when the white man ran away. She risks her life easily—athletically she moves always towards feats that could end in death." Morrison emphasized the point again a page later, writing, "I must emphasize that there are no two Angela Davises. One political, one human. They are one and the same thing. She does not tuck her politics away. Never. Not even in her dreams. Not in the bathtub. Not on the toilet. Not anywhere."

The reviewer's desire to be thrilled while reading the book also frustrated Morrison. She read this as a not-so-subtle critique that the book needed more stories about love and sex. The reviewer referenced *The Autobiography of Malcolm X* often as a book Davis might take as her model. The irony of that reference was not lost on Morrison. "I don't have to remind anyone that Bantam turned down Malcolm's book," she wrote, "but I *am* interested in why particularly since that is the criterion consistently used for this book." Unlike Malcolm X, who "was able to include in his book sex and drugs because both were there and both were important to him," Davis had "no such sensational personal ingredients as drugs and sex to report." The underlying question the report seemed to be asking, too, Morrison thought, was *Where was Angela Davis the woman?* "The fact is," Morrison wrote, "that Angela is not 'feminine.' She responds to life in a manner that can only be described as masculine . . . meaning advertunesome [*sic*], unemotional, logical, fearless, etc. She is not in any way 'a girl.' If this book were about a man certain problems of credibility would never arise. The real question . . . is why doesn't she think and behave like a female?"

Morrison's feeling about the report was clear. The general call for more personal material contradicted the specific calls for more material and more information, all of which were political. "As you can see," Morrison argued, "what fascinates the reviewer is precisely the *political* Angela Davis." Ultimately, Morrison was unmoved by the report. After three and a half pages of insolence, she ended the memo with outright sarcasm: "I find the Bantam report wholly useless to me. . . . How nice it would be if Angela were really Jane Fonda and not Jean [*sic*] d'Arc." Notably, this was no insult to Jane Fonda, who had visited Davis in prison and joined her at rallies. Rather, it was to make the point that Davis transcended gender norms and was determined to turn the tide in what she saw as a war on freedom and democracy.

Even as she threatened to withdraw from the project as editor if Bantam insisted on changes beyond those she intended to make—cutting about two hundred pages from the draft and rewriting some sections for style—Morrison was completely confident that she and Davis were in lockstep. As she reminded Silberman, they had become very close. And even as she saw herself as one of the few people who did not idolize Davis, Morrison knew that Davis would not likely consider another editor. Nor would she relent to reshaping the book the way the report called for. So she continued her work on the book—pruning it, guiding Davis's revisions of it, and working with the copy editors to arrange it.

It was Morrison, in fact, who titled the six chapters and wrote or selected the epigraphs for each.[11] The one-word titles—"Nets," "Rocks," "Waters," "Flames," "Walls," and "Bridges"—were broad enough to give shape to the long chapters held together by the theme. The epigraphs did much of this work. The epigraph for part 1, "The net will be torn by the horn of a leaping calf," was inspired by the biblical verse in Malachi 4:1–2, which proclaims that the arrogant and the evildoer would fall, while the sun of righteousness would rise with healing in its wings. Evil would be destroyed ("Not a root or branch will be left to them"), and the righteous would "leap like calves from the stall." With the epigraph, Morrison extended the metaphorical net dropped on Davis as a fugitive to ensure her capture to include the imperial state that designated her one of America's most wanted criminals. Her victory, then, was but one aspect of the larger struggle to decimate evil. The epigraph for part 2—"I have a home in that rock, don't you see?"—made clear that Davis was equally a citizen of the United States (the infamous Dynamite Hill in Birmingham, Alabama, in fact) and of the world. Morrison chose a line from a Federico García Lorca poem as the epigraph for part 3, "Waters"; a line from a Henry Dumas poem for part 4, "Flames"; and a line from a Wallace Stevens poem for part 5, "Walls." She crafted from her imagination the epigraph for part 6, "Bridges"—"Walls turned sideways are bridges"—to make the point that political struggle, at its core, was about connecting people, not about putting up and fortifying walls to separate them. The political movement Davis's trial made possible, and the trial was covered in part 6, was about the critical work of turning walls into bridges.

With most of the revisions complete, the copyediting team hard at work, and another legal review of the manuscript underway, Morrison began to work with the design team for the book's cover.

But first, there were several ancillary matters she needed to address. In mid-May, Greg Armstrong, the Bantam editor who had worked with George Jackson for *Soledad Brother*, gave an interview to *The Village Voice*, in anticipation of the release of Armstrong's book on Jackson, *The Dragon Has Come*. In that interview, Armstrong previewed the book's revelation that he had captured on tape Jackson's confession of beating the Soledad Prison guard to death. According to Armstrong, Jackson would have wanted the truth about his involvement to be known. "Actually, it would be more precise to say," Armstrong noted, "that he wanted to take credit for it. The same is true for the events at Marin."[12] This claim that Jackson admitted to killing the guard compromised the integrity of the nationwide campaign that had been launched to free him as a political prisoner. Even after Jackson was killed by another prison guard, he was presumed innocent, except for the theft of $70 at age eighteen that earned him an "indefinite sentence," ten years of which he had already served. Of course, Davis's story was intricately linked to Jackson, since it was in his defense that his brother Jonathan acted with guns Davis had purchased. Further, the confession contradicted Davis's depiction of him in her manuscript.

After reading the interview, Geis wrote to Morrison.

> Are you planning to do anything about this interview with Greg Armstrong saying he has George Jackson's confession on tape to killing the guard at Soledad?
>
> I should think Angela ought to acknowledge this somehow, whether to say this comes as a complete surprise to her, or she believes Armstrong's statement is false, or whatever.[13]

Geis, anticipating resistance to making any significant changes to the manuscript already in production, added a handwritten postscript suggesting that Davis would only need to add a paragraph or so in the relevant section of the book. Morrison agreed to have Davis consider adding a paragraph before noting that Davis's first response was "surprise and then extreme anger—at Greg."[14]

The Dragon Has Come was not the only book Morrison had to contend with. Bettina Aptheker was also working on a book about the Davis trial. Unlike Armstrong, however, Aptheker did not claim to offer a bombshell exposé in *The Morning Breaks: The Trial of Angela Davis.* She and Davis had remained close, and out of respect for the impending publication of Davis's book, Aptheker coordinated her book's publication date with Morrison, who had convinced Lou Diskin at International Publishers to delay the release of Aptheker's book. Aptheker was under the impression that Morrison was lobbying for a one-year lag between the two books. There need not be a full year, Morrison suggested, but there were variables they needed to consider. She wrote to Aptheker:

> Angela's book is now complete (more or less). We are still hoping to publish in June: but there may be some delay. . . . If we are able to get book club sales or other kinds of subsidiary rights sales, such sales will require the postponement of the book in terms of it's [*sic*] being available to the public. That is to say, if Book-of-the-Month takes it, for example, one of the conditions for their taking it will be that they have no competition on the open market. In such an event, they would probably run it in their summer list and ask us to publish in September. . . . If what we hope comes true, that other people want to buy it for magazines and book sales before publication, then I suspect our book will be on the market in early fall. It seemed to me that there should be no other book on the subject during the fall months.[15]

The other quandary Morrison had to address delicately was the fact that Davis had initially intended to limit her commentary about the trial to forty or fifty pages. But, in actuality, she had written nearly 150 pages. And even as those pages were cut extensively, there was still a robust section about the trial in the book. It was not an exhaustive documentation, so there was room for both books, just not at the same time. "I will keep you and International informed of our progress," Morrison wrote. "Obviously both of us want the best things for both books and I don't think there will be any obstacles in doing just that."

Whether they admitted it or not, the Armstrong claims about Jackson's confession made everyone at Random uneasy. The number of copies to be printed was reduced from thirty thousand to twenty-five thousand. And Richard Udell, the firm's in-house counsel, pushed to have the manuscript reviewed again for libel. Morrison reminded Udell that they had used comments from an outside attorney, Arthur Abelman, to complete the manuscript and that his second review should come once the book was in final galleys. But "it would be the better part of valor," Udell argued, to have him read uncorrected galleys.[16] So Morrison sent galleys to Abelman, Hollingsworth, and Branton, noting that proofing and revisions were happening simultaneously and entreating them for a speedy review.

Meanwhile, Morrison's preproduction work on the book continued. She arranged to have Philippe Halsman take the cover photo and helped Davis select the clothes for the photo shoot and the interviews they anticipated. Halsman was considered one of the best portrait photographers in the country, having taken pictures of countless celebrities and the photos for more than one hundred *Life* magazine covers. The fact that he was Russian-born was not lost on Morrison either. And his signature style—to position his subjects in such a way that the camera could reveal their character—would make the point that this book would offer some special insight into the Angela Davis everyone thought they knew.

With the cover and promotional photos done, Morrison worked closely with designer Jack Ribik on the cover and finalized the copy for the flap. Morrison also wanted to include photographs of Davis at different stages in her life: one of her as a young child (at fifteen months old), one of Davis with her sister, Fania, dressed in their Sunday best as young girls, one of Davis in her Girl Scout uniform, and one of Davis at Brandeis University in her junior year. The picture of Davis as a Girl Scout was badly torn, however. And though Morrison directed the design team to spare no expense in repairing it, in the end, she had to switch it out with a picture of Davis visiting New York as a young girl.

Morrison was attentive to every detail. She approved the back ad layout for the jacket, which was to have "a hairline of white around each halftone and a black border around that white hairline," and she requested oval frames for the four snapshots above.[17] While she was pleased with the manufacturing in general, she found the cloth binding, color, and design quality "dreadful" and appealed to Silberman to help ensure she had some input in these matters in the future. She was similarly hard on the publicity team. She complained: "The Angela postcard 1) has no space for a message (on the left) 2) places the Geis credit improperly 3) needs a vertical line to separate the address area from the quote/message area—as a normal postcard."[18] In the future, she told Selma Shapiro, she would like to see the layout and copy for publicity items.

Morrison sent galleys to all the major news outlets and to a range of writers asking them for comments. When she secured a quote from Jessica Mitford, the leftist author of the prison reform book *Kind and Usual Punishment*, she added an excerpt of it to the book's back cover and to the appeal letter. She also crafted a special outreach letter for Black venues. The letter made clear Morrison's awareness of how Black readers are sometimes neglected by the sales team. "There are huge problems connected with getting important books into the homes of black people," she wrote, "almost all of which have to do with not owning bookstore chains, book clubs, etc. Because of this, I have to rely (as always the case and is as it should be) on our own people."[19] The letter also invited those receiving it to host a book party to create a space where the books could be sold and to create a fundraising opportunity for the seller. Random House would offer the books at a 40 percent discount. The books could then be sold at regular price, thereby allowing the host to keep the profit. Morrison and Davis were both pleased when *The Black Scholar*, the first journal of Black studies and research and one of the few publications Davis wrote for while in prison, offered a special edition of the book as a subscription premium. Readers could order a one-year subscription to the journal for $15 and receive a copy of the autobiography. The three thousand hardcover copies for this special edition removed the paper jacket and replaced it with the cover art laminated directly onto the book cover.

Two years after Davis's acquittal, *Angela Davis: An Autobiography* was released. There was no disputing that Davis had achieved something unique with the genre. Her attempt to tell a different kind of story was not lost on those who read the book closely, even if some reviewers expressed disappointment in how little about her personal life she divulged. The consistent compliment was that the book's prose was intelligent and readable at once. Some reviewers thought the book was too propagandistic and, conversely, did not divulge enough information about her early life. White critics especially wanted a clear path to her commitment to communism.

Her personal and familial experiences with racism and classism clearly were not enough to explain her decision to assume a career of activism, especially when other class and race theorists did not. What most reviewers appreciated was Davis's firsthand account of her political activity, her capture and imprisonment, and the trial, even if they did not feel she offered a compelling self-portrait that explained why she felt so strongly about Black liberation and, by extension, the liberation of all people. All in all, Geis and Random House were pleased with the book they had produced. In the months leading up to the book's publication, Davis had reduced her travel significantly, in part to ensure that she had ample time to complete the needed revisions on the book. Once it was published, she embarked on a multicity book tour, where she was well received and used the book as a written platform through which she could discuss her views on prison reform, communism, and political prisoners in America.

The Bantam agreement Davis signed for the autobiography included an option for a second book. Her early attempt at a manuscript was two chapters of a book that picked up on the theme of an article she had written for *The Black Scholar* while she was in prison. Published as "Reflections on the Black Woman's Role in the Community of Slaves," the article was the point of entry for a larger conversation about the contributions Black women made to the overarching project of women's liberation. Since publishing *Angela Davis: An Autobiography*, Davis had returned to teaching but also remained in the public eye. When Geis saw a comment about her next book in an article in the April 17, 1978, issue of *New York Magazine*, he appealed to Morrison for any updates. He wrote: "I refer to the following sentence in Orde Coombs's article. . . . '(Davis still does not have her PhD.; the FBI destroyed her thesis, but she is working on a book on racism and sexism

for Random House and this will form the basis of her dissertation.)'"[20] Encouraged by the mention, Geis suggested that they
get together as soon as Davis submitted a manuscript beyond the
two chapters they had seen previously to discuss the possibility of
another three-way publishing arrangement.

Morrison, who had been in touch with Davis, was similarly
encouraged. The idea of publishing a book that set straight the
historical record about Black women and their relation to race
and class struggles appealed to Morrison in every way. She had
a pronounced awareness of the long-standing racial tension that
persisted between Black women and white women in feminist
circles and beyond. In "What the Black Woman Thinks About
Women's Lib," an article *The New York Times* commissioned
Morrison to write in anticipation of the one-year anniversary of
the August 26, 1970, "Strike Day," organized by the National
Organization for Women (NOW), Morrison began to explore
this tension. While the *Times* offered more rounded commentary than other print and television media did at the time of the
march (women were to forgo work and to march instead), the
"Gray Lady" had still neglected to cover, in any meaningful way,
Black women's participation in the march or to include Black
women's perspectives about the demands for gender equality
NOW articulated as a critical element of the strike. Morrison's
essay was meant to help remedy this. "What do black women feel
about Women's Lib?" she asked, before answering her own query.

> Distrust. It is white, therefore suspect. In spite of the fact that
> liberating movements in the black world have been catalysts
> for white feminism, too many movements and organizations
> have made deliberate overtures to enroll blacks and have ended
> up by rolling them. They don't want to be used again to help

somebody gain power—a power that is carefully kept out of their hands. They look at white women and see them as the enemy—for they know that racism is not confined to white men, and that there are more white women in this country, and that 53 per cent of the population sustained an eloquent silence during times of greatest stress. The faces of those white women hovering behind that black girl [Elizabeth Eckford] at the Little Rock school in 1957 do not soon leave the retina of the mind.[21]

Morrison's incisive critique confronted the historical differences between liberation struggles of the two groups of women. In its own way, the essay cleared a path that allowed Morrison to publish, in two years, four books authored or edited by white women that could enrich conversations about gender without reinscribing uneven power dynamics: Karen DeCrow's *Sexist Justice: How Legal Sexism Affects You* and Bettie Wysor's *The Lesbian Myth* in 1974 and Rosalyn Baxandall and Linda Gordon's *America's Working Women* and Gina Luria and Virginia Tiger's *Everywoman* in 1976. Working on a second book with Davis, one specifically on intersections of sexism and racism, was a welcome return to a "Black woman" book.

Morrison and Geis talked at length and agreed that Geis should initiate conversations with Bantam about the Davis contract, which he did immediately. He wrote to Elly Sidel at Bantam to bring her up to date.

So far, only the two chapters you've seen have been received. Toni agrees with us that these need more work, particularly in putting them into a more popular style. . . .
If the book had a title, which it doesn't, it might be *Sexism*

and Racism in America. (My suggested title, not Toni's or Angela's.) This will be a scholarly work, but Toni will try to push it into a popular direction to the extent that may be practicable.

This is not going to be written as a commercially popular book, but I'm convinced it will be an important one. Depending on reviews, the initial sale could be quite substantial, and the book would have excellent long term potential and foreign rights values.[22]

Geis offered Sidel an overview of the book, based on his conversation with Morrison, and he tried to contextualize it amid contemporary conversations about sexism especially. "By coincidence," he wrote, "today's Op-Ed page carries a wonderful essay on the subject [sexism] by Dr. Rosalyn Yalow, a copy of which I enclose." While he did not argue that Davis's book would be the definitive word on the matter, he did remind Sidel that Davis's popularity would work to their advantage. He also felt a contract—one with a $35,000 guarantee (where Bantam paid $25,000 and Random House paid $10,000) would motivate Davis to finish the book.

Morrison and Davis talked at length about the book in early August, and Davis was convinced that she could finish a first draft before the next academic quarter began. Davis was not sold at all, however, on the idea of making the project commercial. And, this time, she could not be convinced otherwise. Morrison warned Geis: "She wants the book to remain very much what it is now: a scholarly examination of the subject of sexism and racism, complete with footnotes, bibliography, etc. I mention this because it will have some impact on your expectations for the book as well as the way in which it should be marketed."[23] To temper his expectations, Morrison also noted that there would be no publicity tour, and sales rights that generated revenue for the autobiography were not at all likely here.

It would be July the following year—1979—before Morrison forwarded Geis a copy of the manuscript, which she was calling *Women and Race*. Davis was teaching a class at San Francisco State called "Women, Class, and Race" at the time she was drafting, and she and Morrison referred to the book by that title at times, too, before settling on *Women, Race, and Class*. Morrison had concerns about the book—chapter 1 needed to be redone, and a final chapter summarizing the book's thesis needed to be written. But, by and large, Morrison thought it was an important book. Its tone was scholarly without being pedantic, and the early reader's report was enthusiastic. As they had done before, Morrison and Davis planned to work on the book in person (in August) to revise the weak chapter 1, to write the final one, and to document and clarify points that needed attention. Geis was similarly satisfied with the draft. What he liked especially was that Davis did not address the reader from a distance but, instead, used first-person narration. Even as the book was undeniably scholarly, it was still interesting and in conversation with important historical contexts. "What Angela is saying," Geis declared, "is important, timely and enduring. Bantam would have to be obtuse not to participate."[24] To their surprise, Bantam declined to exercise the option. And without the obligation to Bantam, Davis saw no need to continue the collaboration with Geis either.

Morrison explored the idea of having Davis sell the book to Random House without Geis and, only at that point, learned that the 1972 contract was between Davis and Bantam. That agreement gave Bantam, in cooperation with BGA, the option for rights to a second book and required Davis to share with Bantam a comprehensive outline and a sample chapter before offering it to

another publisher. The contract also called for reasonable negotiations between Davis and Bantam before involving another publisher. Then, the follow-up contract for the autobiography, dated
January 31, 1973, was between Random House and Bantam. BGA
was not involved in the copublishing agreement. Since Bantam
declined the option for the second book and Geis was not included in the copublishing agreement, Davis was free to negotiate
a contract for her second book with any publisher and without
Geis. Davis was confident that Morrison would negotiate the best
possible contract for her. The two women remained close, and they
had little reason to separate business and friendship. Morrison's
letter to Davis about resolving matters with Geis made this clear.
In the first paragraph, it was all business.

> Let me know as soon as you have gotten in touch with Berney
> Geis. We cannot draw up contract terms until something one
> way or another is resolved. . . . If there are going to be changes
> in personnel, then I need to know what those changes are. . . .
> Call me collect.[25]

The second paragraph was all friendship.

> Also, Toni Cade Bambara says you are due in Atlanta in De-
> cember. If so, I'd like very much for you to get in touch with her.
> You will get on splendidly and her house is a good "home" for
> you. She says to tell you she has a popcorn popper. (I was telling
> her about the benefits of popcorn as well as your and Fanya's
> [*sic*] method of popping it.)

"Love and stuff" is how Morrison signed off. Contrastingly,
while Davis's working relationship with Geis was solid, it had

endured the strain of their differing expectations for the autobiography. Free to act on her own behalf, Davis disentangled her
publishing project from Geis and signed an agreement with Random House directly.

Morrison had the contract proposal drawn up. Davis would receive $25,000—$5,000 upon signing, $5,000 upon acceptance of
50 percent of the manuscript, and the remaining $15,000 upon
submission of a complete and satisfactory manuscript. The firm
would also have an option for Davis's next book. Sales of the
three-hundred-page manuscript were projected between 12,500
and 15,000 copies, and the probable retail price was set for $15
(though it was actually set at $11.95). Morrison also suggested
that foreign publishers were most likely to buy subsidiary rights
and that the paperback edition should have a long life. In short,
the book could make a profit. Importantly, too, it would be "a careful and consistent and intelligent analysis (documentation) by a
scholar and prominent political analyst."[26]

Morrison used the adjectives *careful, consistent,* and *intelligent* expressly to contrast her sentiment about Michele Wallace's *Black Ma-
cho and the Myth of the Superwoman,* which had just been published
and critiqued as more personal experience and opinion than careful
scholarly analysis. In her description of Davis's book for the in-house
editorial fact sheet, Morrison continued to promote the book's virtues.

In this pioneering book, *Women and Race,* Angela Davis examines the historical connection between sexism, racism and
class consciousness. By concentrating (as none of the many
books on slavery do) on the plight of female slaves and female
abolitionists, and by tracing the nature and origins of the split
between them she identified, she identifies the seeds of the
current impasse between black and white feminists.

In careful, powerfully argued chapters, Professor Davis an-
alyzes the role of both women and race (in the context of
industrialism and slavery) with devastating implications for
[the] current movement for social change.[27]

The book offered an analysis of the relation of industrial capitalism to sexism and racism, the historical and continuing tension between racism and feminism, the fallacy of the myth of the
Black rapists and its relation to lynching, the political source of
pro-life and pro-abortion movements, and the class dimension of
women's rights movements. At the height of the contemporary
women's rights movement, Davis offered a historical analysis of
the ways white women feminist practitioners and scholars alike
have struggled to come to terms with racism. The lone exception
seemed to be in the field of education, where Black women and
white women worked closely together. And unlike Wallace's text,
which unrelentingly castigated Black men for upholding patri-
archy, Davis pointed out, citing Black freedmen who supported
women's voting rights, that Black men have historically been the
only male supporters of women's rights. "These and many other
issues," Morrison wrote on the fact sheet, "are raised and clarified
in a text which should become mandatory reading for sociologists,
historians, political scientists and all feminist scholarship."

The book was published in April 1982 as *Women, Race, and
Class*, and it received a bevy of critical attention. But there was also
backlash, with conservatives writing Random House directly to
assail the book. John Lofton, editor of the *Conservative Digest*, for
instance, wrote: "May I ask you please . . . why has Random House
published such undocumented, outrageous assertions?" He also
wanted to know why there was no mention of Davis's affiliation
with the central committee of the Communist Party USA.[28] Gene

K. Bruce, an orthopedic surgeon from San Mateo, California, was similarly miffed: "To identify her [Davis] only as a person who teaches, lives in California, studied at Brandeis University, etc., without any mention of the fact that she holds a senior position as a member of the Communist Party USA . . . does not reflect, I think, truth in advertising." To make his point, Bruce also chided, "It's been a long way down from Bennett Cerf, it seems to me."[29] Publishing *Women, Race, and Class*, in his view, was an outrage and beneath the Random House of old.

Tony Schulte, Random House's second-in-command, invited Morrison to share her thoughts on the critique to inform his reply. Even as Schulte was known for his kindly presence, Morrison was unclear whether Schulte might not have agreed that the omission of Davis's Communist Party USA affiliation was intentional and problematic. So she was incisive in her response. First, Random House took seriously its association with the Freedom to Read Committee. Freedom to read, she declared, also implied the freedom to write. Second, neither the Communist Party nor membership in it was illegal. Davis's affiliation was omitted from the flap copy because her politics were public knowledge, Morrison claimed. Third, the job of the publisher was to judge the merit of the manuscript not the political affiliation of the writer. Fourth, Lofton's specific claim about undocumented assertions refers to the discussion in the chapter "Rape, Racism and the Myth of the Black Rapist." Morrison pointed out that Davis had not invented any statistics or facts in the chapter. Rather, she had provided sources and been in conversation with well-known, common rape literature, including Susan Brownmiller's *Against Our Will*. Finally, rape statistics were readily available for anyone to consider. If Lofton had a problem with Davis's interpretation of them, he would be in good company since they were indeed the source of much scholarly debate.[30]

The reviews of *Women, Race, and Class* were fairly consistent. A core argument of the book, however—that the source of sexual and racial oppression is capitalism—did not land as well or as consistently with reviewers as her other aims did. The book did the hard work of examining the women's movement (in its variations), charting the efforts of Black women in this movement, and critiquing white feminists and Black historians' neglect of the role Black women have played historically in the women's movement. As Davis recalled, Morrison understood from the beginning the significance of the contributions the book could make with its analysis. She helped Davis with the research, and they collaborated to determine the layout of the chapters. Davis's principal motivation was to point out the contributions Black women made to the overarching project of women's liberation. Anyone familiar with Black women's history knew that the so-called women's movement was not actually just a white women's movement. But too few books provided the evidence and analysis. *Women, Race, and Class* took up this challenge as its goal. In the end, while it would be the last book Morrison worked on with Davis—though the two remained good friends and continued to make public appearances together—it would be only one of the many books Morrison edited about women's liberation. She was as committed as ever to ensuring that the historical record reflected a core of approaches to understanding women's liberation movements.

CHAPTER 14

Letting Giants Talk

While *Contemporary African Literature*, the first book Morrison published as an editor, was minimally impactful in terms of establishing her reputation, publishing the anthology had been a rewarding personal literary achievement. Too little attention had been paid historically to African literature in her estimation, and offering readers a sampling of it was, for her, a point of pride. An attending benefit of publishing the anthology was the opportunity to pursue some of the writers included who did not have commitments to another publisher.

A few months before *Contemporary African Literature* was released in 1972, Chinweizu approached Morrison about publishing a project that extended the thesis of that essay. The first draft of the book was done, Chinweizu claimed. It was divided into three sections. The first was a long interpretive essay that reviewed five centuries of Western expansion in the world. The second was a four-part essay that analyzed Africa in relation to precolonial and colonial encounters. The third offered "a comparative historical analysis of Black Africa and Black America." After modest revisions, he speculated it would be 350 pages and could be complete by the end of January 1972.

A native of Nigeria, Chinweizu came to the US to pursue his postsecondary education. He earned a bachelor of science degree in 1967 from MIT, where he studied philosophy and mathematics. In response to the civil war in Nigeria that began that year, he founded and edited the *Biafra Review*. That journal was short-lived (1969–70), but he became associate editor of *OKIKE: An African Journal of New Writing* when it was founded in 1971 and held that post for years. At the time, he was also a PhD student at the State University of New York, Buffalo. The project would serve as his doctoral dissertation.

Morrison's enthusiasm for the book was immediate. The work she had done on the anthology helped foster more curiosity about Africa and the many independence movements afoot on the continent. As political and cultural changes unfolded, more interpretations of colonialism's impact were bound to emerge. A book by a Nigerian writer could only complement already published work that examined the dynamics between the Western and the so-called "non-Western" world. Morrison pitched the idea successfully and sent Chinweizu a contract for what she referred to as *The African Stasis* in November 1971. The title was arbitrary, she admitted. But she was not yet sold on *The West and the Rest of Us*, and *The African Stasis* was better than *Towards a Liberated African Culture*, which was the subtitle Chinweizu used on the proposal. That title was too easily confused with the essay, and she preferred to have a title when she proposed a project for a contract. Referring to a book as "untitled" at that stage, especially for a new author, would guarantee an uphill climb. While Chinweizu had published poetry and essays, he had not yet published a book.

Chinweizu accepted the modest $2,500 advance—$1,000 due

upon signing, $1,500 upon receipt of an acceptable manuscript—and signed the contract. He missed his January 1972 deadline, which was probably unreasonable from the start. By March, he felt compelled to explain the delays to Morrison. But, first, he needed to celebrate the anthology's publication.

> Congratulations on *Contemporary African Literature*. It is really a fine book. It is not just the format, the printing and the pictures (oh! the pictures!) that make it stand out. Even more so is the selection.
>
> As regards my book here's the situation. I've really been in a bad way because of complications from my accident. It really is a pain to try to work under persistent head and eye aches. But however I have managed to grind along. I do have now close to 300 typewritten pages, but the book is not yet done. What I plan to do is send you what I have so you can look at it while I go ahead as best and as fast as I can.[1]

The delays continued since his health had not yet improved steadily. He wrote again in December.

> This is just to reassure you that, even between my bouts with my incapacitating headpains, I'm still going forward with the book. I still plan on handing *The African Stasis* to you in about a month from now, well in time to make your Fall 1973 schedule.
>
> It is a pity that this work has been delayed so long, but when the body zonks out with pain there's nothing one can do but attend it first.[2]

To encourage him along, Morrison suggested that he consider the project as two volumes instead of one. Volume I would be

The African Stasis, and volume II would be *The West and the Rest of Us*.

He delivered the first three hundred pages of the manuscript to Morrison in January 1973, in hopes of making a fall publication date. The additional pages came soon enough for Morrison to send him helpful feedback before her summer vacation but too late for publishing the book in 1973. Morrison's notes focused on work to be done on the manuscript. One problem was the repetition. He said the same thing in different ways with different images, she chided. She had begun to prune the repetition, but she needed him to do this as well in each instance where no new information is given. While Chinweizu had examined the US involvement in Africa in education, Morrison pushed him to consider US encroachment in other sectors.

In his critique of universities in Africa, he argued that their function was "to turn out products useful to imperialists." Were there no points of resistance to the goals among the faculty, no rejection of the "neo-colonial yoke"? He needed to consider this, Morrison insisted. Part 5 needed the most work.

> Part Five is top heavy. You must explain why you focus on and devote so much time to the Senghorian ideas and governt-mental [*sic*] practice. Then, the book would be more effectively closed if you compared Senegal with Guinea? Perhaps, or the workings of some place where you see true liberation in the process of taking shape.[3]

Finally, he needed to rethink the table of contents to make the chapter headings more reader friendly. Morrison made notes to suggest possible ways of dealing with this, but he should avoid letting that delay his revisions. They could work on that more together once the full manuscript was complete.

In January 1974, Morrison nudged Chinweizu about the manuscript. She did not understand the delays. He needed only to add fuller footnotes. He should do this work quickly and send the draft along. She also shared her excitement about the final title. She wrote: "I have come up with a splendid subtitle for the book: *The West and the Rest of Us: White Predators and Black Slaves*. Great yes?"[4] Chinweizu agreed to the title (which they tweaked, ultimately) and finalized the draft. By May, he received the loose galleys with a May 27 deadline to return them so the index could be prepared. In the meantime, Morrison worked on getting blurbs for the jacket. The first came from her friend and fellow writer Chinua Achebe, whom she had seen recently at a party for *OKIKE*, the journal Achebe and Chinweizu worked together on. She also sent review copies to Basil Davidson, Stanley Diamond, Noam Chomsky (with whom Chinweizu had worked at MIT), Julius Nyerere (president of Tanzania), Sékou Touré (president of Guinea), Bettina Aptheker, and Angela Davis.

While she waited for other comments she could use, Morrison began to finalize the jacket cover and copy. Things were moving along smoothly when Chinweizu called Morrison distressed about the jacket and demanding that it be changed. She listened but insisted that it was too late for the changes. She also admitted that she would not change the jacket, even if there was time to do it without incurring costs and delaying the book. Chinweizu was so upset by the conversation that he hung up the phone without saying goodbye. The next day, he sent her a letter, extending an olive branch. "Listen! I can get explosively mad," he wrote, "but with friends my anger soon blows away. How about you?" Perhaps because they were friends before they began to work together on this project, Morrison seemed unbothered by the tussle and accepted his apology. She wrote back casually:

> Now that our author-editor relationship has been baptized and duly anointed with our first spat, we can get on with our business.
>
> It was really awful to have to go to a huge sales conference to present your book with the slammed phone ringing in my ear. But it worked out o.k. I even got the printing up from 7,500 to 10,000 (paper) when the whole mood of the house is 'cut printings and raise prices.' . . .
>
> Maybe my anger improved my delivery. . . .
>
> All's well, Chinweizu. . . .
>
> I can never stay angry at people—only institutions.[5]

Chinweizu was glad to know that she did not take his anger personally and thanked her for the happy news that the first printing would be larger than planned.

Still, he pressed the issue again, this time with more details and in a letter instead of with a call. He claimed to have done informal market tests with his bookseller and book-buyer friends, and the sentiment was clear. They all thought the jacket did not convey the book's contents sufficiently. Morrison had argued that the number of people who bought books impulsively after browsing them was remarkably low. Chinweizu's response was that the number was not as low as Morrison might imagine. He continued: "Even those attracted by reviews do still read the flap copy before leafing through and deciding to buy or not to buy. So a weakness in flap copy can become a terrible weakness in packaging and presentation, and so can retard sales."[6]

By his estimation, the jacket did not summarize the fundamental thesis of the book. It was not immediately clear what was happening in the picture on the cover. A white slaver was trading with an African leader, but the nuances beyond that broad stroke were not easily perceptible. The reader had to review the flap and then return to the cover to notice the unequal exchange between the African and the enslaver. His friends also thought the jacket copy in the draft he received needed to be more straightforward than it was now. What it did say did little to excite the reader, and what it did not say was crucial—that the book used "the African case as a detailed example" of more general commentary about anti-imperialism. His friend's final criticism was about the book's overall gestalt. It appeared "too much as a black book" at a time when American reading interests had shifted from Black liberation books to global anti-imperialism books, in their view. "They feel it is not being packaged right for the American market of the 70s," Chinweizu asserted. Before closing the letter, he returned to the issue of the flap copy, which was the source of his blowup before. If the flap copy was so unimportant, as Morrison claimed it was, it could be deleted. That would force the reader to the table of contents, which was more representative of the book's thesis than what appeared on the jacket.

As a concession, Morrison agreed that the flap copy Chinweizu sent in his December missive was better than what they had previously drafted. She agreed to stress the global points (that the African case was but one) in the advertising copy. If there was ever a second printing in hardcover, she would make sure he saw and approved the revised copy in advance. But that was where her agreement ended. She was unusually patient with his assumptions that she did not understand how to sell books and that she was ill-prepared to promote his book effectively. She balanced her remarks with directness and immodestly veiled condescension.

> I take you and this book very, very seriously. So, I say the following in that vein. Books do not "fail" ultimately because of jackets, pictures, color combinations, etc. Nor do they succeed because of [the] same. It is natural, I know, just before publication to develop some crutches in the heat of anticipation of a possible fail. But you need not do that. Your book is important, classic and powerful.[7]

Being preoccupied with the jacket was a common symptom of "novice's disease," she warned. Then, she used a metaphor she invoked often. A book jacket was mere "frosting on a cake" that "can indeed influence the buyer. But the bakers, the cake judgers and eventually the cake eaters know the difference between frosting and cake. Once they bite, the cake itself will satisfy or disappoint them."

If the book did well, it would be because of his brilliance, she joked. If it failed, it would be because she was an "idiot editor." In short, he should worry less about the jacket and focus more on getting reviews, feature articles, television appearances, radio shows, and news stories so he could promote the book. The publicity team would help, but he could recommend friends and colleagues who might give him book parties or places to read from the book or to give lectures about it. She implored him to trust that she would do everything in her power to help the book be a success. Ultimately, he did trust her. Much like she speculated, readers and critics alike thought *The West and the Rest of Us* was important, classic, and powerful. Fifty years later, the book Morrison had the foresight to help Chinweizu nurture has seen different publishers, but it has never gone out of print.

Working on a second anthology with her friend Quincy Troupe and his collaborator Rainer Schulte gave Morrison another opportunity to expand her list to include books with an international focus. She and Troupe first met through Toni Cade Bambara, whose short stories Morrison had edited. Morrison and Troupe struck up a conversation at a party Bambara hosted at her apartment in Harlem on East 124th Street and became fast friends thereafter. Troupe, who had recently moved to New York after teaching at Ohio University in Athens, had published a collection of poems, *Embryo* (1972), and was the editor of *Watts Poets and Writers: A Book of New Poetry and Essays* (1968) and *Confrontation: A Journal of Third World Literature*. Morrison and Troupe began to talk at the party about the authors who contributed to *Confrontation*. She was unfamiliar with many of them, but her editorial curiosity was piqued. She had become familiar with many African authors through her work on *Contemporary African Literature*, she told Troupe, but she did not have any non-African writers who were from the so-called "Third World" on her list yet. Publishing an anthology of both established and unknown writers from different countries and cultures was, at once, prescient and long overdue. Before the end of the night, she and Troupe agreed to connect again soon to pursue the idea.

Once he agreed to work on the anthology, Troupe invited Rainer Schulte to join the effort. The two had been colleagues at Ohio University, where Schulte directed the comparative literature program from 1965 to 1975 and was the editor of *Mundus Artium: A Journal of International Letters and the Arts*. He had published a book of poems, *The Suicide at the Piano* (1970), and coedited *Continental Short Stories: The Modern Tradition* (1968), for which he also wrote the afterword. Additionally, he had written and produced a play, *Needle Off Center: A Multimedia Show* (1971). Schulte was highly respected in the academic community, having published essays, completed translations, and reviewed books in scholarly journals. Morrison was able to get a contract for the book rather easily. The sales team agreed that there was a market for such a book, and there were two experienced writers and editors in place to guide the project. Contract in hand, Schulte and Troupe divided the task of selecting texts to include. Schulte agreed to select entries by authors from South America, Mexico, the Near East, Japan, Asia, and India, while Troupe would make selections by authors from the Caribbean and Africa. They decided early on not to group the entries by an author's country or continent of origin. Rather than use geographical divisions, they resolved to arrange the anthology thematically.

With more than 150 authors and nearly 600 pages, *Giant Talk* included poetry, short stories, novel excerpts, and folktales to offer a comprehensive examination of literature by writers of color. The idea that the book would focus on "Third World" voices was always present, but the decision to name it *Giant Talk* emerged somewhat out of necessity. Because the Third World Press had a title called *Third World Voices for Children*, Morrison needed to find a title that was reflective of their aims but distinct from other titles that might be related in some way. *Giant Talk* seemed to do the trick. "To me," she told Schulte, "it suggests major talents with a non-establishment voice talking to themselves."[8] The writers were giants, and the ideas they wrote about were grand. Importantly, too, they were in conversation with each other, not with the colonial powers that informed the histories of their countries of origin.

The book's seven sections were chosen to reflect the evolution of Third World writing—"Oppression and Protest," "Violence," "A Crisis of Identity," "Music, Language, and Rhythm," "The Humorous Distance," "Ritual and Magic," and "The Conceptual Voyage." The inclusion of writers from three different continents, including Black authors from North America, spoke to the question of definition. What constituted the Third World exactly? In Schulte and Troupe's view, it included "the world of the politically and economically oppressed and exploited." They also had to address misconceptions about the term:

> Though the world contains an overwhelming number of black and brown people, it is by no means limited to them. . . . A second misconception about the Third World is that it is confined to the poor and educationally deprived. Political and economic oppression observes no polite borders or lines of class demarcation. Third World writers may be African farmers or Latin American academicians.[9]

In their view, any writer who identified with historically exploited people and confronted the establishment on their behalf was a Third World writer.

The task of narrowing the selections and determining which writers to include was a difficult one, made worse by the fact that a paper shortage in 1973 persisted and would, thereby, drive up the cost of the anthology. With Vintage on board to make the paperback of *Giant Talk* its lead book for the month for its simultaneous publication in hardcopy and paperback, cuts had to be made to ensure that the book could be priced reasonably. "I had the terrible experience yesterday of having to price a 500 page hardback book somewhere between $15 and $20," Morrison wrote. "I certainly don't want anything like that to happen to *Giant Talk*, for a $6.95 paperback simply won't do."[10] But with a 44-page introduction, 519 pages of literature, and 22 pages of bibliography and biographical notes, the $20 price point for the hardcover and $6.95 for the paperback was unavoidable.

The anthology was finally finished in the late fall of 1974 and published in October 1975. The review in *Choice* reflected the work the trio had put into organizing it. This "big book shows evidence of great editorial care and taste," the review read. "Among Third World anthologies, it stands out in its level of excellence, variety, and sense of unity." *The New York Times* offered a short review of *Giant Talk*, alongside *The Negritude Poets: An Anthology of Translations from the French*. While the reviewer recognized the "extraordinary variety" in *Giant Talk*, he felt the scope was unwieldly, especially its broad definition of Third World literature.[11] The claim that attended this broad definition—that there are only haves and have-nots—he thought, minimized the racial, ethnic, and cultural differences characteristic of Third World literature. Schulte and Troupe's introduction had argued against this very notion, that broad definitions inherently minimize difference. For them, narrowing the field was a divisive tactic meant to stall the revolution these writers tried to enact. Still, every reviewer agreed that the value and necessity of a comprehensive anthology like *Giant Talk* was indisputable. In the years to come, it became highly referential as awareness and acceptance of multiculturalism continued to grow.

While Morrison hoped *Giant Talk* would broaden readers' cultural exposure, she rightly assumed that Ivan Van Sertima's *They Came Before Columbus* would challenge readers' widely held beliefs about what they thought they knew about Western culture. In many ways, *They Came Before Columbus* revealed Morrison's determination to use her editorship to move Black culture from the margin to the center. Van Sertima was already established as a writer by the time he published the book, having published *River and the Wall*, a book of poems, in 1958 and *Caribbean Writers: Critical Essays* in 1968. He had also compiled a *Swahili Dictionary of Legal Terms*. Born in British Guiana, he attended the School of Oriental and African Studies at the University of London, where he completed his undergraduate studies in African languages and literature and where he began to take his creative writing seriously. After working as a press and broadcasting officer at home and as a journalist in Britain, he became a graduate student at Rutgers University in New Brunswick in 1970. He eventually became a professor at Rutgers and served as chair of the Cultural Linguistics Seminar at Princeton, a program between Princeton, Rutgers, and Lincoln University's Afro-American Studies program. Notably, too, he was a widely recognized literary critic, so much so that the Nobel Committee invited him to nominate a candidate for the prize in literature in 1976.

Morrison first became familiar with the central idea of *They Came Before Columbus* when Van Sertima asked her to write a letter of support for his tenure and promotion file at Rutgers. After explaining to her that he had long critical essays, in addition to his fiction, in his portfolio, he decided to ask fellow writers Wilson Harris and C. L. R. James to write for him instead. "I had, in my absentmindedness thought I had shown you most of my work, which indeed I haven't," Van Sertima wrote to Morrison. "I know you would have done it anyway out of friendship but I feel this is unfair, and an imposition. . . . Please, therefore, ignore letter, requesting same, from the Promotion Committee."[12] Even though Van Sertima decided not to lean on his friend for a letter of reference, Morrison read the early pages of a draft of the untitled novel he had shared with her. While she was under-whelmed by the 12,500-word manuscript, she did find the idea from his master's thesis interesting. Was there more in that vein? she inquired.

Two months later, in December 1971, he sent a full outline for a book that extended the thesis of the five-thousand-word article on Africans in America. Included in the bigger project, he told Morrison, was

> a chapter on the nature of the African and Amerindian bond both before and after the Conquest. It is a little known fact, for example, that Blacks were leaders of Indian rebellions against the Spaniards in the sixteenth century. While the central thread of this book will be wound around the evidence for the propo-sition that Africans visited the American continent before the Spaniards, it will branch off into other fascinating and little known areas of the cultural confrontation and relationship be-tween the African and native American.[13]

It would be three years before Van Sertima made enough progress on the project to share with Morrison a schedule for completing chapters of the book. Morrison was interested in ac-quiring the book for Random House, but until he had more of the draft complete, they only had a gentleman's agreement about publishing it there.

Four years later, when Van Sertima completed the first seven chapters, he and Morrison began to talk about the challenge of making the book accessible for a general audience while also mak-ing a scholarly argument that was impenetrable. He submitted drafts of new chapters and revised old ones based on Morrison's feedback at the same time. He also provided Morrison with periodic updates about the book's progress and outlined how he had handled their shared concerns about audience.

> I have found a way to make this [the chapter he was working on] a lot more interesting by beginning with the mystery of Mu-lan-p'i rather than with the maize so as to whet the reader's appetite. . . .
>
> Not only is the presentation more dramatic and attractive but I have avoided linguistic crosswords. I have abandoned, for example, the section on Shells. . . . No other section rests on philology like the section on shells. . . .
>
> Scrapping [it] is no great loss, considering the body of new evidence which has emerged since I wrote the [earlier] version.[14]

Morrison wanted to avoid the quandary of trying to market anything that looked like a textbook as a trade book with commercial potential. Van Sertima wanted to make a compelling argument that would stand up to the most rigorous scholarly scrutiny, which he knew was inevitable considering his argument—that people of African descent were in the Americas with awareness of it prior to Columbus's "discovery" of the so-called New World. The book had potential for mass-market appeal, especially to readers interested in topics ranging from American history to anthropology. And Morrison wanted to garner that appeal in every way she could.

With enough pages of the draft done to be confident about its impending completion, Morrison was finally able to secure a contract for the book. The arduous process of drafting and revising was time-consuming for Van Sertima. It was also stressful, so much so that his wife wrote to Morrison directly, prompting him to apologize on her behalf. He wrote:

Since I wrote to you last . . . I have had a chance to talk with my wife about the letter she wrote you concerning the contract. I deeply regret both her communication and mine for indeed both grew out of the years of waiting and anxiety. I have been working on this book for five years, the last three almost continuously, night and day. I must apologize for any unpleasantness you may have experienced through her concern over my anxiety.[15]

Van Sertima's wife had no real way of knowing how hard it had been for Morrison to get a contract for the book. As much as she believed in the project, convincing the publisher to take the risk on an intellectually driven book that made a controversial argument as a trade book was another matter.

Morrison labeled the book as "compelling, dramatic, and superbly detailed" on the editorial fact sheet, and she made a point to boast about the dual quality of the writing and the scholarship using familiar figures from history to do so.

With the skill of a novelist, the author recreates some of the most powerful scenes history has to offer: the launching of the great ships of Mali in 1310 . . . ; the sea expedition of the Mandingo king himself in 1311; Cadamosto, the Portuguese explorer's encounter with a fleet of Black sailors carrying poison-tipped arrows. With the fastidiousness of a scholar, he documents the facts of navigation and ship building; the sources of latitudinal and longitudinal coordinates; the scores of cultural analogies found nowhere else except middle America and Africa; linguistic analyses of African languages and ancient Mexican languages; and the very important transportation of plants, cloth and animals from Africa to the Americas.[16]

The book was finally published in fall 1976, and Morrison promoted the book personally in *Publishers Weekly*. She also helped Van Sertima publish "Bad News for Columbus, Perhaps" as an op-ed and teaser on December 4, 1975, in *The New York Times*.

Once the book was released, the reviews of it were similarly titled—"Columbus Discovered America? Random House Book Says Blacks Here First," "How About Abu Bakari II Day? A Rutgers Professor Says Africans Beat Columbus Here by 2,000 Years," "Rich Black Past 'Embarrasses' Europe," and "'Before Columbus': Roots of a Dispute."[17] When a decidedly conservative reader, Glyn Daniel, reviewed *They Came Before Columbus* harshly in *The New York Times*, Van Sertima offered a response, which he shared with Morrison. "Your reply to the *Times* is fantastic!" she wrote to Van Sertima. "I called Mel and told him I want every word of it printed. . . . Here's hoping."[18] The Mel to whom she referred was Mel Watkins, the first Black staff editor for the *Times Sunday Book Review*, with whom she had built an important relationship over the years. Van Sertima's letter was included almost verbatim, along with other letters critiquing the review and Daniel's response to these letters.[19]

They Came Before Columbus overtly challenged widely held contemporary thought about the New World's historicity in general and Africans' relation to the so-called "New World" more specifically. Unequivocally, Van Sertima argued, Africans had extended contact with what would become North America as explorers and then as settlers who contributed meaningfully to early US civilization well before Columbus's "discovery." What Morrison's decision to publish the book revealed was her willingness if not determination to rewrite history more honestly in the tradition of the Black Studies movement, which challenged dominant narratives that mischaracterized, marginalized, and erased African and

African diaspora contributions to world history. The look beyond the domestic and accepted histories of civilization held a unique appeal to Morrison. The interplay between culture-shifting books, literary books, and commercially successful ones exemplified her innovative approach to editing.

The interplay between culture-shifting books and a high-profile celebrity book exemplified her innovative approach to editing. She was determined to prove that commercial success and cultural significance could coexist. She could enrich both the industry and the discourse around the important societal issues she was convinced mattered the most. If she did both well, she would not have to choose.

CHAPTER 15

Beyond *The Black Book*

Scrapbooking Black History

When James Alan McPherson and Miller Williams saw a copy of *The Black Book* for the first time, they were already contemplating a book on railroads and trains. In the same way that large-format books examined the significance of the aircraft carrier, the handgun, and the skyscraper, a book on the railroad could chronicle the historical meaning of railroads and trains in human culture. Of all the technological advances made in recent decades, few were the subject of mythology more richly and frequently than the train. Now, with a clearer sense of what the book might look like, the duo sent a draft of their proposal to Owen Laster at William Morris Agency in New York. When Laster received the proposal in September 1974, there was only one editor he had in mind to share it with: Morrison.

As a well-regarded literary agent known for his ability to

recognize important books, Laster gave the project an advantage it might not have had with a lesser-known agent. Both McPherson and Williams had modest accomplishments Laster could use to sell the project as well. McPherson had published a collection of short stories, *Hue and Cry* (with Atlantic / Little, Brown), and had written for the *Atlantic Monthly*, *Playboy*, *New York Times Magazine*, and *Reader's Digest*. He earned an MFA from the Iowa Writers' Workshop and had taught at the University of Iowa, the University of California, Harvard University, and Morgan State College (later Morgan State University). Williams was a poet who taught science at Wesleyan College before joining the faculty in English at Louisiana State University (upon the recommendation of his friend Flannery O'Connor) to teach poetry. He eventually made his way to the English department at the University of Arkansas, where he became codirector of the program in creative writing and director of the program in translation. Williams had also been a visiting professor of US literature at the University of Chile and a Fulbright professor at the National University of Mexico. He had published three collections of poems—*A Circle of Stone*, *So Long at the Fair*, and *Halfway from Hoxie: New and Selected Poems*.

Morrison thought the book had exciting possibilities. There was no denying that train lore was present in almost every aspect of culture, yet there were no competing documentary histories of railroads and trains. This would make the book relevant and appealing. Before agreeing to take on the project, however, she had three minor suggestions and two major ones she wanted the team to consider. For one thing, she thought they should limit their selections in each section to American experiences. It would be impossible to cover trains and railroads across the globe, and isolated international material (there was a piece on South Africa by

Nadine Gordimer) could not be justified. Nominal consideration of the early English context was understandable, because of its inextricable relation to American experiences. But the focus needed to be tightened otherwise. Morrison also wanted to see more photographs, in volume and variety. Beyond specific types of trains, they should also include trains in art, photographs that included trains, and images of patents related to trains. While she appreciated the literary selections included, there was also focal literature that included commentary about trains and railroads that should be considered.

Two significant challenges would also need to be addressed. One problem was the book had two introductions. Morrison wrote:

> The book should speak with one voice of many things. As authors, you are the voice, and it should be established in one introduction written by the two of you. That might pose some problem because 1) your writing styles differ so greatly and 2) each of you is taking a different tack. Somehow, some way, the subjective reflections of the one must blend with the historiography of the other if the individual reactions of one with the social and technological views of the other. The cooperation seems to me vital—for the material must be more than commentary: it must be cohesive.[1]

The second problem was the book could not be eight hundred pages. A book that size would be cost prohibitive and have a very limited market. Otherwise, she was confident she could get everyone on board at Random House with publishing another documentary history book.

McPherson and Williams conferred with each other and decided that McPherson should provide the response to Morrison. Part of the reason for this was McPherson wanted to provide context on how the book was conceived. The more he observed people's deep-seated fear of innovations in technology, from computers to bioengineering, the more he became interested in the relation between technology and culture in American society. As the nineteenth-century symbol for American progress, the railroad, in McPherson's view, was the best example of what Leo Marx called "the middle landscape." The Black people and immigrants who built the railroad made functional art of it and created an aesthetic that grappled with the argument of the impact of art on machines and the impact of machines on art. McPherson's lengthy articulation of the book's background was meant to give Morrison a sense of why and how the book had been conceived and to explain why his essay was necessary to open the book. Williams's essay, contrastingly, was reflective and captured memories of his experiences of the railroad as a boy growing up in the South. It was more poetic too.

The next area Miller and Williams offered in response to Morrison was in relation to the proposed table of contents. They were both aware of the 1970s rhetoric of racial integration. In addition to their enactment of this—with the white poet and Black fiction writer—they chose literature that would reflect cultural pluralism, an "Omni-American" view of the railroad. Accordingly, they intended to present material from each ethnic group and the railroad. Having two introductions, in their view, also accomplished this notion of plural views on the same topic. This notwithstanding, they were willing to reconsider the table of contents, but they defended their interest in using material beyond America. McPherson laid this argument out clearly.

As you point out, the inclusion of the story by the South African Nadine Gordimer may be stretching the border a bit; yet I would rather include materials from South Africa and Australia than materials from England. My reason is this: As I point out in my introduction, my interest is in seeing how people on that level of the folk responded to the railroad; and it strikes me that, unlike America, Australia and South Africa (colonies which developed into nations), England already had an ongoing folk tradition, one grounded in the remote past. Only in America, Australia and South Africa were pioneers and machines thrown together, and only in these places were there pressures to modify old traditions and assumptions in order to make something new—to forge new aesthetic connections between men and machines.[2]

McPherson and Williams agreed that there could be more photographs and greater variety, that there should be more folk literature, and that the size of the book needed to be more manageable. They ended the letter with the suggestion that Amtrak might help them call attention to the book. The company had begun its passenger service in May 1971 and was trying to encourage people to ride their trains. Marketing the books there and in classrooms would help make the point that the texture of people's experiences might differ from one another regionally and otherwise, but, ultimately, all Americans had something in common.

Morrison noted that while she had a great deal of enthusiasm for the theory McPherson articulated as justification for two introductions, she was not convinced that would work. She reiterated her point. "A good introduction ought to be what you want the book to be," she wrote, "an integrated piece which takes *both* experiences and modes of expression into account."[3] A reader or reviewer should be able to browse the introduction and know what to expect. This prompted a query about the book's organization, its use of headnotes to contextualize the literature, and its mechanics (page numbers, trim, number of photos, etc.). She also needed pages of a representative section to share with the designer, production manager, and lead salesman. Getting this team on board was important since the editor in chief would need more than her editorial enthusiasm to make an informed publishing decision.

This time Williams wrote back, just before Christmas, and included a sample section on the westward expansion of railroads. Morrison responded in the new year that she was impressed with the material and would be in touch shortly. When he had not heard from her by mid-February, Laster sent her a gentle reminder. They had spoken in late January, and Morrison had suggested that an offer was forthcoming in a matter of days. She wrote back quickly.

> Let me assure you that a) I am "determined" to take *Railroad* and b) I'm doing the best I can. But I got stuck with out of date figures and now need more and newer ones. So, not to cause any duress, let me continue with production costs on the material and . . . if you like, I'll send the original copy to you for showing elsewhere simultaneously. My preference, of course, is that you hang in there with me.[4]

Once she had the updated figures, she made her pitch to Silberman. The design would be simple—black-and-white photos, drawings, sheet music, and text. She had a significant section of the manuscript already, so she could trust that the authors could deliver on what they proposed. They had access to archives of "all the railroad people" (from Amtrak to railroad unions) and had been given passes to travel anywhere by train to conduct their research. In addition to the built-in market at train stations and promises of promotion by Amtrak, passenger train travel was coming back and would likely be a point of interest and celebration during the bicentennial year. Silberman agreed to the terms Morrison proposed—an $8,000 advance (with Random House retaining world rights)—so in late April, she could finally offer McPherson and Williams the awaited contract for *Railroad: Trains and Train People in American Culture.*

Once the first full draft of the manuscript was submitted in June, she worked with McPherson and Williams to identify changes she wanted to see and gaps in the manuscript. There were songs with wonderful lyrics that also needed to be included in the section of railroad songs. The biggest gap, she noted, was the lack of commentary about the Brotherhood of Sleeping Car Porters in the chapter on unions. McPherson and Williams agreed with all Morrison's points and agreed to add a biographical piece on A. Philip Randolph to reference the Brotherhood of Sleeping Car Porters. Even as Randolph's work fell outside of the time frame they had articulated for the section on unions and czars, they agreed that adding it to the end of this section would be appropriate. Once they did, Williams added a special note to Morrison about it. "Thanks for getting on to this," he wrote. "Now that it's done, it scares me to think that we might have gone to press without the Brotherhood of Sleeping Car Porters in the book."[5] The final late addition was material on Conrail, the freight train company the federal government created to provide funding for bankrupt railroad companies in 1974.

By August, the project had gone to the copy editor, and Morrison began to consider design ideas. Her suggestions for the design team about the book's layout revealed her vision for the book.

This book . . . will resemble *The Black Book* but be more orderly in its design: large trim, double col-text, interesting use and placement of photographs, etc. . . .

The Sidetracks, placed after each Chapter, contain various kinds of material for a freely designed but self-contained unit. . . .

"Sidetrack" heads should have the same weight in design as the chapter heads—but they can have a different design feature.[6]

She also added information about the page numbering, photo captions, and placement of introductory material. The book went to production in January, just in time to be ready for a fall publication date and gift-giving season. The editorial fact sheet announced its contents—material on freedom and troop trains, robber barons and railroad bandits, the great trains like the *Phoebe Snow* or the *Yellow Dog*, great train songs and literature, railroad and train folklore, great train wrecks, union strikes, and frontier wars. Everything the sixty-three thousand registered "train buffs," the five hundred thousand train union members, and a general audience wanted to know about trains was there.

Along the way, Morrison developed a relationship with McPherson—fiction writer to fiction writer. It was clear to Morrison from his detailed, thoughtful, and lengthy letters that McPherson was sagacious. He was cerebral about most things, dogged about others. He and Morrison finally met in July 1975 when Morrison was in Monterey to meet with the National Endowment Committee. McPherson drove from San Francisco to meet with her in person and to share some ideas about how contemporary music—the O'Jays' "Love Train" especially—dealt with the train motif. They connected in person again in April 1976 when McPherson visited New York, after moving to Baltimore, Maryland, at the end of 1975. Even the brief time they shared together getting to know each other better helped Morrison understand those times when McPherson, who was normally pleasant even if verbose, was testy. He wrote Morrison, for instance, to reiterate his desire to have the sentence about his considering himself an "Omni-American" (as Albert Murray used the term) included in his biography for the dust jacket. "This is very important to me, as it is tied to the project on which I am presently at work," he noted. And while his academic affiliation had switched to the University of Virginia, he had wanted to ensure that his time at Morgan State was included to help publicize the fact that the school had attained university status.

His next letter was less solicitous.

This morning I received from Random House the proofs for the dust jackets of the book. I note that Miller Williams's name preceeds [*sic*] mine as co-author of the book. Who made the change and why was it made?

I do not consider this a minor point. . . . the book was my idea from the very first. I am led to assume that someone there decided that the order of names was a matter of race. This saddens me.[7]

If the change could not be reversed, McPherson declared, he would seek an injunction to have his name removed completely from the authorship. "Miller can carry the book on his own," McPherson wrote. He had called Morrison earlier in the day before mailing the letter and did not expect to hear back from her. When he did, he quickly sent off another letter to append the one he knew Morrison would likely find offensive. In the second letter, he wrote: "I hope that our conversation has put an end to what for me was a pretty tense and hectic experience. I also hope that this letter reaches you very soon after my first letter." The first letter was written in anger, he admitted, and their conversation had cleared things up. He still hoped to have the arrangement outlined in writing, for the record and for the sake of his old law school buddy whom he had consulted when he noticed the error.

The fact that she knew the letter was coming and they had resolved the problem did little to avert Morrison's annoyance with the first letter. Flummoxed, she wrote:

> I will probably always be befuddled about what you imagine this publishing company to be and about your reasons for ascribing sinister motives to a copyediting mistake of placing your name after Miller Williams. I can only assume you had some bad experiences with other publishers.
>
> We make errors, Jim, and I am sure that I will never be wholly free of that frailty. What I (we) don't do is spend time thinking up silly ways to tell the world on a book jacket that one of our own authors is racially inferior to his co-author and/or has done "less" work. . . . But more than the misunderstanding, I regret the absence of trust which is the single most important ingredient to exist between author and editor. I wish you thought I deserved it.[8]

She confirmed that the changes were being made in production, so the dust jacket would read "James Alan McPherson and Miller Williams." The cloth cover of the hardback would be changed in subsequent editions, if there were any. Wanting to avoid any further miscommunication (and taking the opportunity to levy sarcasm), Morrison noted that on the back of the paperback, Miller Williams's picture was on the left and McPherson's on the right. So, Williams's name would obviously be first since his picture was on the left. There would be no change there.

The book sold well—almost 14,000 paperback and 1,300 hardcover copies in its first few months—and the early reviews were complimentary. McPherson made a point to offer, again, a mea culpa to Morrison and to share his thoughts about the finished product. "It is really a beautiful book, Toni: visually and in design and layout," he wrote. "Although I have barked and growled at some things (this is an aspect of my personality), I'm very pleased with how things turned out. . . . You're probably the only editor in the country with sympathy for the work Miller and I were attempting."[9] In McPherson and Williams's view, the book owed its success as much to Morrison as to anyone. She had embraced it, improved and nurtured it, and promoted it with generous enthusiasm. The feeling of satisfaction was mutual. *Railroad* was a well-done book, she thought. Importantly, too, it was further proof that the formula she had first used for *The Black Book* had not lost its charm. That was a good thing, because another scrapbook project was already in process.

The spring 1977 release of Jim Haskins's *The Cotton Club: A Pictorial and Social History of the Most Famous Symbol of the Jazz Era* was, for Morrison, an unfortunate reminder of just how long the road to publication could be for a book. Four years had passed since Morrison first proposed the idea to her editor in chief. In June 1973, she pitched the idea of offering her friend Haskins a three-book contract—one with Aretha Franklin and Haskins, where Franklin offered reflections on a series of photographs that chronicled her life, a second one with Haskins and Duke Ellington and his music, and a third on the project Morrison and Haskins were calling the *Cotton Club Papers*. "Here is a run-down of these contracts," she wrote in an interoffice memo to Silberman, "so when we talk you will have the background."

Mr. Haskins is the author of twelve or more books . . . who has easy access to and trust of certain people I want to sign. He is involved in these projects first as a writer and second as a trusted liaison.

1. *The Cotton Club Papers*: The author has the photos, clippings and correspondence of an enormous private collection. He also has interviewed major figures who appeared there (he will do more). Rather than the picture book plus essay I originally wanted, this book is a book-book—with photos supplementing a major text.
2. The Aretha thing we have not talked about. Several intensive attempts to get her story have been unsuccessful. She has been very reluctant to talk. Now, apparently, she will—by reminiscing over photos. . . . Haskins—again—will put it together and write the afterword. . . . Her story will be marvelous and there is *no* other book on or by her.
3. The Duke thing: We have selected twenty (out of over 600) songs that can be printed, played, sung, etc.

I'll wait to see you this evening.[10]

As always, Morrison had done her homework. The Aretha Franklin book would not be a typical memoir, but it would have wide appeal, especially on the heels of the release of her live gospel album *Amazing Grace*, which sold more than two million copies after its June 1972 release. The Ellington book, Morrison noted, would be similar to *Music and Lyrics: A Treasury of Cole Porter*, which G. Schirmer, Inc., published in 1972. The published books on songs and lyrics by Noël Coward could also be considered among the comparable titles. Ellington was of particular interest because he seldom allowed his written music to appear in print. *The Cotton Club Papers* were from a private collection and could, therefore, offer an exclusive history of the famous Harlem nightclub.

Despite her best efforts, Morrison could not convince Silberman that signing up all three books was the best path forward. He was willing to have Morrison pursue the *Cotton Club Papers* but only after she got design and sales on board. Even before they met to talk about the three books, Silberman had pushed Morrison to round out her plans for how the firm would handle the Cotton Club project. "In order to get this book to the point of contract," he wrote, "we need to do what we did with *The Black Book*: first to get a proposal that indicates what the book will be and second to bring it to a point where we can get the cooperation of the sales department on a printing."[11] He also thought the sales estimates (twenty-five thousand paper and cloth) were too high. Morrison followed Silberman's advice and, armed with a design and sales plan, proposed a single-book contract for *The Cotton Club*. The contract was finalized, and Haskins began to work on the project in due course.

Haskins earned his reputation as a writer rather unconventionally. While teaching a special education class at PS 92 in New York, he began keeping a diary of his experiences working with ten-year-olds who had disabilities and who were not being served well in the New York public school system. After Grove Press published his *Diary of a Harlem Schoolteacher* in 1969, he began to write biographies about Black people for juvenile readers. As he completed his research, he became more interested in writing books on the Black history that shaped the lives of his subjects. By the time he and Morrison began to work on *The Cotton Club*, he had written on topics ranging from anti-war revolutionaries and street gangs to witchcraft and consumer movements.

For two years, Morrison and Haskins met regularly in her office to work on the manuscript. Morrison preferred working with authors in person when she could. Haskins and his wife lived in an apartment on Riverside Drive, close enough to the Random House offices that he could meet Morrison there easily and enjoy the comradery her office afforded. They worked together to determine the content and organization, but she left the writing to Haskins. Once the layout was done, Morrison offered feedback about how he might tighten and enliven the language to give readers the feeling of discovery of the era, even as they had Haskins as their guide. The "ponderous and repetitious prose" needed attention, for one thing. "I have marked and queried Chapter 1 as an example of the kind of thing I mean," Morrison wrote.[12] A second writing could eliminate this.

He rewrote chapter 1, as Morrison advised and to her satisfaction. And he keyed the photos—some of which he had chosen and some of which Morrison had chosen—to specific pages in the manuscript. Still, there were more images to decide between and others yet to be secured. Some illustrations needed to be shot by the firm's photo department so they could be included in the book. He and Morrison also had to decide what to do with the London Palladium illustrations, new photos he received since their last meeting about content, and the photos from the Museum of the City of New York picture collection Haskins intended to send along in two weeks or so. The bigger challenge was finding prints for photographs that would ensure sufficient variety in the images and representation of all the best-known Cotton Club personalities.

Once the book was done, the 170 pages of pictorial and social history was not the book they had proposed—Morrison, in particular, had pitched it to Silberman as a "gossipy" book that offered insight into an untold story—but it was unique enough still for them to be pleased with it. Haskins was a gifted writer who, with "wit and clarity," put the Cotton Club in context, from its owners and audiences to its performers and their music. Most of the pictures were from a private collection and, therefore, not available elsewhere. The thing that made the book unique—the photos—also made it more expensive to produce, however. Not long before the book was published, in fact, Haskins asked Morrison if they could renegotiate the contract with respect to illustration fees. They were more than he anticipated and more than he could afford to pay out of pocket. Morrison's response was clear. "What you propose is quite out of the question," she exclaimed.

> We cannot renegotiate the contract because you don't want to assume the costs of photos in your book as agreed upon. Perhaps it will make a difference to know that all such costs are deducted from future earned royalties of the book—there is no exprectation [*sic*] of bills paid by you out-of-pocket. Also, the additional photos, I'm sure are very much worth it in the long run—they should increase sales.[13]

She followed her letter up with a call to explain how payment would work and to dissuade him from thinking that renegotiation was a possibility. After their talk, he settled down.

The Cotton Club was finally published October 27, 1977. Earlier in the month, the publicity department alerted major media outlets, especially those with Black audiences, that Haskins was available for interviews. Promotional material described *The Cotton Club* as "an extraordinarily-handsome photo and text memoir of the so-called 'good old days' up in New York's Harlem." The club's fame was tied to remarkable performances by Black talent there, on the one hand, and its exclusivity to white audiences on the other. This irony gave the book a unique appeal. It was an inside view of an "exclusive" space. Publicity focused as much on Haskins as it did on the book. It announced the book's author as thirty-four-year-old Jim Haskins, who spent more than four years putting the book together.

The promotional media letter closed with information about how to request review copies and how to schedule Haskins for interviews. A second, more targeted version of the letter included specific cities and dates where he would appear as part of a book tour. Haskins made appearances in DC at the end of October and in New York, Boston, Chicago, and Cleveland in November. In each city, he did as much radio and TV as his schedule would allow. One final boon was the fact that a newly imagined Cotton Club reopened in January 1978, less than three months after the book's release. The club bought one hundred paperback copies of the book to sell at the concession stand. And Haskins was a part of the club's publicity plans, along with celebrities like Lena Horne and Cab Calloway. Random House also sent complimentary copies to the Black press and culture keepers. "The appearance of this nostalgic book coincides with the opening of the new 'Cotton Club,'" the club's public relations lead Ellen DeBard wrote. The venue would capture the spirit and glamour of the '30s while making it open to all patrons. An expert chef and staff had been hired to create dinner specials each night, and their valet parking service was buttressed by "a fleet of 1978 white Cadillacs" that offered limousine service for a nominal fee.

The Cotton Club sold modestly and was celebrated critically for its detailed account of the social context and history of the period it covered—from the club's opening in 1920 to its closing in 1935, following the Harlem riot. Though it reopened on West 48th Street, it was never as popular as when it was at 142nd and Lenox; and it eventually closed in 1940. *The New York Times Book Review* heaped praise on the book, calling it a "detailed, instructive and entertaining work," a "lavishly illustrated" and "handsome" book.[14] It would be years, however, before the book reached the potential Morrison and Haskins thought it had. In 1984, it inspired the American crime drama film, *The Cotton Club*, directed by Francis Ford Coppola. The more immediate energy publishing *The Cotton Club* created in 1977 was related to its being the latest book Morrison edited that gave general audiences unique insight into Black culture and history.

For years, she and Rudolph "Rudy" Lombard toyed with the idea of publishing a cookbook that featured storied New Orleans chefs. A native of New Orleans, Lombard was the director of La Cuisine Creole, Inc., an association of minority chefs, cooks, and caterers in the New Orleans area. La Cuisine enabled the members of the group to have a bargaining position they would not have as independent culinary workers, created opportunities for them at the many fairs in New Orleans they might otherwise be excluded from, and provided them with pensions that enabled them to retire. This latter point was significant because many of them were ineligible for social security since they had often been paid under the table most of their careers, from their earliest jobs working in kitchens, mostly as dishwashers, until they achieved some status as chef.

In addition to directing La Cuisine Creole, which was more about providing recognition and support to the chefs than about profit, Lombard was the president of Lombard and Associates, Inc., a minority–affirmative action consulting firm. He earned his PhD from the Maxwell School of Citizenship and Public Affairs at Syracuse University and built his career planning public works and teaching. Over the years, he was planner and principal for the Claiborne Avenue Design in New Orleans, director of the Freedmen's

Hospital on Drug Abuse and Addiction at Howard University in Washington, DC, and program director for the Interracial Council for Business Opportunity and Association for Commerce and Trade in New York. He had also been a longshoreman in New Orleans while finishing his undergraduate degree at Xavier University.

In some ways, he was a kind of everyman—able to move freely in whatever spaces he found himself. The common thread was his commitment to Black people and Black culture, especially in his hometown of New Orleans. While Lombard was also a gourmet chef himself, he insisted on bringing a premiere New Orleans chef, Nathaniel Burton, to the project as its coauthor. Burton was a native of McComb, Mississippi, and got his start as a busboy and dishwasher at the old Hotel New Orleans on Canal and Crozat Streets. He eventually became the chef at the Caribbean Room at the Pontchartrain Hotel in New Orleans and then executive chef at Broussard's Restaurant in the French Quarter. Under his direction, Broussard's became one of the most celebrated restaurants in New Orleans, and it featured many of the dishes Burton created over the years. Burton was the legendary elder who was well regarded among his peers and his mentees alike. He trained students at culinary institutes in the United States, lectured at several universities for their hotel and restaurant management programs, and consulted with culinary institutes and restaurants in France.

At the end of March 1976, Morrison and Lombard finally began to talk in detail about the proposal for the book they were calling *Great Black Chefs of New Orleans*. They agreed that Lombard would write the introduction and collect materials from the chefs—recipes, personal stories, restaurant lore, and ideas about the art and craft of food culture. For purposes of negotiating a contract, Morrison needed a manuscript, which they decided would be an interview with Burton, the book's coauthor. She received the taped interview of Burton in mid-May and wrote to Lombard excitedly.

> I received the two tapes of your interview with Mr. Burton and I am very pleased. There is quite a bit of good general information in them and substantial detail. My compliments to you both.
>
> Our next step is to have the tapes transcribed. I can edit the transcription and it, along with the introductory material you wrote, plus a short introduction of Mr. Burton will be enough to submit for final approval.[15]

Morrison received the transcript in July, along with the names of eighteen additional chefs who might be included in the book. It would be September, however, before Morrison gathered all the information she needed to move the project forward. Once she did, she wrote to Silberman:

> Herewith the contract proposal for the *Black Chefs of New Orleans* book we discussed some time ago. Dr. Lombard is a native of New Orleans, and an amateur gourmet cook who has the confidence of all those proud, secretive premier chefs in New Orleans. . . .
>
> Mr. Burton is the undisputed King of New Orleans chefs—(he rules the Broussard kitchens) and the man people have followed from restaurant to restaurant over a period of 50 years. His presence in the book has assured it [*sic*] success and the full cooperation of the other black chefs.
>
> The style is a chatty, personal one as though each cook is talking to the reader alone. . . .
>
> It's a tremendous idea and the material is delicious.[16]

Whether it was a novel or a cookbook, Morrison always appreciated any stylistic or aesthetic approach that made readers feel they were being let in on a secret. The cookbook did this in two ways—the familiarity the reader (whom Morrison imagined was Black) would feel when reading the interviews and the trade secrets the chefs shared in the book that they had not shared elsewhere. Whether the dishes were Black, Creole, Classic French, or Italian, they were all prepared with a distinctive New Orleans style. The interviews and recipes were "crammed with inside information, tips, secrets," and with "the trade information which excellent cooks almost never share."

Silberman thought the book was a good idea and approved the contract right away. Lombard and Burton agreed to the $6,000 advance and returned the contracts in November. Morrison presented the project at the first editorial meeting of the year. It would have two parts: the conversations and the recipes. The preface could define the uniqueness of the cuisine, which they might call "New Orleans Creole Black." The recipes section would have subsections for each genre—main dishes, salads, desserts, sauces, and the like. In addition to the recipe index, back matter would include a list of ingredients and equipment and where these could be purchased. Finally, they would need a picture of each chef and at least one picture of all the chefs together. "The enthusiasm for the book is overwhelming—you can't imagine," Morrison wrote to Lombard.[17] All he needed to do was to produce the requested materials, and they were on their way. If all the material was in by March, they could have the book published in time for Christmas sales that year.

Despite an on-time delivery of the first draft of the manuscript in March, the project missed the winter publication season because of the volume of additions and revisions that needed to be made. Since they missed Christmas sales, Morrison slowed the project down to a normal pace. She sent Lombard a complete draft of the manuscript to review in July 1977. She wrote: "You can go over all this but I think it is most efficient if your and the other chefs' fastidious examination of it come after the copy editor is through. . . . And since we have to assume that our buyers are all novice cooks, a lot of stuff has to be spelled out in kindergarten fashion."[18] She provided an example of what she meant. In the shrimp marguery recipe, for instance, the ingredients list included three pounds of boiled shrimp. To the right of the ingredients list was a note about the boiled shrimp: add one tablespoon cayenne pepper and two tablespoons salt to water and boil for 8 to 10 minutes. Morrison moved all the ingredients to one side and wrote the instructions out explicitly. She scratched through the first line of directions, which simply indicated that the shrimp should be placed in a pot 8 inches or deeper. The new directions read: "Shell and clean the shrimp. Put aside. Bring 3 quarts of water to a boil. Add cayenne pepper, salt and shrimp. Boil for 8 to 10 minutes. Drain and place shrimp in 8 inch deep pot." Morrison was delighted getting her cooking hands dirty, even if it was just on paper.

Morrison also cautioned that all recipes should use fresh food instead of allowing for shortcuts. It was extra work for the cook to use fresh food, but it would add an element of legitimacy to the recipes and thereby to the cookbook. Where the shrimp marguery recipe called for one can of mushrooms *or* one pound of fresh mushrooms, for example, she deleted the can option from the list of ingredients. If a recipe called for a quart of cream sauce, she added a page reference to a cream sauce recipe. This was a significant addition that needed to be made—all sauces mentioned needed recipes. Burton agreed to supply these. The rationale here was that this was the first time these recipes had been written down in most instances. The only way to make the case for their authenticity was to avoid substitutes at all costs. "The recipes given out to patrons bear no resemblance to what and how they actually prepare the food," Morrison noted as a selling point for the book. "Even the owners don't know the real recipes or how it is prepared."[19] In short, the book's greatest asset was its rare and inside look into the chef's kitchen.

For every entry, Morrison made the edits or added notes she thought were necessary to make the recipes as user-friendly as possible. She also worked with the copyediting team to standardize the typing. All measurements were to be spelled out and used uniformly in a recipe (tablespoons should not be *tbsps.*, and wet and dry measurements should all be in the same units instead of wet *cups* and dry *pounds*). Every recipe was to include approximate serving sizes. Ingredients needed to be listed in order of preparation. And every recipe that required baking should prompt the reader to prepare the pan and oven first in the instructions. Small details for tricky recipes also needed to be included. Morrison was not convinced the chocolate almond bars would hold together, so she cautioned them to test the recipe. And it would be important to add a note to the fruit and nut bars recipe. To have them hold together, they needed to cool before they were iced and then served. With this project, she was more than an editor. She was an editor who also knew her way around the kitchen.

When she advised the copyedit and design team, Morrison noted that the various types of speech (informal and formal) in the chefs' narratives should be maintained. The same was true for the word choices that gave the recipes that distinct New Orleans flavor. They should maintain the word *rib* and not replace it with *stalk*; they should keep *paw* instead of *whole garlic tuber* and *green onions* instead of *scallions*, she noted. Part 2 of the book, which contained the recipes, should have four major type elements, which she identified on a sample recipe. The type elements could be different as long as they were open and stylish: "but not too cute to read easily."[20] Since all the chefs' photos were black and white, the artwork would need to be highly creative, reflective of the flavor of New Orleans but without relying heavily on the clichés of the city.

In September, Morrison sent Lombard copies of the interior design for the book (which at this point they were calling *14 Master Chefs of New Orleans*). It was shaping up nicely, Morrison commented. But the final work on the recipes still needed attention. She had done as much as she could in previous drafts, but it was not enough.

> We have decided that the work that still has to be done on the recipes—setting them up in fastidious detail—cannot be done in the house. It is, of course, the authors' responsibility to do all of that. . . . I thought I could still get it done with Pat's and the copy editor's help but the fact is, it needs a professional's touch who has the time and expertise to execute it.
>
> Rather than have it redone by you, and rather than have you traipse back and forth to the chefs—all of which will delay the book until another season—we will hire someone to do the work.[21]

A freelancer could do it well and quickly, and they would charge the expense to the royalty account. Morrison was right that a freelancer was the best option if the book was to stay on its revised publication schedule. Lombard and the chefs were all preoccupied with preparations for the two-day event they dubbed "Creole Feast." It included food tastings, cooking demonstrations, and traditional jazz performances. The event concluded with a banquet honoring Burton and hosted by *Roots* author Alex Haley and actress Denise Nicholas. Following the October celebration, which was highly successful in every way, Morrison and Lombard began to refer to the cookbook by the same title as the event: *Creole Feast*.

Morrison readied the editorial fact sheet, which announced *Creole Feast: 15 Master Chefs of New Orleans Reveal Their Secrets* as the first cookbook created "by the chefs who actually cook the food in the famous New Orleans restaurants."[22] The marketing strategy relied on promoting the authenticity of the recipes.

If you have ever fallen in love with a dish, asked for the chef's recipe and, after following it scrupulously, had it turn out differently or fail entirely, it's probably because the cook didn't write the recipe in the first place—the owner did; or because 1 or 2 subtle but crucial ingredients were omitted; or because the "house" recipe has been altered a dozen times by the cooks themselves. *Creole Feast* solves that problem.

In addition to recipes of favorite dishes at New Orleans's best restaurants, the book promised to reveal the secrets of the chefs' cooking methods. By reading their narratives, you could learn all kinds of tricks of the trade—how to keep biscuits fresh and soft longer, how to clear stock without straining it, or how to tell when fried chicken is done, the hardest task of all. Some dishes had different recipes—there were four different hollandaise sauces by four different chefs. The takeaway, in short, was *Creole Feast* "outdistance[d] all previous creole cookbooks in every way."

The book was finally published at the end of September 1978, in good time for Christmas sales, a year later than planned. The publicity team got an unexpected boost when the liquor brand Hiram Walker invited a few of the chefs to create a recipe using a praline liqueur Hiram Walker was launching. Morrison alerted Carol Schneider of this opportunity to promote the book in January. "Their plans are to bring three or four chefs to New York February 14 and have them cook for fifty to seventy-five food editors at a New York restaurant," Morrison wrote. "I think we should try to get as much additional media exposure as possible for the book. Of course, this is Hiram Walker's own promotion activity but it will be of great help for pushing the book."[23] Of the four chefs who "brought a taste of Mardi Gras to New York City," three were included in the cookbook. They prepared Creole staples to 125 guests at the Tower Suite in the Time-Life Building. In addition to the original entrées and desserts the chefs created to feature the new praline liqueur, some of the dishes on the buffet had recipes in *Creole Feast*.

Creole Feast sold well quickly (sixteen thousand copies) and went into its second printing in less than a year. Morrison's hands-on approach to the project paid off. Notably, that kind of active engagement continued after the book was published. In April 1979, she made a special request to accounting to authorize the early payment of author royalties, which were not due until August. When the request was met with hesitancy—"Our policy is to hold on until the last possible minute," she was told—she pressed the case.

> I understand the reluctance to do this sort of thing, but I think this is a case where an exception is warranted.
>
> The author of *Creole Feast* organized major Black chefs in New Orleans into the first real and only corporation. . . .
>
> Their organization is alive but barely. They need funds

immediately to operate and keep the whole structure from falling apart. This money (due in August) could save the life of the organization and August will be way too late.[24]

She prevailed and happily sent the check for $7,838.92 along with the royalty statement to Lombard in mid-May.

For Morrison, publishing *Creole Feast* was a labor of love. Like *The Black Book*, *Railroad: Trains and Train People in American Culture*, and *The Cotton Club*, *Creole Feast* celebrated a hallmark of Black culture—in this instance, the culinary arts—and codified traditions on the one hand and venerated those whose extemporaneous work kept them alive on the other. As much as the books focused on a communal impulse, they also relied on their authors' specific expertise to create them uniquely. Morrison's gift as their editor was to ensure that the books reflected the best of the traditions and experiences they tried to capture. The books also reflected her broader philosophical stance on the importance of storytelling in understanding the past. The scrapbook was a genre that could articulate the intricacies of Black experiences. Disparate elements could coexist and converse, mirroring the multifaceted nature of history itself. Through her editorial choices, Morrison emphasized that history is a living, breathing entity shaped by the stories we tell and how we tell them. Publishing these books helped brandish her reputation as a culture worker whose productivity as an editor could be rivaled only by her rising prominence as an important writer.

CHAPTER 16

Daring to the End

W hen *Song of Solomon* was published with critical acclaim in 1977, Morrison declared to herself and to
anyone who would listen that if the book proved to
be more than a literary success—meaning a financial one—she
might finally get the nerve to stop working full-time as an editor
and give her best hours in the day to her writing instead. She had
been working in some job or another since she was twelve years
old, after all. She wanted to stop stealing time to write. If she kept
this pace, it would be years before she would have enough time to
complete her next novel. "I want to stop writing around the edges
of the day . . . in the automobile and places like that," she joked,
during the 1978 interview "A Day with Toni Morrison," but with
no less candor. "I want to sit down in the middle of the day and
spend five hours at it and not feel guilty that I've taken some time
away from a full-time job." She would get to that point, eventually, but not without adding more books to the already long list of
important books she edited first.

Now that she was coming into the office only one day a week,

Morrison was highly selective about the books she published. She continued to work with authors she had recruited to her list and who had pending books under contract (including her work on Bambara's first novel, *The Salt Eaters*, and Forrest's third, *Two Wings to Veil My Face*), but there was no denying her time as an editor was winding down. When she made an exception to work with an author not already on her list, it was usually because the book would not demand too much of her time. In 1979, she published Michael Raeburn's *Black Fire!*, a book that had been recently published in London by Julian Friedmann Publishers. And in 1983, she published William Hinton's *Shenfan: The Continuing Revolution in a Chinese Village*, which chronicled the lives of Chinese peasants after the collectivization of 1948.

James Baldwin had been instrumental in getting her to publish *We Are Everywhere*—he also wrote the introduction to the US edition. And Jean Pohoryles had handed Morrison *Shenfan* before Pohoryles left Random House. It would be Helen Knopf who would coax Morrison into working with Leonard Ray Teel on Erma Calderon's *Erma: A Black Woman Remembers* (1981) at the same time Morrison was drafting her fourth novel, *Tar Baby*, and Gayl Jones, though indirectly, who had a hand in Morrison's decision to edit Nettie Jones's *Fish Tales*. Each book, though vastly different in content and genre, reflected a perfect blend of experience and innovation. Even as she worked on them part-time while balancing the demands of her career as a writer, she offered the books the same meticulous attention to detail and passion for storytelling that defined all the years of her editorship.

As time at Random House came to an end, it was evident to all—colleagues, collaborators, and readers alike—that Morrison's editorship had been something truly remarkable. What began almost serendipitously evolved over the years into something far more profound. Her role as editor was not just a matter of overseeing content—it was about creating a space where creativity could be nurtured and flourish when an author showed genuine interest in that kind of collaboration. She also benefited greatly from a spirit of cooperation she helped cultivate at Random House. Though she never shied away from challenges to her editorial authority, she also went to great lengths to nurture talent among her peers and to create a space where designers and layout specialists, copy editors and proofreaders, and marketing and publicity professionals could work together as equals. Every decision was infused with purpose—one that valued substance and depth over all else.

In an industry marked more and more by commercial pressures as the years progressed, Morrison's editorship was marked by an aesthetic authenticity. Her time at the firm coincided with a time of shifting cultural, political, and technological changes, and she was keenly attuned to these forces. She understood that the role of an editor was not simply to curate content, but to reflect and sometimes challenge the world around them. So many of the publications she brought into print became a mirror to the era—capturing the nuances of its complexities and responding to its demands. Still, her approach to content was both timely and timeless. She pushed boundaries by embracing emerging voices, upending widely held "truths," and reflecting the pulse of the moment with as much depth and integrity as her authors would allow. She set new standards for what good editorial practice could achieve. Through the books she published and the editorial vision she crafted for herself, Morrison left for us a legacy we are only now beginning to understand fully, a legacy that will be felt long after the final page is turned.

Titles Edited by Toni Morrison

Contemporary African Literature (1972)

The People's Handbook of Medical Care (1972)

To Die for the People (1972)

Gorilla, My Love (1972)

The Case for Black Reparations (1973)

Cultural Relativism: Perspectives in Cultural Pluralism (1973)

There Is a Tree More Ancient Than Eden (1973)

Grow or Die: The Unifying Principle of Transformation (1973)

Some Sweet Day (1974)

From Memphis & Peking (1974)

An Ordinary Woman (1974)

Ark of Bones (1974)

Play Ebony, Play Ivory (1974)

Look What They Done to My Song (1974)

Breakfast in the Ruins (1974)

Sexist Justice (1974)

The Lesbian Myth (1974)

The Black Book (1974)

Angela Davis: An Autobiography (1974)

Corregidora (1975)

Giant Talk (1975)

The Greatest (1975)

Bill Cosby's Personal Guide to Tennis Power (1975)

The West and the Rest of Us (1975)

Generations (1976)

Jonoah and the Green Stone (1976)

Eva's Man (1976)

America's Working Women (1976)

Everywoman (1976)

Making It from 40 to 50 (1976)

Railroad: Trains and Train People in American Culture (1976)

They Came Before Columbus (1976)

The Cotton Club (1977)

The Seabirds Are Still Alive (1977)

The Bloodworth Orphans (1977)

White Rat (1977)

Things That I Do in the Dark (1977)

Creole Feast (1978)

Tragic Magic (1978)

We Are Everywhere (1979)

Rope of Wind (1979)

The Salt Eaters (1980)

Erma (1981)

Women, Race, and Class (1981)

Shenfan (1983)

Fish Tales (1984)

Two Wings to Veil My Face (1984)

Acknowledgments

L ong before *Toni at Random* had a name, "I was living with it and imagining its reality."[1] I began thinking about this project in 1997 while in a graduate seminar with Eleanor W. Traylor at Howard University. The course examined the fiction of four of the writers Toni Morrison edited at Random House Publishing Company—Toni Cade Bambara, Henry Dumas, Gayl Jones, and Leon Forrest. While in that seminar, I had begun to contemplate my dissertation topic. I suggested that I had been thinking seriously about examining Morrison's editorship with a focus on these writers for the dissertation, and Eleanor (whom I call Dr. T. out of respect) said to me, almost flippantly, something like, "Miss Thang: You're good, but you're not that good. A project like that will take you years. Pick an author and get on with it." Young and foolish, I plotted ahead contrarily with confidence. Realizing a swift and utter conceptual defeat two months later, I quietly decided on Bambara and resolved that I would save the editorship project for the post-dissertation book. I proclaimed my decision to my would-be advisor. Her eyes said, "Maybe you're not as bright as I thought you were." Her words were something like, "Do the dissertation on Forrest and then the book on Forrest and save the book on the editorship until after tenure." We debated, as much as you can debate with a dissertation advisor who also happens to be Eleanor Traylor.

There is no way to describe her, really. But her import to this project cannot be understated. Neither this book nor these acknowledgments are about either of us, except both are. The very seminar out of which this project was birthed was a function, quite literally, of her friendship with Toni Morrison. They taught together at Howard, where they became fast friends and each other's interlocutors. Their closeness sustained every test of time, so much so that she gave one of only two eulogies at the private family memorial for Morrison—the other was by Angela Davis. Toni Cade Bambara captured the bounty of Dr. T.'s intellect many times over but most strikingly in a letter to Morrison after she had published Bambara's first novel.

> Read Miz Ella Noir's review of *Salt*. Good God. . . . That woman is dangerous. Do you know what will happen when she . . . starts publishing articles more regularly? EVERYbody who ever thought they knew a damn thing about literature will shut the fuck up, which of course will be delightful in many ways.[2]

I belabor the point of Miz Ella Noir, Eleanor, Dr. T.'s brilliance here for two reasons—I owe most of the success that may emerge from this book to her commitment to Black literary and cultural traditions as a master teacher who was generous enough to pass on to me a project that she was far better equipped to complete than I was. She chose to transform culture with teaching and public-facing acts instead of writing books at the speed of her mind. Her collected essays, which I hope will be published soon, make clear that Bambara was right. I have no delusions about the role Dr. T.

played in getting me access to Morrison for the interviews and informal exchanges that helped shape the breadth and depth of this book. Learning from and thinking with her over the past twenty-five or so years has been the singularly most impactful experience in my life as an African American literature scholar. She's a light for me in more ways than one.

The first time I mentioned the project to Morrison was at the 2005 Leon Forrest Lecture at Northwestern University. My book on Forrest had just come out, and she had been thinking a lot about Forrest in preparation for her talk. As one of too few scholars who had written about Forrest extensively, I was confident I could hold my own in the conversation. The "lean" book on Forrest was done, I told Morrison. My plan now was to shift my attention to the project on her work as editor at Random House. She offered enough immediate encouragement that I decided after that exchange that I needed finally to commit to this book—the sooner the better. Fast-forward a few months, and I found myself on the train from DC to Princeton, anxiously rehearsing the questions I carefully crafted for what was to be our first interview about her editorship. I arrived early at her office on Nassau Street for the meeting, which was scheduled at 3 p.m. and was to last for one hour.

I had my plan mapped out. I knew how much time I wanted to spend on each question. I knew that Bambara, Dumas, Forrest, and Jones were not the only writers whose books Morrison edited. But now a converted pragmatist, I decided to focus exclusively on her work editing fiction by Black authors. That narrowed my list significantly. In a coda of sorts, maybe I would talk about some of the other literature she had edited—poetry by June Jordan, Lucille Clifton, and Barbara Chase-Riboud and the literature anthology by Quincy Troupe and Rainer Schulte. I had a plan.

Almost two hours later, Morrison was still talking freely, and I was too into the stories about her editing nonfiction writers to be completely dismayed by the fact that her most revealing comments were about her work with Muhammad Ali, Angela Davis, Bill Cosby, and Huey P. Newton and her role in publishing *Contemporary African Literature* and *The Black Book*. What she had shared about the literary writers was abbreviated comparatively. Commentary about each author came with distinct expressions, complimented by hand gestures and effusive body language. It was so clear that she was proud of the work she had done. She reveled in the opportunity to remember those days. Maybe it was the look on my face—a mix of interest and concern—that prompted her to say that we could talk more about the other authors another time. Unsure of how that would happen exactly and ever mindful to not be presumptuous or to impose on others' hospitality, I thanked her for her time and prepared to leave. As I gathered my things, she remarked that she was glad I was writing a book on the editorship. "That was hard, important work that no one really talks about," she noted. She also said she would help in any way she could. That continued to be true over the years. We committed to talking again soon.

In our next interview, we talked about editing in broad strokes instead of with the specificity I needed. Bambara's narrative strategy was cinematic scenes, moving from object to object. Forrest's was spiral. What they had in common was an attempt to do something with time. We went from long stories to one-word answers. Determined to get more of what I hoped for, I asked, "What did you see as your specific task as editor?" With Gayl Jones, she suggested, she would have to ask questions about characters every fifty to eighty pages. With Forrest, she would cross out whole lines at a time because he was so verbose, or note words that appeared too often, and figure out how to keep the song but release some of the words. Editing Bambara was different from editing all the other writers. "Her lines were so tight, you couldn't get in and move them. But you didn't need to. She self-edited; she'd have lines drawn all over the paper." Morrison laughed heartily. "All you had to do with her was copyedit—make sure things matched up and fill in abbreviations, acronyms, and her shortcuts."

In that moment, I learned what I began to call the magic of "the other Toni." We had talked before about her shared name with Bambara and the way Bambara's mother cleverly referred to them both as "the other Toni" depending on the occasion. Whenever she talked about "the other Toni," Morrison's mood lightened. Their friendship was so splendid and Bambara so enjoyable that, for me, she became a waymaker, a path to openness. The pump now primed, I asked Morrison to talk about the difference in editing fiction and nonfiction. With fiction, she explained, she could help the writer play with his or her vision. But with nonfiction, the author would have an idea, and the most she would have to do was help clarify it. Other times, she would make sure the arguments were fulfilled and sustained and that the footnotes were accurate and appropriate. There was no one way to edit; good editors did what the writer or the text demanded.

By our next conversation, my focus sharpened but widened. I had imagined the book as being about the writers and the fiction and Morrison's editing of them. That I could do fairly quickly. That, however, was not what Morrison had in mind. Like a good teacher, she refused to say it outright and waited for me to realize what this book would have to be—a book about the authors and the books, yes, but more importantly, a book about the visible and invisible work of an editor. This could be no run-of-the-mill academic book. It would need to explore and explain, make connections and inferences, and show and tell. A few months after Paula Giddings's *Ida: A Sword Among Lions* (2008) was released, Morrison asked if I had seen the book. I assured her that I had. "Now that's a book," she replied. Well-researched, sweeping narrative, vivid telling, 832 pages—point made, no pressure.

Many years later, *Toni at Random* is finally what Morrison suggested implicitly in our earliest conversations it would be—a book that examines the full editorship, from her earliest days at L. W. Singer, when she edited textbooks, to her final days at Random House, where she remained senior editor until she left the company permanently to pursue her own writing full-time. While her influence on the depth of this book was indirect, her guidance on the title was explicit. We were at one of Dr. T.'s famous New Year's Day salons when Morrison asked about my progress on the book. "It's coming along but slowly," I said honestly. I did not bother to explain how many demands there were on my time and how debilitating those demands could be. I looked for a bright side. Recalling a previous conversation we had about titles—how hard and important it is to get them right—I did have that one achievement to brag about. The title would be *The House That Toni Built at Random*, I proudly declared. She nodded satisfyingly then said, "Smart but too long." After a pause, she said, "*Toni at Random*." She repeated it; then I said it; then we repeated it, turning it over in our minds while saying it aloud to see if it fit. It did. I owe more than a thanks to this ancestor—*dọbalẹ*.

Writing can be, all at once, a fulfilling and a lonesome process. But in key moments and in important ways, dozens of people can step in and make it better. There are many such moments and people without whom writing this book would have been impossible to complete. Howard is one big briar patch. What good fortune it was for me to land there as a student and then, some years later, to return as a faculty member. The late Cheryl Wall was the first person I ever heard talk at length about Toni Morrison's editorship. She was Howard, too, of course. I am indebted to her scholarship and so fortunate to have known her as a scholar. I hope she is pleased with the work I have done here. I am fortunate enough to have "grown up" as a faculty member at Howard with some wonderful people. My Howard colleagues give me life. I owe a debt of gratitude to the members of the first reading group I was in at Howard—Terri Adams, Greg Carr, Kenyatta Gilbert, Greg Hampton, Jules Harrell, and Dawn Williams. Greg Carr and I had the great pleasure of coleading the Freshman Seminar in Arts and Sciences for more than ten years. His influence and the influence of those we convened in that intellectual space on my thinking and my approach to this book cannot be overstated. *Medaase*, my friend.

My extended Howard family is deep: I am grateful for my colleagues who serve on the dean's council and for our provost for all their support and collegiality. Jennifer A. Jordan, David Green, Shauna Morgan, Jennifer Williams, Tricia Elam, Kenton Rambsy, Tony Medina, Carole Boyce Davies, Kyr Mack, Barbra Chin, Trevon Pegram, Kendra Parker, Tanya Hardy, Sandra Shannon, Constance Ellison, Linda Jones, Miriam Okine Davies, Darlene Taylor, Bernard Richardson, Ron Hopson, Eric Walters, Mario Beatty, Valethia Watkins, Amy Yeboah Quarkume, Nikkole Salters, Khalid Long, Ben Talton, Mike Ralph, and Joshua Myers make me proud to be on the faculty at Howard. Many people read parts of this book in draft and gave me critical feedback. Josh is one of two people who read every word. Janis

Mayes is the other. Thank you both for the time you spent laboring over every sentence.

The only time I have worked on this book full-time is the year I had an HBCU fellowship at Duke University's John Hope Franklin Humanities Institute (FHI), planfully, the year before I became chair of English. I laugh aloud now at my naivety in thinking I could out-write administrative work. I enjoyed my time at Duke as an inaugural FHI fellow along with Fatimah Tuggar and Jelani Favors. They were good sounding boards, so I thank them and the FHI team that surrounded us, including the late Srinivas Aravamudan. I later had an NEH HBCU faculty fellowship to work on the book in summers. That made a big difference.

Remarkably, I have been doing this work now long enough to be able to call the scholars whose work I admired before I joined the professoriate friends. Maryemma Graham, Paula Giddings, Deborah McDowell, Karla FC Holloway, Farah Jasmine Griffin, Mary Helen Washington, and Angelyn Mitchell are giants in my eyes still, and I am grateful for their embrace. Paula and Farah, along with Tayari Jones, were among the first readers of the book after its first editorial review. They boosted my confidence at that crucial moment when the book was done but I was not convinced it was done, done. Soyica Diggs Colbert, Robert Patterson, Zandria Robinson, and the reading groups Robert and Soyica convened at Georgetown kept me honest and on task.

I am so grateful that every author Morrison edited I contacted said yes to my request for an interview. Quincy Troupe (my #GramFam) and his wife, Margaret, invited me to their home one Saturday afternoon for some wonderful Senegalese food and even more wonderful conversation. Angela Davis, Barbara Chase-Riboud, Gina Luria Walker and Virgina Tiger, Arthur Frank, and John McCluskey were gracious with their time and memories of working with Morrison as their editor. I had the good fortune of multiple background conversations with Charles Harris and Marie Brown, both editors who were Morrison's contemporaries. They deserve their own stories I hope someone will write soon. And Rene Boatman has supported this project every step of the way. I appreciate every person in the village.

The College Language Association is the single most important professional organization there is for scholars of color who teach languages and literature. My CLA family is large, but a few people stand out even among family. Warren Carson, Donna Akiba Harper, Geneva Baxter, Yakini Kemp, Reginald Bess, Elizabeth West, Tara Green, Thabiti Lewis, Tony Bolden, Carol Henderson, Jervette Ward, James Davis, Antonio Tillis, Trudier Harris, Sandra Govan, Joanne Gabbin, and Daryl Cumber Dance make every annual conference and the time in between a delight. I presented part of this research there over the years, and it's better because of it.

During my year as president of MLA, this project regularly competed with my duties as an officer. I appreciate the council, Paula Krebs, and the MLA senior staff, for their patience and unwavering encouragement.

At a crucial moment in the life of this book, Adam J. Banks redirected my anxiety and talked me through the mental blocks that accompany being a department chair and interim dean and then a dean who also wants to be a serious scholar. Our running joke was "Everybody can't be Larry Jackson," meaning we cannot all write big, good books early or mid-career. But everybody should try. That said, I must thank Lawrence P. Jackson (the Larry we can't all be), too, for being a model and inspiration. John Valery White, who helped me get through the LSU years with his abiding friendship, came through for me again in the clutch with a careful close read of the first half of the book that sharpened it in important ways. You deserve an editor's credit, my friend.

Because this book was more than ten years in the making, it had the benefit of many research assistants, many of whom have gone on to earn PhDs. Melanie Chambliss, Rosa Ponton, Stacey Cohen, Corey Lamont, Tiffany Walker, Dawn Henderson, Thomas Addington, Aja Kennedy, and Cecily Duffie worked on this book over the years. Their foundational work on all things tangential made the book better. Similarly, a few seminars I taught helped clarify what I was trying to do. Thanks are due to these students: Khaliah Peterson-Reed, Jasmine Wilson, Alexis Boyd, Dominique James, Sheena Garrant Mason, Dawn Henderson, Aja Kennedy, Thomas Addington, Adonis Williams, Joe Heidenescher, Alexis Harper, Jimisha Relerfod, Jordan Lindsey, Bryan Jenkins, Cecily Duffie, Carmen Crusoe, Forrest Yerman, Christin Smith, Brenton Brock, and Catherine Saunders.

My sincere thanks to Judith Curr and the teams at HarperCollins/ Amistad for their expertise and dedication to this book.

The project had more editors than is normal for an author— Tracy Sherrod acquired the book for Amistad, Jen Baker and Daniella Wexler worked on it for a short time, and Abby West brought it home. In a full-circle moment, I was guided wonderfully by editorial assistant Makayla Tabron, a Howard English alum whom I recommended for a position at Amistad when I learned she was interested in publishing. I can't say enough about how gentle and deliberate Abby and Makayla have been. When I was still a little uncertain about how well I could make the turn from academic to trade writing, Abby assured me that a paper she heard me give at the fiftieth anniversary of the Phyllis Wheatley Poetry Conference at Jackson State University was proof that I could write a trade book. That reassurance and the fact that she made time to come to the conference and to the panel for our first in-person meeting let me know she was the real deal. Johanna Castillo at Writers House was completely invested in helping me navigate this project from the first time she heard about it. I am grateful that she believed in its potential until the end. I consider the Toni Morrison Society a familial scholarly home. I appreciate TMS founder Carolyn Denard and her commitment to only the highest hills of excellence more than she can ever know.

Nothing replaces being ably guided early on in a huge archive. At Howard, Joellen El-Bashir was a godsend. Richard Jenkins, Amber Junipher, Ishmael Childs, Sonja Woods, Clifford Muse, and Tewodros Abebe were helpful in important ways. At Columbia, Tara Craig was supportive without fail. Texas State University librarians Katie Salzmann and Stevie Davis sent me everything the library had on Toni Morrison's correspondence with Bryan Woolley when the COVID-19 pandemic made travel impossible. At Spelman, Holly Smith and Kassandra Ware guided me through the Toni Cade Bambara papers, which is one of the best collections an African American literature scholar could dream of.

Friends and family have sustained me: Ruth R. Jackson, Sonya Sims, Shively Smith, Satira Corbitt, Sidra Smith, Bryon Garner, Shawnee Callier, Robert Reed, Adeyinka Pierce, William Watkins, Derek Hicks, Obbie Franklin, Jon and Michelle Robinson, Daniel Black, Sam Livingston, Nathaniel Norment, Shalonda Turner Simoneaux, Edwidge Danticat, Catherine Adams, Lakshmi Krishnan, Jamila Minnicks, Bettina Williams, Johnny Cleckley, John and Linda Newson, Kim Walk, and Evetta and Michael Spencer. You know what you did. To every Walk and Williams I've ever known, I hope I've made you proud.

Academics are not always lucky enough to have life partners who read. I hit the jackpot. William H. Lamar IV is an incredibly gifted storyteller and a remarkable wordsmith. He not only endured the sacrifices of time away from us I spent on this book; he helped me understand how best to frame the telling. I am grateful for his love and laughter and for the family we now share, William and Eartha Lamar, Marty Lamar, and Calvin, Kerri, Caleb, and Karys Anderson.

In 2014, my father succumbed to colon cancer after a stage IV diagnosis in 2011. I loved him as much as I loved any human. I have said it often, and I meant it every time: When he died, "part of my soul went with him." Then, in 2017, two short months after a bone marrow cancer diagnosis, my mother became an ancestor. She was/is the center of my universe. I am still finding my way in the world without her physical presence. Every day I remind myself how fortunate I am to have had such wonderful parents, and those parents gave me my sisters, who, along with their families, are my joys. Gia Williams, Jann Williams-Buchanan, Charlie Buchanan, Tommi Caston, Marvin Caston, and Thomas and William Caston: I hope everyone is lucky enough to know love like ours.

Notes

CHAPTER 1: "WE'RE ALL WE GOT"

1. The video is from the publishing panel of the 1976 Institute for the Arts and Humanities Second National Conference of Afro-American Writers at Howard University held April 22–24, 1976. The conference theme was "Beyond Survival: 200 Years of Black Literature, 1776–1976." It is a part of an unprocessed collection at Moorland-Spingarn Research Center at Howard University in Washington, DC. Digitizing the proceedings from the conference was made possible through an NEH HBCU grant.

CHAPTER 2: FINDING HER FORM

1. The narrator has this to say about the character Sula in the novel of the same name: "Had she paints, or clay, or knew the discipline of the dance, or strings, had she anything to engage her tremendous curiosity and her gift of metaphor, she might have exchanged the restlessness and preoccupation with whim for activity that provided her with all she yearned for."

CHAPTER 3: THERE NEEDS TO BE A RECORD

1. *Toni Morrison: The Pieces I Am* (00:42:06–00:43:19) cites the ad as appearing in the January 14, 1965, issue of *The New York Review of Books*.

2. Singer had been founded in 1924 by Leland W. Singer. In time, it became one of the top publishers of elementary to high school textbooks in the United States. After Leland Singer's death in 1944, his wife,

Frances, took over the company and managed it until 1960, when she sold it for 150,000 shares of Random House stock.

3. *Toni Morrison: The Pieces I Am*, 00:50:29–00:50:51.

CHAPTER 4: ESCAPING THE CHRYSALIS

1. UW News press release from the University of Wisconsin News and Publications Service, dated January 29, 1969. The course offering was also covered in an article titled "New Class on Black Culture" in *Capital Times* on January 31, 1969, p. 29, and again on February 3, in an article titled "UW Tries Different Ideas for Blacks," p. 4. Retrieved from the university archives by Mackenzie Ryan, assistant university records officer and compliance specialist.

2. Susan McHenry, "Lady Laureate: Meet the Great Toni Morrison in an Exclusive BIBR Kitchen-Table Chat," *Black Issues Book Review* (November 1, 2003). Morrison reiterated this point to me in one of our interviews where she pulled the book from her shelf to show me with great pride the first book she published as the acquiring editor. She also makes the point about the gaze and the assumed white reader in interviews and in *The Pieces I Am*.

3. Lacy wrote of this experience in *The Rise and Fall of a Proper Negro: An Autobiography*. Like Angelou's *All God's Children Need Traveling Shoes*, which Random House published, Lacy's autobiography celebrated Ghana as the Pan-African home that allowed Black expatriates to find and express a liberated Black self.

4. Interoffice memo, dated February 17, 1971. Unless otherwise specified, all interoffice memos and letters are from the Random House Collection in the Rare Book and Manuscript Library at Columbia University.

5. Interoffice memo, dated February 17, 1971.

6. Edris Makward and Leslie Lacy, eds., *Contemporary African Literature* (Random House, 1972), 1.

7. Makward and Lacy, eds., *Contemporary African Literature*, 4.

8. Books published by members of the so-called "radical left" had consistently sustained the interest of the reading public. John Simon is cited as editor for *Stokely Speaks* on the initial contract, while Alice Mayhew was the editor listed on the October 30, 1970, editorial fact sheet. Morrison's involvement in the publication of *Stokely Speaks* was informal. Still, in *Ready for Revolution: The Life and Struggles of Stokely Carmichael (Kwame Ture)*, Carmichael (Ture) cited her as his editor for *Black Power* and *Stokely Speaks* (130). Simon was also the editor for *Black Power*,

which Random had published in 1967, while Hilary Maddux was the editor for George Jackson's *Blood in My Eye*.

9. Letter from John J. Simon to Raymond Procunier, dated December 3, 1968; letter from Raymond Procunier to John J. Simon, dated December 20, 1968.

10. Letter from David G. Lubell to James Silberman, dated October 5, 1971.

11. Interoffice memo from Toni Morrison to Jim Silberman, n.d.

12. Interoffice memo from Toni Morrison to Jim Silberman, n.d.

13. Editorial fact sheet for *To Die for the People*, n. d.

14. Letter from Toni Morrison to Huey P. Newton, dated May 23, 1972.

15. The third book was Arthur and Stuart Frank's *The People's Handbook of Medical Care*, published in 1972. The book shared with the public general medical knowledge and, more important, information subcultures needed to survive, including medical draft counseling and treatment plans for medical issues emerging from civil disobedience.

CHAPTER 5: TAKING FLIGHT

1. Kurt Newman, "Reparations Roundtable: On Boris Bittker's *The Case for Black Reparations*," US Intellectual History (blog), July 9, 2014, https://s-usih.org/2014/07/reparations-roundtable-on-boris-bittkers -the-case-for-Black-reparations.

2. Huggins and Seale were indicted, but the jury for their trial was deadlocked. Since there was no retrial, charges were dismissed.

3. Letter from Boris Bittker to Toni Morrison, dated September 25, 1972.

4. Letter from Toni Morrison to Boris Bittker, dated September 28, 1972.

5. Bittker, for example, was the first scholar to seriously "address the federal and state treatment of the 'third sector'—the terrain of philanthropy and nonprofit organizations. His eight articles in this field included a 1969 essay providing the first thoroughgoing defense of the exemption of churches from federal, state, and local taxation" (John G. Simon, "Let Us Count the Ways: A Tribute to Boris Bittker," *Yale Law Journal* 115 [2006]: 751–54).

6. Boris I. Bittker, *The Case for Black Reparations* (Random House, 1973), 7. It is worth noting that the body of legal scholarship, mainly published in law review journals, in the early 2000s, is heavily influenced by Bittker's work. Ta-Nehisi Coates's thinking builds on this body of

scholarship. In that sense, a fairly direct line can be drawn from Bittker's argument to Coates's.

7. Review of *The Case for Black Reparations*, *Kirkus Reviews* (January 15, 1973), 86; review of *The Case for Black Reparations*, *The New Yorker* (March 10, 1973), 135; review of *The Case for Black Reparations*, *Stanford Law Review* (June 1973), 927.

8. Letter from Frances Herskovits to Toni Morrison, dated October 29, 1971.

9. Letter from Sidney W. Mintz to Toni Morrison, dated December 15, 1971.

10. Letter from Toni Morrison to Frances Herskovits, dated February 25, 1972.

11. Letter from Frances Herskovits to Toni Morrison, dated March 3, 1972.

12. Letter from Toni Morrison to Frances Herskovits, dated February 25, 1972.

13. Letter from Toni Morrison to Donald Campbell, dated May 24, 1972.

14. Review of *Cultural Relativism: Perspectives in Cultural Pluralism*, *Choice* (June 1973), 690; Morris Forslund, "Review: *Cultural Relativism: Perspectives in Cultural Pluralism*," *Library Journal* (February 1973), 430; review of *Cultural Relativism: Perspectives in Cultural Pluralism*, *Kirkus Reviews* (December 1, 1972), 1388.

15. Margaret Mead, "Review: *Cultural Relativism: Perspectives in Cultural Pluralism, by Melville J. Herskovits, Frances Herskovits*," *American Journal of Sociology* 79 (March 1974): 1326–30.

16. Letter from Toni Morrison to George Land, dated May 16, 1972.

17. Letter from Toni Morrison to George Land, dated June 1, 1972.

18. In addition to the books mentioned in this chapter and the previous one, Morrison also published *The People's Handbook of Medical Care* in 1972; a short story collection, *Gorilla, My Love*, by Toni Cade Bambara in 1972; and Leon Forrest's first novel, *There Is a Tree More Ancient Than Eden*, in 1973. I discuss these books and Morrison's extended work with Bambara and Forrest in later chapters.

CHAPTER 6: THE SIMPLEST LIFE IS A TRIUMPH: MAKING *THE BLACK BOOK*

1. *Toni Morrison: The Pieces I Am*, 1:00:35.

2. Toni Morrison, "Rediscovering Black History: It's Like Growing Up Black One More Time," *New York Times Magazine*, August 11, 1974.

3. Morrison, "Rediscovering Black History."

4. Letter from Toni Morrison to Bill Cosby, dated July 31, 1973. Morrison would go on to publish Bill Cosby's *Personal Guide to Tennis Power, Or, Don't Lower the Lob, Raise the Net* in 1975.

5. Contract proposal dated May 22, 1972.

6. Letter from Toni Morrison to Bill Cosby, dated July 31, 1973.

7. Letter from Toni Morrison to Bill Cosby, dated July 31, 1973.

8. Copy of radio spot scripts for *The Black Book* promotions.

9. Copy of template letter from Toni Morrison to recipients who received promotional copies of *The Black Book*.

10. Toni Morrison, "Behind the Making of *The Black Book*," *Black World* 23 (February 1974): 86–90.

11. Barbara Campbell, "New Book Bridges Gap in Black History," *New York Times*, March 5, 1974. The archived version of the article includes more details and, accordingly, is slightly longer than the print version.

12. Morrison, "Rediscovering Black History."

13. Interoffice memo, n.d. The *Big Event* series began in fall 1976, two years after *The Black Book*'s publication.

14. Morrison, "Rediscovering Black History."

15. Campbell, "New Book Bridges Gap."

CHAPTER 7: THE TWO TONIS

1. Linda Janet Holmes, *A Joyous Revolt: Toni Cade Bambara, Writer and Activist* (Praeger, 2014), 49.

2. Linda Janet Holmes and Cheryl A. Wall, eds., *Savoring the Salt: The Legacy of Toni Cade Bambara* (Temple University Press, 2008), 89.

3. Thabiti Lewis, ed., *Conversations with Toni Cade Bambara* (University Press of Mississippi, 2012), 9–10.

4. Lewis, *Conversations*, 128.

5. Lewis, *Conversations*, 128.

6. Editorial fact sheet for *Gorilla, My Love*, dated April 17, 1972.

7. Boyd, *Savoring*, 90.

8. Letter from Lucille Clifton to Toni Morrison, dated June 6, 1972.

9. C. D. B. Bryan, "The Best American Short Stories of 1972," *New York Times*, October 15, 1972, BR31.

10. Anatole Broyard, "2 Writers Revolutions Apart," *New York Times*, October 11, 1972, 41.

11. Editorial fact sheet for *The Sea Birds Are Still Alive*, which they were calling *The Organizer's Wife and Other Stories* at the time, dated September 7, 1976.

12. Lewis, *Conversations*, 59.

13. Lewis, *Conversations*, 131.

14. Jacqueline Trescott, "Black Writers in the '70s," *Washington Post*, May 6, 1977, D1, D5; Jessica Harris, review of *The Sea Birds Are Still Alive*, *Essence*, June 1977, 31; Bruce Allen, "Bambara's 'Straight-up Fiction,'" *Chicago Tribune*, March 27, 1977; Mary Helen Washington, "Blues Women of the Seventies," *Ms.*, July 1977, 36, 38; *Booklist*, March 1977, 90.

15. Ruby Dee, "Review: *The Sea Birds Are Still Alive*," *Freedomways* (Summer 1977): 102–4.

16. Barbara Mahone, "A Handsome Family Quilt," *First World* (May/June 1977): 40–42; Margo Jefferson, "Blue Notes," *Newsweek*, May 2, 1977, 76; Robie Macauley, "New Feminine Talents, New Feminine Concerns," *New York Times*, March 27, 1977, 267.

17. Letter from Toni Cade Bambara to Toni Morrison, n.d.

18. Lewis, *Conversations*, 65.

19. Letter from Toni Cade Bambara to Toni Morrison, dated September 16. No year is noted but the letter responds to a letter from Morrison to Bambara dated September 8, 1977.

20. Holmes and Wall, *Savoring the Salt*, 90.

21. Holmes and Wall, *Savoring the Salt*, 90.

22. Editorial fact sheet for *The Salt Eaters*, dated March 15, 1979.

23. Interoffice memo from Toni Morrison to Tony Wimpfheimer, dated March 17, 1979.

24. Interoffice memo from Toni Morrison to the design and copyediting department, dated July 30, 1979.

25. Letter from Toni Morrison to Toni Cade Bambara, dated May 31, 1979.

26. Untitled, undated letter. A handwritten note indicates "11/15," which we can presume refers to November 15. The typed first line on the page reads "Note: For Review Copies Only."

27. Letter from Toni Morrison to Michael Dirda, dated December 3, 1979.

28. Letter from Toni Cade Bambara to Stephanie Dowrick, dated March 23, 1981.

29. Lewis, *Conversations*, 56.

30. Lewis, *Conversations*, 79.

31. Letter from Toni Cade Bambara to Toni Morrison, n.d.

32. Lewis, *Conversations*, 133.

33. Holmes and Wall, *Savoring the Salt*, 92.

34. Holmes and Wall, *Savoring the Salt*, 93.

35. Toni Cade Bambara, *Deep Sightings and Rescue Missions* (Knopf, 1999), viii (preface).

36. At the time, Bambara did not have an agent. So Morrison essentially acted as editor and agent for her friend. Morrison would later help Bambara secure Joan Daves as her agent.

37. Letter from Toni Cade Bambara to Toni Morrison, n.d.

38. Holmes and Wall, *Savoring the Salt*, 91.

CHAPTER 8: LEON FORREST AND THE COLLECTIVE COMPLEXITY OF BLACKNESS

1. "Ezekiel, Notes Towards a Suicide; Poem" appeared in the June 1966 issue of *Negro Digest*. *Theatre of the Soul* was produced at Parkway Community House in November 1967.

2. Letter from Leon Forrest to Toni Morrison, n.d., presumably in late 1970. Morrison recalled meeting Forrest shortly after she had published *The Bluest Eye* (personal interview with Toni Morrison, November 9, 2007).

3. Personal interview with Toni Morrison, September 21, 2005.

4. Letter from Toni Morrison to Leon Forrest, dated January 7, 1972.

5. Letter from Toni Morrison to Leon Forrest, dated July 21, 1972.

6. Personal interview with Toni Morrison, September 21, 2005.

7. Letter from Leon Forrest to Toni Morrison, n.d.

8. Letter from Leon Forrest to Toni Morrison, n.d.

9. Editorial fact sheet for *There Is a Tree More Ancient Than Eden*, dated November 6, 1972.

10. Letter from J. Saunders Redding to Toni Morrison, dated May 7, 1973.

11. The Troupe and Bambara quotes are included on an interoffice memo from Toni Morrison to Selma Shapiro, dated January 16, 1973.

12. Interoffice memo from Jim Silberman to Toni Morrison, dated February 20, 1973.

13. Review of *There Is a Tree More Ancient Than Eden*, *Publishers Weekly*, March 26, 1973, 68; review of *There Is a Tree More Ancient Than Eden*, *The New Leader*, July 9, 1973, 15; review of *There Is a Tree More Ancient Than Eden*, *Library Journal*, May 1973, 1599.

14. Anatole Broyard, "Everything's on My Mind," *New York Times*, June 8, 1973, 37.

15. "Two Views: *There Is a Tree More Ancient Than Eden*," *Black World*, January 1974, 66–70. The Baker review is simply styled as *I* and appears on pages 66–69; the Gilbert review is styled as *II* and appears on page 70.

16. Letter from Leon Forrest to Toni Morrison, n.d.

17. Letter from Toni Morrison to Leon Forrest, dated December 10, 1974.

18. Letter from Toni Morrison to Leon Forrest, dated February 10, 1975.

19. Letter from Toni Morrison to Leon Forrest, dated June 1, 1976.

20. Editorial fact sheet for *The Bloodworth Orphans*, dated October 22, 1976.

21. Letter from Leon Forrest to Toni Morrison, dated April 7, 1982.

22. Letter from Toni Morrison to Leon Forrest, dated December 13, 1982.

23. Letter from Toni Morrison to Leon Forrest, dated December 13, 1982.

24. Letter from Toni Morrison to Leon Forrest, dated June 13, 1983.

CHAPTER 9: THE EXTRAORDINARINESS OF ORDINARY BLACK WOMANHOOD

1. Letter from Toni Morrison to Barbara Chase-Riboud, dated November 1, 1973. Morrison convinced the team to print five thousand copies instead of one thousand five hundred. As she feared, sales were low, and Random House had a tough time even getting bids on the remainders.

2. Personal interview with Barbara Chase-Riboud, July 10, 2020.

3. Editorial fact sheet for *From Memphis & Peking*, dated November 6, 1973.

4. Barbara Chase-Riboud, *From Memphis & Peking* (Random House, 1974), 63–64.

5. Letter from Barbara Chase-Riboud to Toni Morrison, dated November 8, 1973.

6. Letter from Toni Morrison to Barbara Chase-Riboud, dated November 15, 1973.

7. Letter from Barbara Chase-Riboud to Toni Morrison, n.d.

8. Letter from Toni Morrison to Barbara Chase-Riboud, dated December 4, 1973.

9. Letter from Barbara Chase-Riboud to Toni Morrison, dated October 10, 1973.

10. Letter from Toni Morrison to Barbara Chase-Riboud, dated October 16, 1973.

11. Letter from Toni Morrison to Barbara Chase-Riboud, dated October 16, 1973.

12. Letter from Barbara Chase-Riboud to Toni Morrison, n.d.

13. Handwritten letter from Toni Morrison to Barbara Chase-Riboud, n.d. I note here that no typed copy of the letter was in the file. Since all other letters were typed (without the handwritten copy preserved), I must note the possibility that the letter was not sent at all or was not sent as drafted.

14. Alvin Aubert, "Review of *From Memphis and Peking*," *Library Journal*, June 1974, 1716; review of *From Memphis & Peking*, *Kirkus Reviews*, March 15, 1974, 337; Angela Terrell, "Moving from Sculpture to Poetry, But 'Always in a Circular Motion,'" *Washington Post*, July 7, 1974, H1.

15. Letter from Toni Morrison to Barbara Chase-Riboud, dated December 12, 1974.

16. Letter from Toni Morrison to Barbara Chase-Riboud, dated December 12, 1974.

17. Chase-Riboud, *From Memphis & Peking*, 64, 66.

18. Letter from Toni Morrison to Barbara Chase-Riboud, dated December 12, 1974.

19. Personal interview with Toni Morrison, November 9, 2007. Morrison also notes this in the foreword to *The Collected Poems of Lucille Clifton 1965–2010* (BOA Editions, 2015).

20. Letter from Toni Morrison to Lucille Clifton, dated November 5, 1973.

21. Lucille Clifton, *Good Woman: Poems and a Memoir, 1969–1980* (BOA Editions, 1987), 141.

22. Letter from Toni Morrison to Lucille Clifton, dated November 5, 1973.

23. Letter from Lucille Clifton to Alice Mayhew, dated July 9, 1970.

24. Letter from Toni Morrison to Lucille Clifton, dated March 4, 1975.

25. Lucille Clifton, *Generations: A Memoir* (Random House, 1976),

29. Clifton spells her father's name as *Sayles* but spells her great-grandfather's name as *Sale*.

26. Clifton, *Generations*, 14.

27. Clifton, *Generations*, 33.

28. Clifton, *Generations*, 57.

29. Clifton, *Generations*, 22, 58.

30. Clifton, *Generations*, 79.

31. Interoffice memo from Toni Morrison, n.d.

32. Editorial fact sheet for *Generations*, n.d.

33. Jordan's publications before 1977 included *Who Look at Me* (T. Y. Crowell, 1969), *Soulscript: Afro-American Poetry* (Doubleday, 1970), *The Voice of the Children* (Holt, Rinehart and Winston, 1971), *Some Changes* (E. P. Dutton, 1971), *His Own Where* (T. Y. Crowell, 1971), *Fannie Lou Hamer* (T. Y. Crowell, 1972), *Dry Victories* (Holt, Rinehart and Winston, 1972), *New Days: Poems of Exile and Return* (Emerson Hall, 1974), and *New Life: New Room* (T. Y. Crowell, 1975).

34. Interoffice memo from Toni Morrison to Jim Silberman, dated June 22, 1975. Jordan provided Morrison with sales figures for *Soulscript*, *Who Look at Me*, and *His Own Where* in an interoffice memo dated June 19, 1975.

35. Letter from Toni Morrison to June Jordan, dated July 29, 1975.

36. Letter from June Jordan to Toni Morrison, dated July 30, 1975. June Jordan Collection (JJC), housed at the Schlesinger Library at Harvard University.

37. Letter from June Jordan to Toni Morrison, dated July 30, 1975. JJC.

38. Letter from June Jordan to Toni Morrison, dated July 30, 1975. JJC.

39. Letter from Toni Morrison to June Jordan, dated October 27, 1975. JJC.

40. Letter from Toni Morrison to June Jordan, dated November 17, 1975.

41. Letter from June Jordan to Toni Morrison, dated November 28, 1975.

42. Letter from June Jordan to Toni Morrison, dated June 16, 1976.

43. Letter from June Jordan to Toni Morrison, dated June 16, 1976.

44. Letter from Toni Morrison to June Jordan, dated June 29, 1976.

45. Interoffice memo from Gerald E. Hollingsworth to Toni Morrison, dated September 9, 1976.

46. Interoffice memo from Toni Morrison to Jason Epstein, dated December 21, 1976.

47. According to Morrison, her editorial relationship with Jordan was further strained by Jordan's last-minute dissatisfaction with the book's title. As Morrison recalled, Jordan thought it implied masturbation, but it was too late to change the title. Personal interview with Toni Morrison, November 9, 2007.

48. June Jordan's invitation to Audre Lorde, dated January 29, 1977. Audre Lord Papers, Spelman College Archives. For a detailed account of the Sisterhood meeting, see Courtney Thorsson, *The Sisterhood: How a Network of Black Women Writers Changed American Culture* (Columbia University Press, 2023).

49. Interoffice memo from Toni Morrison to Milly Marmur, dated December 17, 1979.

CHAPTER 10: WILL THE CIRCLE BE UNBROKEN?

1. Personal interview with Toni Morrison, September 21, 2005.

2. Personal interview with Toni Morrison, September 21, 2005.

3. Personal interview with Toni Morrison, September 21, 2005.

4. Interoffice memo from Toni Morrison to Jim Silberman, dated April 13, 1973.

5. Editorial fact sheet for *Ark of Bones*, dated April 19, 1974.

6. Form letter of invitation from Toni Morrison for Dumas book party, dated September 17, 1974.

7. Letter from Hale Chatfield to Toni Morrison dated September 24, 1974.

8. Letter from Hale Chatfield to Albert Erskine, dated October 14, 1974.

9. Letter from Hale Chatfield to Albert Erskine, dated October 14, 1974.

10. Letter from Hale Chatfield to Toni Morrison, dated November 6, 1974.

11. Letter from Carole A. Parks to Toni Morrison, dated October 31, 1974.

12. Letter from Toni Morrison to Carole Parks, dated November 7, 1974.

13. Letter from Toni Morrison to Hoyt Fuller, dated October 30, 1974.

14. John Deck, "A Rich Talent: *Ark of Bones*," *New York Times*, October 20, 1974, 35.

15. Letter from Eugene Redmond to Toni Morrison, dated January 8, 1975.

16. Letter from Toni Morrison to Eugene Redmond, dated September 17, 1975.

17. Letter from Toni Morrison to Eugene Redmond, dated September 17, 1975.

18. Quincy Troupe, "The First and the Last: Review of *Jonoah and the Green Stone*," *The Soho Weekly News*, May 13, 1976.

19. "Review of *Jonoah and the Green Stone*," *Kirkus Reviews*, March 15, 1976, 341.

20. For the most detailed account of Dumas's life and the murky circumstances surrounding his death, see Jeffrey B. Leak, *Visible Man: The Life of Henry Dumas* (University of Georgia Press, 2014).

21. Personal interview with John McCluskey, June 2, 2021.

22. Personal interview with Toni Morrison, September 21, 2005.

23. "Nairobi Night" appeared in the January 1973 issue of *Black World*. McCluskey refers to the story as "Nairobi Nights." It appeared in the table of contents in the issue of *Black World* as "Nairobi Nights," but the story as printed on page 54 of the issue bears the title "Nairobi Night."

24. Reader's report for *Look What They Done to My Song* by Pat Fogarty, dated May 11, 1972.

25. Personal interview with John McCluskey, June 2, 2021.

26. Letter from John McCluskey to Toni Morrison, dated October 11, 1973.

27. Letter from Toni Morrison to John McCluskey, dated November 19, 1973.

28. Letter from Toni Morrison to John McCluskey, dated November 19, 1973.

29. Letter from Toni Morrison to John McCluskey, dated November 19, 1973.

30. The concern about *Look What They Done to My Song* as the novel's title was related to the song "What Have They Done to My Song, Ma?" by Melanie Schekeryk. In-house counsel Richard Udell recommended obtaining permission from the song's publisher. Random House also had to add an errata slip to the first 3,500 copies of the novel to reflect acknowledgment of three lines of lyrics from "Drifting Blues" and four lines of lyrics from "Stormy Monday Blues." Interoffice memo from Richard Udell to Toni Morrison, dated September 4, 1974.

31. Alicia Metcalf Miller, "McCluskey of CWRU," *Cleveland Plain Dealer*, October 27, 1974; Russell Atkins, "John McCluskey's Blues," *Cleveland Magazine*.

32. Letter from Toni Morrison to John McCluskey, dated February 13, 1975.

33. Letter from Toni Morrison to John McCluskey, dated February 13, 1975.

34. Brown recounts his working relationship with Morrison in an interview with Edwidge Danticat after *Tragic Magic* was reissued in 2021 in McSweeney's Of the Diaspora series.

35. Interoffice memo to the design and copyediting department from Toni Morrison, dated January 23, 1978.

36. Back ad copy in draft for *Tragic Magic*, dated July 31, 1978.

CHAPTER 11: GREEN WITH ENVY

1. Toni Morrison, "Toni Morrison on a Book She Loves: Gayl Jones's *Corregidora*," in *What Moves at the Margin* (University Press of Mississippi, 2008), 109–10.

2. Letter from Toni Morrison to Gayl Jones, dated October 29, 1973.

3. Letter from Toni Morrison to Gayl Jones, dated October 29, 1973.

4. Letter from Toni Morrison to Gayl Jones, dated October 29, 1973.

5. Letter from Gayl Jones to Toni Morrison, dated November 8, 1973.

6. Interoffice memo from Toni Morrison to Jim Silberman, dated November 12, 1975.

7. Back jacket copy for *Corregidora*, n.d.

8. Editorial fact sheet for *Corregidora* (revised version), dated October 8, 1974.

9. Letter from Alice Walker to Toni Morrison, dated February 13, 1975.

10. Morrison, "Toni Morrison on a Book She Loves," 110.

11. Christopher Lehmann-Haupt, "Women in Pain . . . or Giggling," *New York Times*, April 21, 1975, 27.

12. Maya Angelou, "The Long, Sweet Contemplation of Revenge," *LA Times Book Review*, June 1, 1975.

13. Letter from Gayl Jones to Toni Morrison, dated March 25, 1975.

14. Letter from Gayl Jones to Toni Morrison, dated March 25, 1975.

15. Letter from Gayl Jones to Toni Morrison, dated August 1, 1975.

16. Letter from Gayl Jones to Toni Morrison, dated August 1, 1975.

17. Letter from Toni Morrison to Gayl Jones, dated November 14, 1975.

18. Letter from Gayl Jones to Toni Morrison, dated December 1, 1975.

19. Editorial fact sheet for *Eva's Man*, dated October 1, 1975.

20. Letter from Alice Walker to Toni Morrison, dated December 11, 1975.

21. Letter from Alice Walker to Toni Morrison dated December 11, 1975. "The Collector of Treasures" appeared in *Ms.* in 1977 and was published by Heinemann in a collection of the same title later that year.

22. Letter from Jean Stafford to the publicity department, dated January 15, 1976; letter from Selma Shapiro to Jean Stafford, dated February 9, 1976.

23. Gayl Jones, "About My Work," in Mari Evans, *Black Women Writers: 1950–1980: A Critical Evaluation* (Anchor Press, 1984), 233.

24. D. Keith Mano, "How to Write Two First Novels with Your Knuckles," *Esquire*, December 1977, 62.

25. Letter from Toni Morrison to Gayl Jones, dated January 5, 1977.

26. Letter from Toni Morrison to Gayl Jones, dated March 2, 1977.

27. Mel Watkins, "Books: Accent Put on Negative in Short Stories by Gayl Jones," *New York Times*, December 28, 1977, 60.

28. Toni Morrison, *Conversations with Toni Morrison*, ed. Danille Taylor-Guthrie (University Press of Mississippi, 1994), 133.

29. Toni Morrison, *Toni Morrison: Conversations*, ed. Carolyn C. Denard (University Press of Mississippi, 2008), 143.

30. Interoffice memo from Toni Morrison to Jason Epstein, dated September 1, 1977.

31. Letter from Toni Morrison to Gayl Jones, dated September 2, 1977.

32. Letter from Peter Matson to Toni Morrison, dated December 21, 1977.

33. Letter from Toni Morrison to Gayl Jones, dated November 1, 1978.

34. Interoffice memo from Robin Straus to Toni Morrison, dated November 3, 1978.

35. Letter from Toni Morrison to Gayl Jones, dated November 6, 1978.

36. Letter from Bob Higgins to Gerald Hollingsworth, dated February 20, 1979.

CHAPTER 12: BOXING THE CHAMP IN

1. Karl Meyer, "A Defiant Clay Weighs In as an Author," *Washington Post*, January 7, 1970; and Henry Ramont, "In This Corner, Cassius Clay, the Author," *New York Times*, January 7, 1970.

2. Letter from Richard Durham to Verne Moberg, dated November 17, 1969.

3. Letter from Richard Durham to Verne Moberg, dated November 17, 1969.

4. Harris recounted this story in part in a personal interview with me on June 2, 2011, and also in greater detail in his interview for the *History Makers*, the largest African American video oral history collection.

5. Letter from Richard Durham to James Silberman, dated September 14, 1970.

6. Letter from Richard Durham to James Silberman, dated September 10, 1971.

7. Letter from James Silberman to Herbert Muhammad, dated September 27, 1972.

8. Letter from Richard Durham to James Silberman, n.d. (received October 12, 1972).

9. Notes on Ali manuscript, n.d. Morrison's note is presumably written to Silberman.

10. Notes on Ali manuscript, n.d. Morrison's note is presumably written to Silberman.

11. Letter from Richard Durham to James Silberman, dated January 11, 1973.

12. Interoffice memos from James Silberman to Toni Morrison and from Toni Morrison to James Silberman, dated January 16, 1973.

13. Letter from Muhammad Ali to James Silberman, dated January 29, 1973.

14. Letter from Toni Morrison to Richard Durham, dated February 11, 1973.

15. Letter from Richard Durham to James Silberman, n.d. (copied to Morrison on May 24, 1973).

16. Letter from Richard Durham to James Silberman, dated April 10, 1974.

17. Letter from Toni Morrison to Richard Durham, dated May 7, 1974.

18. Letter from Muhammad Ali to James Silberman, n.d.

19. Toni Morrison, "Muhammad Ali's Editor Tells . . . Why the Crowd Roars," promotional material for *The Greatest*, n.d.

CHAPTER 13: FREE ANGELA

1. Letter from Toni Morrison to Bettina Aptheker, dated June 27, 1972.

2. Eric Pace, "Miss Davis Signs to Write Memoir," *New York Times*,

October 20, 1972, 33, https://www.nytimes.com/1972/10/20/archives/miss-davis-signs-to-write-memoir-california-radical-accepts.html.

3. Letter from Bernard Geis to James Silberman, dated October 4, 1972.

4. Outline of *The Education of a Revolutionary*.

5. Interoffice memo from James Silberman to Toni Morrison, dated May 7, 1973.

6. Interoffice memo from Toni Morrison to James Silberman, dated May 10, 1973.

7. Personal interview with Angela Davis, July 20, 2021.

8. The notes (dated January 5, 1974) appear on lined paper in a folder as "Queries" without attribution. Rene Boatman, Morrison's longtime assistant, and I agree that the script is undeniably consistent with Morrison's.

9. Toni Morrison, "Who Is Angela Davis?," *New York Times*, October 29, 1972, BR48.

10. Interoffice memo (subject: Bantam Report—Angela Davis) from Toni Morrison to Jim Silberman, dated February 1, 1974.

11. Personal interview with Angela Davis, July 20, 2021.

12. Eileen Lottman, "Armstrong Revelation: George Jackson Confession," *Village Voice*, May 16, 1974, 35.

13. Letter from Bernard Geis to Toni Morrison, dated May 22, 1974.

14. Letter from Toni Morrison to Bernard Geis, dated May 24, 1974.

15. Letter from Toni Morrison to Bettina Aptheker, dated March 13, 1974.

16. Interoffice memo from Richard Udell to Toni Morrison, dated May 29, 1974.

17. Interoffice memo from Jan Tigner to Toni Morrison, dated July 31, 1974; interoffice memo from Toni Morrison to Jan Tigner, dated July 31, 1974.

18. Interoffice memo from Toni Morrison to Selma Shapiro, dated October 18, 1974.

19. Form letter from Toni Morrison, dated October 23, 1974.

20. Letter from Bernard Geis to Toni Morrison, dated April 11, 1978. Geis refers to the article "Angela Davis Keeps the Faith" by Orde Coombs.

21. Toni Morrison, "What the Black Woman Thinks About Women's Lib," *New York Times*, August 22, 1971, section SM.

22. Letter from Bernard Geis to Elly Sidel, dated June 12, 1978.

23. Letter from Toni Morrison to Bernard Geis, dated August 2, 1978.

24. Letter from Bernard Geis to Toni Morrison, dated July 26, 1979.

25. Letter from Toni Morrison to Angela Davis, dated October 8, 1979.

26. Contract proposal for *Women and Race*, dated November 28, 1979. The book is contracted with the title *Women and Race*. It is published as *Women, Race, and Class*.

27. Editorial fact sheet for *Women and Race*, dated March 9, 1981.

28. Letter from John Lofton to Bob Bernstein, dated March 31, 1982.

29. Letter from Gene K. Bruce to Random House, dated May 18, 1982.

30. Interoffice memo from Toni Morrison to Tony Schulte, dated June 1, 1982.

CHAPTER 14: LETTING GIANTS TALK

1. Letter from Chinweizu to Toni Morrison, dated March 21, 1972.

2. Letter from Chinweizu to Toni Morrison, dated December 12, 1972.

3. Letter from Toni Morrison to Chinweizu, dated July 17, 1973.

4. Letter from Toni Morrison to Chinweizu, dated January 28, 1974.

5. Letter from Chinweizu to Toni Morrison, dated November 1, 1974; letter from Toni Morrison to Chinweizu, n.d.

6. Letter from Chinweizu to Toni Morrison, dated December 2, 1974.

7. Letter from Toni Morrison to Chinweizu, dated December 5, 1974.

8. Letter from Toni Morrison to Rainer Schulte, dated September 17, 1974.

9. Quincy Troupe and Rainer Schulte, eds., *Giant Talk* (Random House, 1975), xxiii.

10. Letter from Toni Morrison to Rainer Schulte, dated September 17, 1974.

11. Review of *Giant Talk*, *Choice*, February 1976, 1566; Jack Slater, "Review of *Giant Talk* and *The Negritude Poets*," *New York Times*, November 30, 1975, 56.

12. Letter from Ivan Van Sertima to Toni Morrison, dated October 27, 1971. Toni Morrison Collection (TMC) at the Firestone Library at Princeton University.

13. Letter from Ivan Van Sertima to Toni Morrison, dated December 6, 1971. TMC.

14. Letter from Ivan Van Sertima to Toni Morrison, dated January 17, 1975.

15. Letter from Ivan Van Sertima to Toni Morrison, dated September 10, 1975. TMC.

16. Random House editorial fact sheet for *They Came Before Columbus*, dated March 18, 1976. TMC.

17. The headlines appear, respectively, in *Publishers Weekly*, *People* magazine, *Sepia*, and *The Washington Post*.

18. Letter from Toni Morrison to Ivan Van Sertima, dated March 17, 1977.

19. Glyn Daniel's review, "America B.C.," appeared in *The New York Times Book Review* on March 13, 1977, 8, 12. Van Sertima's letter appeared on May 1, 1977. Watkins was staff editor from 1968 until 1985.

CHAPTER 15: BEYOND *THE BLACK BOOK*: SCRAPBOOKING BLACK HISTORY

1. Letter from Toni Morrison to Miller Williams and James McPherson, dated November 11, 1974.

2. Letter from James McPherson to Toni Morrison, dated November 16, 1974.

3. Letter from Toni Morrison to James McPherson and Miller Williams, dated December 5, 1974.

4. Letter from Toni Morrison to Owen Laster, dated February 14, 1975.

5. Letter from Miller Williams to Toni Morrison dated July 7, 1975.

6. Interoffice memo from Toni Morrison to copyedit/design team, dated January 20, 1976.

7. Letter from James McPherson to Toni Morrison, dated September 13, 1976.

8. Letter from Toni Morrison to James McPherson, dated September 20, 1976.

9. Letter from James McPherson to Toni Morrison, dated November 14, 1976.

10. Interoffice memo from Toni Morrison to Jim Silberman, dated June 20, 1973.

11. Interoffice memo from Jim Silberman to Toni Morrison, dated May 15, 1973.

12. Letter from Toni Morrison to Jim Haskins, dated December 17, 1975.

13. Letter from Toni Morrison to Jim Haskins, dated April 27, 1977.

14. Jervis Anderson, "Review of *The Cotton Club* by Jim Haskins and *Fats*

Waller by Maurice Waller and Anthony Calabrese," *New York Times*, November 20, 1977, BR8.

15. Letter from Toni Morrison to Rudy Lombard, dated May 14, 1976.

16. Interoffice memo from Toni Morrison to Jim Silberman, dated September 27, 1976.

17. Letter from Toni Morrison to Rudy Lombard, dated January 6, 1977.

18. Letter from Toni Morrison to Rudy Lombard, dated July 20, 1977.

19. Interoffice memo from Toni Morrison to Jean McNutt, dated August 15, 1977.

20. Interoffice memo from Toni Morrison to the copyediting and design department, dated July 20, 1977.

21. Letter from Toni Morrison to Rudy Lombard, dated September 1, 1977. Here, Morrison refers to Pat Chu, her assistant.

22. Editorial fact sheet for *Creole Feast*, dated March 15, 1978.

23. Interoffice memo from Toni Morrison to Carol Schneider, dated January 8, 1978. The year is likely an error that should be 1979.

24. Interoffice memo from Toni Morrison to Sandy MacGregor, dated May 7, 1979.

ACKNOWLEDGMENTS

1. I tip my hat here to Margaret Walker, who pens this line in the opening paragraph of the essay "How I Wrote *Jubilee*," which appears in *How I Wrote "Jubilee" and Other Essays* (Feminist Press, 1990), 50.

2. Letter from Toni Cade Bambara to Toni Morrison, n.d. TMC.